NK 3/16

BWB

D0493858

Please return or renew this item by the last date shown.

Libraries Line and Renewals: **020 7361 3010**

Web Renewals: www.rbkc.gov.uk/renewyourbooks

KENSINGTON AND CHELSEA LIBRARY SERVICE

William Faithorne's engraving of Sir William Davenant (1673).

SONG.

1.

THe Lark now leaves his watry Neſt
    And climbing, ſhakes his dewy VVings;
He takes this VVindow for the Eaſt;
    And ſo implore your Light, he Sings,
Awake, awake, the Morn will never riſe,
Till ſhe can dreſs her Beauty at your Eies.

2.

The Merchant bowes unto the Seamans Star,
    The Ploughman from the Sun his Seaſon takes;
But ſtill the Lover wonders what they are,
    VVho look for day before his Miſtreſs wakes.
Awake, awake, break through your Vailes of Lawne!
Then draw your Curtains, and begin the Dawne.

Davenant's most anthologised poem, from *The Works of Sr William D'avenant Kt* (1673).

Shakespeare's Bastard

THE LIFE OF
SIR WILLIAM DAVENANT

SIMON ANDREW STIRLING

The
History
Press

An ART & WILL Book

To Kim,
eudail de mhnathan an domhain

Front cover image: © iStock
Back cover image: Detail of portrait, said to be of William Davenant as a young man.
Reproduced by kind permission of the Rector and Fellows of Lincoln College, Oxford.
© Keith Barnes, www.keithbarnesphotography.co.uk

First published 2016

The History Press
The Mill, Brimscombe Port
Stroud, Gloucestershire, GL5 2QG
www.thehistorypress.co.uk

British Library Cataloguing in Publication Data.
A catalogue record for this book is available from the British Library.

ISBN 978 0 7509 6107 3

Typesetting and origination by The History Press
Printed in Great Britain

Contents

Acknowledgements

I would like to thank the following: the Rector and Fellows of Lincoln College, Oxford; my colleagues and students at the University of Worcester; Keith Barnes; Mike Jones at Rare Old Prints; Julian Smith at The White Bear; the vicar and churchwardens at St Leonard's, Beoley; Jacqueline Rattray and Johanna Franklin at Goldsmiths; Richard Peach; Steve and Julie Wadlow; the late Michael (Lord) Birkett; Lee Durkee; Dr Joanne Paul; Ceilidh Lerwick; Dr Alan Ogden; Anna Davies; Shana and Sid; Al Petrie; my parents, Norman and Brenda, for the books; Janet and John Ford at Tudor World, Stratford-upon-Avon, for helping to fund the research; the Historical Honeys; Rebecca Rideal; my editors, Mark Beynon and Juanita Zoë Hall, and the team at The History Press; and, as ever, Kim and Kiri.

Preface

On 26 February 1936, members of the Davenant Society gathered to celebrate the 330th anniversary of the birth of Sir William Davenant. They met in the recently restored Painted Chamber, in what had been the tavern run by Davenant's parents, where they were treated to an 'informal address' by Edgar Cardew Marchant, sub-rector of Lincoln College.

Marchant observed that Davenant's was 'indeed a career of strange vicissitudes, of many ups and downs, mainly downs: and shows him to have been a man of unlimited resource, undaunted courage, and unruffled good temper. When one has read the account of his life, one does not know whether to guffaw with laughter or to weep; so grotesque is it, yet so pathetic.' But on the subject of Davenant's paternity, he was in no doubt:

> The story that William Davenant was the illegitimate son of Shakespeare has no basis of fact. Scott in his *Woodstock* jests upon this possibility, but Scott was too good an antiquarian seriously to have accepted such a story. The only original authority is Aubrey, who almost certainly wrote the story when he was drunk. I hope the society will dismiss it from their minds.

E.C. Marchant's 'informal address' was hardly a model of accuracy. In almost the same breath as his blunt dismissal of the 'son of Shakespeare' story he argued that the apostrophe in Davenant's name – 'D'Avenant' – was 'a fancy of his third wife, Lady Davenant, who was a Frenchwoman; it was used by him only in the later part of his life'. In fact, Davenant was using the apostrophe a good quarter of a century before his third marriage. Marchant was also strangely ill-disposed towards much of Davenant's work – 'I cannot carry in my mind the plot of any one of Davenant's plays'; 'the epic [*Gondibert*] as a whole is completely unreadable'; 'to the last years of Davenant's life belong the deplorable adaptations of Shakespeare' – and managed to get the date of Ben Jonson's death wrong.

Marchant was senior honorary member of the Davenant Society and sub-rector of Davenant's old Oxford college. And yet he could not bring himself to remember the plots of Davenant's plays or to give credit where it was due. With friends like that, one might think, Davenant had no need of enemies.

No evidence of any kind was adduced to support Marchant's contention that the 'story that William Davenant was the illegitimate son of Shakespeare has no basis of fact'. No evidence was given because none had been looked for. The most compelling question about Davenant – was he, as he apparently claimed to have been, the illegitimate son of Shakespeare? – was repudiated on no grounds whatsoever: 'I hope the society will dismiss it from their minds.'

It had not always been so. During his lifetime, and in the years that followed, Davenant's relationship with Shakespeare was much talked about. Reputable figures – many with connections to Davenant's Oxford – accepted that Sir William had probably been the product of an illicit liaison between the Bard of Avon and the buxom mistress of the Taverne. Then it became *streng verboten* to consider the possibility that Davenant was Shakespeare's son. Not that any evidence had come to light to quash the rumours. Academic intolerance demanded that the story be rejected out of hand.

I became interested in Sir William Davenant while working on *Who Killed William Shakespeare? The Murderer, The Motive, The Means* (The History Press, 2013) and soon discovered that I liked him. He was undoubtedly brave, resourceful, industrious and loyal. Moreover, biographies of Davenant are few and far between. Bearing in mind his status as England's second poet laureate, his role in the English Civil War and his theatrical innovations, it seemed that he had been unjustly overlooked by biographers. I guessed that the main reason for this neglect was the awkward matter of his paternity, since any biographer would have to broach the subject, and this would require either a blanket denial (without evidence) or a serious engagement with the story, which might be detrimental to one's career prospects. Best to leave well alone.

But Davenant deserves to be taken seriously, as does the question 'was he Shakespeare's son?' This book is an attempt to answer that question. To avoid a biography that feels too front-loaded – the most pertinent part being the very start of his life – I resolved to arrange it backwards. Thus, Part One ('Restoration') recounts Davenant's final years, after the return of King Charles II. The second part ('Revolution') covers Davenant's activities immediately before, during and after the Civil War. Part Three ('A Young Man in London') explores the beginnings of Davenant's theatrical career, while Part Four ('A Child in Oxford') concentrates on the links between the young Davenant, and his parents, and William Shakespeare, working towards the final section ('1605') in which the extraordinary love affair between Shakespeare and Davenant's mother is revealed.

Much of the book grew out of, and builds upon, my research for *Who Killed William Shakespeare?* There have been developments since that book was written: Steve Wadlow introduced me to his remarkable portrait, which I believe to be of Shakespeare; Goldsmiths, University of London, published my paper on 'The Faces of Shakespeare'; and at the time of writing moves are underway, led by a team from the University of Staffordshire, in conjunction with a Channel 4 documentary, to determine whether or not the Beoley skull is indeed the 'veritable skull of William Shakespeare'. Some of the information presented in *Who Killed William Shakespeare?* has been duly revised. For example, I previously claimed that Shakespeare had dallied with Jane Sheppard-Davenant at Banwell in Somerset; further research has convinced me that I was wrong, and that the Shakespeare–Jane–Southampton love triangle actually unfolded on the outskirts of Bristol.

Wherever possible I have quoted from the earliest available written source or publication (the main exceptions to this rule being Samuel Pepys's *Diary* and John Aubrey's *Brief Lives*, the originals of which are too idiosyncratic to be readily comprehensible) but I have amended the typography, standardising the uses of 'u' and 'v' and avoiding the long 's' which can make *wise* look like *wife*, and so on.

With the 400th anniversary of Shakespeare's death upon us, the time has come for a reassessment of the life and achievements of the man who liked to be thought of as Shakespeare's bastard: Sir William Davenant, poet laureate and Civil War hero.

Simon Andrew Stirling

INSIDE OF THE DUKES THEATRE
in Lincoln's Inn Fields.
as it appeared in the reign of King Charles II.

This view represents the stage of the above Theatre, and its very elegant frontispiece, during the perform-
ance of a scene from Elkannah Settle's Empress of Morocco. The Theatre itself was deserted twelve
years after its foundation, for the one in Dorset Gardens; being found too small and incommodious
for the company that visited it. Part of it was discovered by the late fire in "Bear Yard". Its size
must have been extremely small, compared with our present Theatres.

Inside the Duke's Theatre, Lincoln's Inn Fields (1673).

PART ONE

Restoration

1660—1668

O Rare Sir Will Davenant

amuel Pepys spent the morning of Thursday, 9 April 1668 in his office on Seething Lane, just west of the Tower of London. He popped home for dinner at midday, and then it was back to the Navy Office to write some letters. He slipped away in the afternoon to visit his bookseller, John Martyn, at the sign of the bell in the churchyard of St Paul's Cathedral. From there, he made his way westwards to Lincoln's Inn Fields – or, as he put it, 'up and down to the Duke of York's playhouse, there to see, which I did, Sir W. Davenant's corpse carried out towards Westminster, there to be buried'.

The house in which Sir William Davenant had lodged was attached to the rear of the theatre and could be reached via an alleyway. Pepys watched the mourners clustering on the street as the coffin was brought out. 'Here were many coaches and six horses,' he observed. A private coach was an expensive way to travel, costing about 5s to hire for the day or (as Pepys himself was soon to discover) upwards of £50 to buy outright. There were also, he noted with distaste, 'many hacknies, that made it look, methought, like the buriall of a poor poet'.

The hackney coach was the ancestor of the London taxicab – still known as a 'hackney carriage' – and cost about 18d to hire for the first hour. Pepys clearly felt that the presence of so many hackneys lowered the tone.

The diarist had been at the king's playhouse, two nights before, when the news reached him of Davenant's sudden death. He took time out of his hectic schedule to see Sir William leave the Duke of York's playhouse for the last time. Pepys had not always been complimentary about Davenant's productions, but he admired the man. A portrait, painted by John Hayls two years before Davenant's death, shows the 33-year-old Pepys glancing – gelatinous eyes looking a bit strained – over his left shoulder, a handwritten sheet of music in his hand. The tune was his own, set to the words of a song by Sir William Davenant. The industrious Mr Pepys was proud of his composition.

The cortège finally departed from the theatre, heading towards the Strand. 'He seemed to have many children,' wrote Pepys in his diary, 'by five or six in the first mourning-coach, all boys.' Sir William in fact had eight surviving sons by his third wife, the eldest then being about twelve. The sight of so many healthy boys no doubt cut Pepys to the heart: he longed for a son, but he and his French wife were, and would remain, childless.

He did not follow the funeral procession but sought solace by walking down to the Strand where, amidst the bustle of the New Exchange, he met the attractive widow of a naval lieutenant. Pepys rode with Mrs Burroughs to Hyde Park, kissing her, but they 'did not go into any house'. Rather, as he 'set her down at White Hall' he presented her with a Valentine's gift 'for the last year before this, which I never did yet give her anything for'. His fumbling with Mrs Burroughs in the four-wheeled carrosse seems half-hearted, the belated gift of twelve silver half-crown coins 'wrapt in paper' lacking both romance and imagination.

Pepys returned to the office and kept himself busy, practising musical scales before supper, but his usual ebullience was lacking. The death of Sir William Davenant, the sight of those hackney coaches jostling outside the theatre, and all those young sons dressed in black, had left him morose and unsettled. Even petting a pretty widow in a carriage could rouse little more in him than a deflating sense of guilt.

John Aubrey knew Davenant's family in Oxford. 'I was at his funeral', wrote Aubrey twelve years after the event. 'He had a coffin of walnut tree. Sir John Denham said it was the finest coffin that ever he saw' – which might not have been the smooth compliment it appears to be. Aubrey was disappointed not to see a laurel wreath placed on the coffin.

Samuel Pepys holding his musical composition to Davenant's words.

'His body was carried in a hearse from the playhouse to Westminster Abbey, where at the great west door, he was received by the singing men and choristers, who sang the service of the church to his grave.'

> We brought nothing into this world, and it is certain we can carry nothing out. The Lord gave, and the Lord hath taken away …

The walnut coffin was carried the length of the nave to the south transept, where the grave was already prepared. It had previously housed the remains of Thomas May, Davenant's sometime rival for the post of poet laureate. May's outspoken support for Oliver Cromwell's dictatorship ensured that his bones were removed from the abbey when King Charles was restored to the throne.

> I held my tongue, and spake nothing: I kept silence, yea, even from good words; but it was pain and grief to me.
> My heart was hot within me, and while I was thus musing the fire kindled: and at the last I spake with my tongue …
> Deliver me from all mine offences: and make me not a rebuke unto the foolish.

The small gravestone of white marble was inscribed *O RARE S. WILLIAM DAVENANT*. John Aubrey recorded the inscription as '*O rare Sir Will. Davenant*' and remarked that it was written 'in imitation of that on Ben Jonson'. Jonson had been buried, in an upright position, on the north side of the nave, under a lozenge-shaped slab which read *O RARE BEN JOHNSON*. The sentiment, in both instances, was Catholic.

Jonson's only true religion had been Ben Jonson. Davenant was a Catholic convert, although his faith was essentially pragmatic. John Aubrey claimed that Sir William privately believed religion would eventually settle into 'a kind of ingenious Quakerism', combining inspiration with social equality.

'*Orare Sir Will. Davenant*' – 'Pray for Sir William Davenant.'

It was a measure of the turbulence of recent times that a staunch Catholic like Richard Flecknoe had written in praise of Cromwell, the Puritan figurehead, in 1650 (*The idea of His Highness Oliver …*, dedicated to Cromwell's son). Flecknoe redeemed himself, ten years later, by penning his *Heroick Portraits* of Charles II and other members of the Stuart dynasty. He also wrote plays and enjoyed putting together fantasy casts of actors, but he was deeply critical of the immorality of the stage.

'Sir William D'avenant being dead, not a Poet would afford him so much as an Elegie', proclaimed Flecknoe in a 'Poetical Fiction' entitled *Sir William Davenant's Voyage to the other World: with his Adventures in the Poets' Elizium*. Davenant had alienated his fellow poets, Flecknoe suggested, by seeking to 'make a Monopoly of the Art' and striving 'to become Rich.' According to Flecknoe, only one poet, 'more Humane than the rest, accompany'd him to his Grave with this Elogium':

Now Davenant's dead, the Stage will mourn,
And all to Barbarism turn:
Since He it was this later Age,
Who chiefly civiliz'd the Stage.

After five quatrains of routine praise, Richard Flecknoe followed Sir William on his posthumous progress.

Believing Davenant to be rich, Charon the ferryman demanded a handsome reward for piloting him across the Styx, only to discover that the poet laureate was so poor he couldn't afford the ordinary fare. The poets already inhabiting the Elysian Fields were surprised to see him, his death having received no publicity at all, and were unhappy to be joined by one who had disparaged such paragons as 'Homer, Virgil, Tasso, Spencer, and especially Ben. Johnson ... Nay, even Shakspear, whom he thought to have found his greatest Friend, was as much offended with him as any of the rest, for so spoiling and mangling of his Plays.' Jack Donne, the son of John Donne, was especially aggrieved to see Davenant and railed against him with such venom that Sir William grew exasperated. The two poets 'Fell together by the ears: when but imagine / What tearing Noses had been there / Had they but Noses for to tear'.

Famously, Davenant's nose had been ruined by syphilis.

The fight between Sir William and 'his old Antagonist Jack Donn' was broken up by the celestial police and Davenant was hauled before a tribunal. Momus, the savage critic, appeared for the prosecution.

Davenant told the heavenly judges that 'he was a Poet Laureate, who for Poetry in general has not his fellow alive, and had left none to equal him now he was dead'. In his 'Plays or Dramatick Poetry' he had plumbed the depths of tragedy and scaled the heights of tragicomedy:

And for his Wits, the Comick Fire
In none yet ever flam'd up higher:

But coming to his Siege of Rhodes,
It outwent all the rest by odds;

And somewhat in't that does out-do
Both th' Antients and the Moderns too.

Momus countered, arguing that Davenant's plays were 'never so good', but it was unbecoming of their author to commend them as he did – and besides, he had marred more plays than he had made; his 'Muse was none of the Nine, but only a Mongrel, or By-blow of Parnassus'; and 'finally, he so perplexed himself and [his] Readers with Parenthesis on Parenthesis, as, just as in a wilderness or Labyrinth, all sense was lost in them.'

15

And as for his Life and Manners, they would not examine those, since 'twas supposed they were Licentious enough: onely he wou'd say,

He was a good Companion for
The Rich, but ill one for the poor;
On whom he look'd so, you'd believe
He walk'd with a Face Negative:
Whilst he must be a Lord at least,
For whom he'd smile or break a jeast.

The judges took pity on Davenant. Since he had left the Muses for Pluto – betraying his poetic gifts for monetary gain – he was condemned to live in Pluto's Court, where he was appointed 'Superintendent of all their Sports and Recreations'. As he had flourished in this world, entertaining a profligate king and his dissolute courtiers, so he would in the next.

Such was the judgement of Richard Flecknoe. Sir William had overestimated his own talent and achievements: he was good, but not that good. He had pandered to the mighty and slighted better poets than himself, Ben Jonson in particular. Worse, perhaps, he had spoiled and mangled the plays of Shakespeare, whom he particularly admired. It all smacked of a talent ruthlessly exploited but ultimately wasted.

And there had been no mention of his death in the weekly gazettes. No 'Cryers of Verses and Pamphlets' had broadcast his obituary.

Davenant was succeeded as poet laureate by John Dryden – another Catholic convert – who had no time for Flecknoe's anti-theatrical posturing. Dryden had collaborated with Davenant on an adaptation of Shakespeare's *The Tempest*, which they subtitled *The Enchanted Island*. This was one of those plays which, in Flecknoe's view, Davenant had mangled and spoilt.

The Enchanted Island was first performed at Sir William Davenant's theatre precisely five months before he died. The script was published in 1670 with a preface by Dryden, dated 1 December 1669. Davenant 'was a man of quick and piercing imagination', wrote Dryden, who went on to praise Sir William in terms which would delight a modern-day producer: 'my writing received daily his amendments, and that is the reason why it is not so faulty, as the rest which I have done without the help or correction of so judicious a friend':

And as his fancy was quick, so likewise were the products of it remote and new. He borrowed not of any other; and his imaginations were such as could not easily enter into any other man. His corrections were sober and judicious: and he corrected his own writings much more severely than those of another man, bestowing twice the time and labour in polishing which he us'd in invention.

Davenant, then, was the consummate professional. Dryden refused to treat him with the same 'ingratitude' that others had shown to him: 'I am satisfi'd I could never have receiv'd so much honour in being thought the Author of any Poem how excellent soever, as I shall from the joining my imperfections with the merit and name of *Shakespear* and *Sir William Davenant*.'

When the critic and biographer Gerard Langbaine included a section on Davenant in his *Account of the English Dramatick Poets* (1691), Sir William's lasting reputation seemed assured. He was a 'Person sufficiently known to all Lovers of Poetry, and One whose Works will preserve his Memory to Posterity', having been 'Poet Laureate to Two Kings, whose Memory will always be Sacred to all good, loyal, and witty Men'. Most of his plays had 'appeared on the Stage with good applause, and been received with like success in Print', and then there were his poems, 'amongst which Gondibert an Epick Poem has made the greatest noise.'

Gondibert had been dedicated to the philosopher Thomas Hobbes, who not only accepted the dedication but replied with an 'extraordinary Compliment' to Davenant: 'The Virtues you distribute in your Poem, amongst so many Noble Persons, represent (in the Reading) the image but of One Man's Virtue to my fancy, which is your own.' The addition of commendations by 'two of our best Poets' – Edmund Waller and Abraham Cowley – should 'have proved a sufficient Defence and Protection against the snarling Criticks', thought Langbaine. But Davenant was never without his detractors. Four 'eminent Wits' (most notably, Sir John Denham, who commented on how fine Sir William's walnut coffin was, and Jack Donne, with whom Davenant brawled in Flecknoe's poetic Elysium) had published 'several Copies of Verses to Sir William's discredit' to be printed with the second edition of *Gondibert* in 1653.

Still, Davenant had risen above the many 'Railleries [that] were broached against him by his Enemies'. It was true that his coffin had 'wanted the Ornament of his Laureate's Crown':

> But this omission is sufficiently recompenc'd by an Eternal Fame, which will always accompany his Memory; he having been the first Introducer of all that is splendid in our English Opera's, and 'tis by his means and industry, that our Stage at present rivals the Italian Theatre.

Regardless of his critics, Davenant had earned his rightful place in the Pantheon.

Samuel Carter Hall agreed. In the first volume of his *Book of Gems: The Poets and Artists of Great Britain* (1836) Hall observed that Davenant's 'poetical reputation' rested almost entirely on *Gondibert*, 'which he, unfortunately, left unfinished', and that 'critics have remarkably differed as to its merits.' Davenant had set out to 'produce an epic on a plan altogether original, "an endeavour to lead Truth through unfrequented and new ways, by representing Nature, though not in an affected, yet in a new dress". However beautiful in parts, though, the poem as a whole had failed. 'A single error therefore, a false step at the outset, deprived Davenant of "what his large soul appears to have been full of, a true and permanent glory."'

Hall concluded: 'Davenant is now little read; his fame scarcely outlived his days. But posterity, in neglecting him, has not done justice; and it was a silly verdict that condemned him for having rehearsed "A theme ill-chosen in ill-chosen verse".'[2]

The fault lay not with Davenant's talent, but with changing attitudes – as Robert Anderson put it in his *Works of the British Poets* (1795): 'The epic poem of Gondibert is unquestionably the noblest production of his genius; and would do honour to any writer of any age or country. The fate which it has experienced conveys reproach upon the inconstancy of national taste …'

The national taste left Davenant behind. His entry in the 11th edition of *Encyclopædia Britannica*, Volume VII, published in 1910, described *Gondibert* as a 'cumbrous, dull production' whilst admitting that the epic 'is relieved with a multitude of fine and felicitous passages, and lends itself most happily to quotation'. This grudging concession was followed, however, by a damning verdict:

> The personal character, adventures and fame of Davenant, and more especially his position as a leading reformer, or rather debaser, of the stage, have always given him a prominence in the history of literature which his writings hardly justify. His plays are utterly unreadable, and his poems are usually stilted and unnatural. With Cowley he marks the process of transition from the poetry of the imagination to the poetry of the intelligence; but he had far less genius than Cowley, and his influence on English drama must be condemned as wholly deplorable.

Alfred Harbage, in his 1935 biography *Sir William Davenant: Poet Venturer*, referred to his subject as 'one of the disreputables of literary history' and 'a quixote – courageous, loyal, sincere, rather naïve, but withal shrewd and resourceful.' Sir William was 'a poet in his heart. He brought to the shrine of the Muses a devotion of which the other Caroline writers were incapable. And this devotion was expressed in actual works, for Davenant possessed energy and initiative unparalleled in the enervated circle of which he formed a part.'

'We prefer to read Milton', wrote Harbage, questionably. 'Yet we should prefer to have made a journey with Davenant.'

Sir William was, as Harbage remarked, 'the chief conduit through which Shakespearean stage tradition has reached us today'. Davenant straddled the chasm of the Cromwellian Protectorate, linking the pre-Commonwealth theatrical world with the mannered Restoration stage. He was one of the most innovative and influential impresarios in theatre history, a Civil War general, poet laureate and political prisoner, devoted royal servant and enemy of the state. To dismiss his contribution to British drama, or indeed to history, as 'wholly deplorable' is unreasonable and unwarranted.

Why has Davenant's reputation suffered so badly?

At first glance, he cuts a comic figure. Opposite the title page of *The Works of Sir William D'avenant*, published five years after his death, was printed an engraving by William Faithorne, based on a lost portrait by John Greenhill. The engraving shows Sir William in neoclassical mode, a laurel crown capping the tumbling curls of his periwig. The mask-like visage is the face of a fool. The eyes, which gaze off to the left, have a guileless vacancy about them. But what really stands out is the misshapen button nose with its gaping left nostril. The dose of syphilis which Davenant caught from a dark-haired beauty in Westminster had ravaged the appendage, collapsing the bridge and turning his nose into a snout.

Faithorne's engraving is the only accepted image of the poet laureate, and it is all too easy to see it as the portrait of an amusing pretender, a pygmy who would be a giant. And yet, there is another portrait, less well known, which presents a very different image of the man – more sensitive, more serious – before his nose was sacrificed to 'a terrible clap'.

Nevertheless, to judge Davenant's achievements on the basis of his unfortunate engraving is at best unworthy. It is also convenient, for by sneering at Sir William, commentators have excused themselves from having to engage sensibly with the most intriguing aspect of his story.

The problem begins with John Aubrey, who attended Sir William's funeral in 1668. Aubrey's potted biography of Davenant, which formed part of his *Brief Lives*, included a startling revelation: 'Mr William Shakespeare was wont to go into Warwickshire once a year, and did commonly in his journey lie at this house [the Davenants' tavern] in Oxford, where he was exceedingly respected':

> Now Sir William would sometimes, when he was pleasant over a glass of wine with his most intimate friends, e.g. Sam Butler (author of *Hudibras*),[3] etc – say, that it seemed to him that he wrote with the very spirit that Shakespeare [wrote], and seemed contented enough to be thought his son: he would tell them the story as above, in which way his mother had a very light report.

John Aubrey knew the Davenant family well. He added, '(I have heard parson Robert [Sir William's elder brother] say that Mr W. Shakespeare has given him a hundred kisses.)'

Aubrey passed the original drafts of his *Brief Lives* to his Oxford contemporary, Anthony Wood, who was himself the source of another rumour. This was written down by the antiquarian William Oldys in the eighteenth century:

> If tradition may be trusted, Shakspeare often baited at the Crown Inn or Tavern in Oxford, in his journey to and from London. The landlady was a woman of great beauty and sprightly wit, and her husband, Mr. John Davenant, (afterwards mayor of that city,) a grave melancholy man; who, as well as his wife, used much to delight in Shakspeare's pleasant company. Their son, young Will. Davenant, (afterwards Sir

William) was then a little school-boy in the town, of about seven or eight years old, and so fond also of Shakspeare, that whenever he heard of his arrival, he would fly from school to see him. One day an old townsman observing the boy running homeward almost out of breath, asked him whither he was posting in that heat and hurry. He answered, to see his *god*-father Shakspeare. There's a good boy, said the other, but have a care that you don't take *God's* name in vain.

Oldys had heard this anecdote from none other than the diminutive poet Alexander Pope, who died in 1744 and who claimed to have heard the tale from the great actor Thomas Betterton, who had worked closely with Davenant. Pope told the story at a dinner hosted by the Earl of Oxford, when the conversation had turned to the subject of the Shakespeare monument in Westminster Abbey, which Pope had helped to erect in 1741. By all accounts, Pope believed the story to be true.

The Shakespeare scholar George Steevens (died 1780) refused to credit the rumour on the slender grounds that Sir William's 'heavy, vulgar, unmeaning face' simply could not have been that of a son of Shakespeare (the curse of Davenant's nose striking again). By way of contrast, Alfred Harbage noted in 1935 that men in the eighteenth century 'were holding his [Davenant's] portrait beside Shakespeare's, and finding in the two a marked resemblance!' And they were right to, for reasons which will become clear.

Thomas Hearne, a sober and scholarly antiquarian of Oxford, added to the scandal in a note dated 30 July 1709:

> 'Twas reported by tradition in Oxford, that Shakespear, as he used to pass from London to Stratford upon Avon, where he lived and now lies buried, always spent some time in the Crown tavern in Oxford, which was kept by one Davenant, who had a handsome wife, and loved witty company, though himself a reserved and melancholly man. He had born to him a son, who was afterwards christened by the name of William, who proved a very eminent poet, and was knighted, (by the name of sir William Davenant,) and the said Mr. Shakespear was his godfather, and gave him his name. (In all probability he got him.) 'Tis further said, that one day going from school, a grave doctor in divinity met him, and asked him, 'Child, whether art thou going in such hast?' To which the child replyed, 'O, sir, my godfather is come to town, and I am going to ask his blessing.' To which the Dr. said, 'Hold, child! You must not take the name of God in vaine.'

Same joke, differently told. Hearne rehearsed the longstanding Oxford tradition that Will Shakespeare was Sir William's godfather, but then he went further – '(In all probability he got him.)' This was a mere forty years after Davenant's death.

The rumours persisted, becoming an irritant to those scholars who, in the late eighteenth century, were determinedly transforming Shakespeare into the epitome of patriotic English virtues. It was an era in which the living, breathing Shakespeare was being swept aside to make way for 'the universal genius'. Awkward details had to be omitted from his biography so that the 'god of our Idolatry' could mount his pedestal. Few details were more embarrassing than the rumours that 'Immortal Shakespeare' had fathered an illegitimate son.

As Shakespeare was elevated into a grotesquely artificial – and strangely immaterial – paragon, so his godson was slandered. Thus, the anonymous contributor to *Encyclopædia Britannica* brought his bigotry to bear:

> It was stated that Shakespeare always stopped at this [the Davenants'] house in passing through the city of Oxford, and out of his known or rumoured admiration of the hostess, a very fine woman, there sprang a scandalous story which attributed Davenant's paternity to Shakespeare, a legend which there is reason to believe Davenant himself encouraged, but which later criticism has cast aside as spurious.

This assessment might carry some weight if 'later criticism' had come up with any evidence to justify its prejudice.

The simple fact is that Will Shakespeare and Sir William Davenant were the victims of scholastic projections and chauvinism. For Shakespeare the demi-god to rise, Davenant with his funny nose must fall. Judgement was passed without the distraction of a trial. Shakespeare was everything; Davenant nothing.

Edmund Gosse encapsulated the unforgiving mood in 1880:

> There is not a more hopelessly faded laurel on the slopes of the English Parnassus than that which once flourished so bravely around the grotesque head of Davenant. The enormous folio edition of his works, brought out in 1673 in direct emulation of Ben Jonson, is probably the most deplorable collection of verses anywhere to be found, dead and dusty beyond the wont of forgotten classics. The critic is inclined to say that everything is spurious about Davenant, from the legend that connects his blood with Shakespeare's to the dramatic genius that his latest contemporaries praised so highly. He is not merely a ponderous, he is a nonsensical writer, and having begun life by writing meaningless romantic plays in imitation of Massinger, and insipid masques in the school of Ben Jonson, he closed his long and busy career by parodying the style of Dryden.

Which is to mistake character assassination for literary criticism.

Sir Walter Scott made hay with the gossip with his Civil War romance, published in 1826 under the title *Woodstock, or The Cavalier: A Tale of the Year Sixteen Hundred and Fifty-one*. In the twenty-fifth chapter, the future King Charles II is posing as a page named Louis Kerneguy:

> 'Why, we are said to have one of his [Shakespeare's] descendants among us – Sir William D'Avenant,' said Louis Kerneguy; 'And many think him as clever a fellow.'

'What!' exclaimed Sir Henry – 'Will D'Avenant, whom I knew in the North, an officer under Newcastle, when the Marquis lay before Hull? – why, he was an honest cavalier, and wrote good doggerel enough; but how came he a-kin to Will Shakspeare, I trow?'

'Why,' replied the young Scot, 'by the surer side of the house, and after the old fashion, if D'Avenant speaks truth. It seems that his mother was a good-looking, laughing, buxom mistress of an inn between Stratford and London, at which Shakspeare often quartered as he went down to his native town; and that out of friendship and gossipred, as we say in Scotland, Will Shakspeare became godfather to Will D'Avenant; and not contented with this spiritual affinity, the younger Will is for establishing some claim to a natural one, alleging that his mother was a great admirer of wit, and there were no bounds to her complaisance for men of genius.'

'Out upon the hound!' said Colonel Everard; 'would he purchase the reputation of descending from poet, or from prince, at the expense of his mother's good fame? – his nose ought to be slit.'

'That would be difficult,' answered the disguised Prince, recollecting the peculiarity of the bard's countenance.[4]

Sir Walter had done his homework. The artist and antiquarian Charles Kirkpatrick Sharpe had written to Scott on the anniversary of Davenant's death, 7 April 1819: 'I have been much amused with Will. Davenant, who you were so good as to give me. Some of his poetry is very smooth and charming, with now and then old-fashioned wild flight, very seldom to be met with now. I perceive that Pope stole a great deal from him, as he did from Shakespeare, who, if I remember right, was reported to have been his papa.'

The reports had circulated widely, emanating from the London theatre-land and the cloisters and watering-holes of Oxford. John Aubrey and Anthony Wood, Thomas Hearne and William Oldys, Thomas Betterton and Alexander Pope had all discussed the story; the eminent Shakespeare scholar Edmond Malone believed it, as did Thomas Warton, the clergyman, schoolmaster and 'second Professor of Poetry' at Oxford, who communicated his memories of the rumour to Malone.

Robert Southey – Poet Laureate for 30 years before his death in 1843 – repeated the story with a grimace:

The father was a man of melancholy temperament, the mother handsome and lively; and as Shakspeare used to put up at the house on his journeys between Stratford and London, Davenant is said to have affected the reputation of being Shakspeare's son. If he really did this, there was a levity, or rather a want of feeling, in the boast, for which social pleasantry, and the spirits which are induced by wine, afford but little excuse.

Only a maverick would dare to depart from the scholarly consensus. One such was Augustus Montague Summers, a clergyman from Bristol who served as a curate at

Bitton and Bath before converting to Catholicism. His fascination with the occult was matched by his abiding interest in Restoration theatre. In *The Playhouse of Pepys*, published in 1935, Montague Summers brought an all-too-rare openminded-ness to the Shakespeare-Davenant conundrum:

> The tradition that William Davenant was Shakespeare's son is, of course, impossi-ble to establish. From the very nature of the case those most concerned – if indeed any save the father and mother knew the facts – would keep silence, although Davenant himself in merry mood was wont to make reference to his paternal ancestry, and the truth cannot be certainly ascertained at this time of day, although myself I see no reason at all why the story may not be accepted.

Maybe it was Summers's Catholicism which set him apart from the more puri-tanical commentators who refused to countenance the possibility that 'immortal' Shakespeare had sired Sir William Davenant. Elsewhere, and in France especially, the matter was less controversial. It even formed the subject of a play, *Davenant*, by Jean Aicard, which was performed by the Comédie Française when they visited London in the summer of 1879.

Victor Hugo dropped a bombshell in 1864. The novelist was then thirteen years into his exile from the France of Napoleon III. His lengthy *William Shakespeare* essay incorporated a short and colourful biography, which included the following snippet (translated by Melville B. Anderson):

> Shakespeare went from time to time to pass some days at New Place. Half-way upon the short journey he encountered Oxford, and at Oxford the Crown Inn, and at the inn the hostess, a beautiful, intelligent creature, wife of the worthy innkeeper, Davenant. In 1606 Mrs. Davenant was brought to bed of a son, whom they named William; and in 1644 Sir William Davenant, created knight by Charles I, wrote to [Lord] Rochester: 'Know this, which does honour to my mother, I am the son of Shakespeare'; thus allying himself to Shakespeare in the same way that in our days M. Lucas [de] Montigny has claimed relationship with Mirabeau.

The dead weight of academic disapproval had forced the rumour into the shadows, and Davenant with it. He became the laughing stock of English literature and is now largely forgotten. But if Victor Hugo was right, and Sir William's boast was true, then England's second poet laureate was the result of a remarkable pairing.

> Know this, which does honour to my mother –
> *I am Shakespeare's son.*

2

His Sacred Majestie's Most Happy Return

*T*here must have been a sense of history repeating itself.

A fleet of warships crossed the English Channel, just as a similar fleet of twenty vessels had crossed the Channel thirty-five years earlier. Back in 1625 they had sailed to Boulogne to fetch Henrietta Maria, the youngest daughter of Henri IV and Marie de Médicis and now the bride of King Charles I. In 1660, they arrived at Scheveningen, the little fishing port which served as a harbour for The Hague, to collect the sons of Henrietta Maria – foremost amongst them, King Charles II.

The flagship boasted three decks and eighty guns. Launched in 1655, it was known as the *Naseby*. Samuel Pepys was on board, officially to serve his kinsman, Sir Edward Montagu, who had been appointed admiral, and unofficially to record the events in his diary.

King Charles boarded the *Naseby*. He was over 6ft tall, with a dark complexion and a 'wide ugly mouth'. With him were his brothers, James Duke of York and Henry Duke of Gloucester, as well as his sister Mary and her son William, Prince of Orange, and his aunt Elizabeth, sometime Queen of Bohemia. Pepys kissed their hands and observed that there was an 'infinite shooting off of the guns'.

The king and his brother James spent that afternoon of 23 May 1660 on the quarterdeck, changing the past. The *Naseby*, named after a decisive victory for Parliament in the Civil War, became the *Royal Charles*. The *Richard*, named after Oliver Cromwell's son, became the *James*. The *Speaker* (of the House of Commons) was renamed *Mary* after Charles's sister, the Princess Royal. Ships whose names recalled some hateful memory of defeat, such as the *Dunbar* and the *Winsby*, were rebranded *Henry*, after Charles's youngest brother, and *Happy Return*. The *Bradford* became HMS *Success*. That done, King Charles and his brothers set sail for England.

The wind was fair, the weather fine. The king was restless, pacing 'here and there, up and down', wrote Pepys, 'very active and stirring.' He reminisced about his escape from Worcester in the autumn of 1651, when he had waded through mud for three days and four nights 'with nothing but a green coat and a pair of country breeches on', his borrowed shoes making his feet so sore, 'he could hardly stir'. For six weeks he had been a fugitive, skulking in barns and copses. When he finally reached France he looked 'so poorly' that people checked the rooms he had been in 'to see whether he had not stole something or other'. The king's tales brought Sam Pepys close to tears.

By the next day, the sombre and reflective mood had lifted like a sea mist. Pepys found himself walking on the deck with 'persons of honour', including Tom Killigrew – 'a merry droll, but a gentleman of great esteem with the King' – whose sister had borne the exiled king a daughter. True to form, Killigrew told a dirty story.

Thomas Killigrew was an undereducated courtier who liked to vaunt his illiteracy. He was also a playwright, his principal contribution to the drama having been a bawdy piece entitled *The Parson's Wedding* (Pepys described it as 'an obscene, loose play'). But Killigrew was well connected. His cousin, Henry Jermyn, had just been created 1st Earl of St Albans. A devoted and beloved favourite of the king's mother, Jermyn was either an ingenious spymaster who had helped to bring about the restoration of the English monarchy or a vainglorious meddler who invariably got in the way, depending on your point of view. Undoubtedly, though, Jermyn was one of the most influential figures around, and among those who had worked closely with him was the poet Sir William Davenant.

Killigrew was no match for Davenant as an artist, although that mattered little. Tom Killigrew and his father had served the king's father and grandfather. Through his mother, Killigrew was related to Sir Francis Bacon and to William Cecil, 1st Baron Burghley and chief adviser to Queen Elizabeth I. He had followed Prince Charles into exile in 1647, and in 1651 – the year of Charles's crushing defeat at Worcester – he became the king's representative in Venice. The 'merry droll' had reason to expect a handsome return on his loyalty and would soon become Davenant's rival for mastery of the London stage.

The White Cliffs were sighted on the morning of 25 May. The king and his brothers breakfasted on the staple food of the seaman: pease porridge, boiled beef and salted pork. Charles measured his height against a ship's beam and gave instructions that the mark he had made should be gilded. He also gifted £500 to the officers and crew of the *Royal Charles*.

They landed at Dover, like Charles's mother a generation earlier. The king went ashore with his brothers. Pepys followed in another longboat with one of the king's spaniels 'which shit in the boat, which made us laugh and me think that a King and all that belong to him are but just as others are'.

King Charles was warmly greeted by General Monck, who had done so much to secure the king's return. The townsfolk of Dover had turned out en masse – as Pepys remarked, 'infinite the crowd of people and the gallantry of the horsemen, citizens, and noblemen of all sorts.' A local gentleman wrote rather feverishly that 'there never was in any nation so much joy both inwardly felt and outwardly expresst, as was in this Kingdom from the day of His Majestie landing at Dover.'

Charles did not stop at Dover but took a coach to Canterbury, 14 miles inland, where his parents had spent their first night together in 1625. The roads were lined with the maidens and militiamen of Kent, cheering wildly. Ahead of the king, all the way to London's Tower Hill, went the gunfire and cannonades. Fires blazed on the hilltops, so that 'All England but one Bonfire seems to be', in the words of the poet Abraham Cowley.

After Sunday service in Canterbury Cathedral, King Charles moved on to Rochester, where he abandoned his coach and rode on horseback to Blackheath. The army had been drawn up there by General Monck. Morris dancers cavorted. In all, about 100,000 people had gathered to welcome his majesty.

The king took four days to travel from Dover to Deptford. The leisurely pace meant that Charles entered the capital on 29 May – his 30th birthday.

'This day came in his majesty Charles the Second to London after a sad and long exile, and calamitous suffering both of the king and the church, being seventeen years', wrote the diarist, John Evelyn. Bareheaded, with his brothers on either side of him, Charles rode through Southwark and then, following the Lord Mayor, crossed London Bridge to enter the city at two in the afternoon. Evelyn described 'a triumph of above 20,000 horse and foot, brandishing their swords and shouting with unexpressible joy: the ways strewed with flowers, the bells ringing, the streets hung with tapestry, fountains running with wine.' Three hundred gentlemen in doublets of silver, and 300 more in velvet cloaks, all with their liveried servants, walked in the procession, as did the soldiers in buff coats, the Sheriff's men in red cloaks, the aldermen in their scarlet gowns and the members of the City of London Livery Companies wearing golden chains. Ladies waved and cheered from windows and balconies; trumpets blared and cannons roared. Music was heard everywhere as 'myriads of people' flocked through the thoroughfares. The stragglers passed through the city at nine in the evening.

John Evelyn 'stood in the Strand and beheld it, and blessed God ... for such a restoration was never seen in the mention of any history, ancient or modern ... nor so joyful a day, and so bright, ever seen in this nation'.

By the time the king reached the palace of Whitehall at seven o'clock he was tired, dazed and somewhat deafened. In response to the flattering speeches of the Speakers of the House of Lords and the House of Commons, Charles smirked: it must have been *his* fault he had been out of the country for so long, since there seemed to be no Englishman 'who did not protest that he had ever wished for his return'.

John Dryden, the 28-year-old poet and soon-to-be playwright, celebrated the 'Happy Restoration and Return of His Sacred Majesty Charles the Second' in a poem he published that June:

> For his long absence Church and State did groan;
> Madness the pulpit, faction seized the throne:
> Experienced age in deep despair was lost,
> To see the rebel thrive, the loyal cross'd

Like many, Dryden was tainted by association with the Cromwellian regime. He hopefully entitled his poem *Astraea Redux*. Astraea, the Greek goddess of justice, innocence and purity, had been 'brought back':

> At home the hateful names of parties cease,
> And factious souls are wearied into peace.
> The discontented now are only they
> Whose crimes before did your just cause betray

Dryden was anxious to ingratiate himself with the 'happy prince' who had promised to punish only his father's murderers, and so *Astraea Redux* sought to exonerate those collaborators who were 'reform'd by what we did amiss':

> Oh happy age! oh times like those alone [...]
> When the joint growth of arms and arts foreshow
> The world a monarch, and that monarch *you*.

John Dryden was not yet Poet Laureate. That honour had been bestowed on William Davenant by King Charles the first, twenty-two years earlier.

Davenant published his own 'POEM upon His Sacred Majestie's most happy Return to His Dominions' that same month. Like Dryden, Sir William averred that justice and religion had disintegrated in the chaos of insurrection and martial law. But truth and wisdom, tempered by experience, had thankfully been restored:

> And now your Nations shall with early Eyes,
> Watch the first Clouds e're storms of Rebels rise.
> Though *Orators* (the People's *Witches*) may
> Raise higher Tempests then their skill can lay [...]
> Yet can they not to full rebellion grow;
> Not knowing how much now the People know;
> Who from your influence have attain'd the wit
> Not to proceed from *grudgings* to a *Fit*.

Such thoughts were no doubt suited to the hour. They were, however, overly optimistic. Whilst the first signs of unrest – those rumbling 'grudgings' which could be worked up into a revolutionary 'Fit' – might now be recognisable, and the republican experiment had failed, the days of the Stuart monarchy were numbered.

Sir William Davenant had already spent more time on earth than his godfather, William Shakespeare. He was 54, and his best days lay ahead of him. Five years into his third marriage, he had begun to produce that crop of sons which Pepys would notice eight years later at Sir William's funeral. The eldest, christened Charles in honour of the exiled king, had been born in about 1656.

The hated Parliament, which had twice imprisoned Davenant, voted itself out of existence on 16 March 1660, having prepared the legislation for a 'free parliament' which would formally invite Charles II to return and claim his throne. The next day Davenant obtained a pass permitting him to travel to France. In the light of subsequent events it seems unlikely that he was hurrying to join the king, who was then in Brussels. His intended destination was probably the Château de Colombes, a few miles north-west of the centre of Paris. This neoclassical villa overlooking the Seine had been bought in 1657 by Anne of Austria, the widowed mother of King Louis XIV, as a home for Henrietta Maria, the widowed mother of King Charles II, and it was here that Henrietta spent much of her time with Henry Jermyn, whose constant service to the Queen Mother had earned him the title Earl of St Albans.

Davenant had been described as a 'Servant of Her Majesty' as far back as 1635. His widow would later recall that her royal namesake 'did Graciously take him into her Family', and he had remained the queen's loyal servant. He had also dedicated his comedy, *The Platonic Lovers*, to Henrietta's favourite in 1635. From that time on, the tiny, delicate Henrietta Maria and the broad-shouldered, overweight Henry Jermyn had effectively been Davenant's joint patrons, and he had shared many of their misfortunes. Between them, in the years to come, Davenant and Jermyn would establish what we now think of as London's West End.

The line between servant and spy was a fine one. Like his friend Abraham Cowley, Davenant was almost certainly part of Jermyn's network of Royalist agents. If Sir William did cross the Channel in March 1660 it would have been to bring the latest news from London and to find out how he could best serve Henrietta Maria and her favourite at this propitious time.

Whether he travelled to Paris or not is unclear. What is known is that, towards the end of that month, Davenant took on the lease of a tennis court.

Lincoln's Inn Fields is the largest public square in London. Sandwiched between High Holborn and the Strand, where the River Thames makes a sharp turn to the east, the fields adjoined the gardens belonging to Lincoln's Inn, one of the four Inns of Court where gentlemen studied to practise law.

It was a fashionable part of town. By day, people walked in the fields; by night, illicit couples fornicated there. Linen was laid out on the grass to dry. Trained bands of militia were drilled in the open air.

Immediately to the south lay the 'Lesser' or Little Lincoln's Inn Fields where, in the summer of 1656, Sir David Cunningham sold a parcel or two of land along the verge of the 'causeway leading from the New Market place towards Lincoln's Inn' to a lawyer named Horatio Moore and a gentleman called James Hooker. Moore was acting for his mother-in-law, Anne Tyler, who lived in nearby Fetter Lane, and her new husband, Thomas Lisle, whose name was kept out of the transaction because, as a former servant to the king, he was 'obnoxious to the powers' of Cromwell's government. Anne Tyler and James Hooker quickly set about building a tennis court which jutted out into the open fields to the east of Lord Brudenell's coach-house and stables, on the north side of the causeway which would eventually become known as Portugal Street.

It was not a tennis court in the modern sense of the term. The racket sport played there was real or 'royal' tennis, requiring an enclosed space with high walls and a lofty ceiling. Though Thomas Lisle had kept himself in the background during the legal exchanges, the new tennis court took his name. It was featured in Wenceslaus Hollar's engraving of 1657 as a rectangular construction with a row of windows set high up in the plain walls and two 'houses' attached to the north.

The exiled royals had seen tennis courts used for theatrical performances in continental Europe. Davenant's confidence in the king's imminent return, and a subsequent boom in public entertainment, is reflected in the fact that, just three years after it opened, and two months before Charles II triumphantly arrived in London, he entered into a contract to lease Lisle's Tennis Court in Lincoln's Inn Fields for the purpose of converting it into a playhouse.

Tom Killigrew had been made a Groom of the Bedchamber, giving him intimate access to King Charles. On 9 July 1660 Killigrew obtained permission to 'Erect a Playhouse with Players for his Ma[jes]ty'. The Attorney General was required to prepare a bill, ready for the royal signature, which would allow 'our Trusty and Wellbeloved Tho. Killegrew Esq … to erect one Company of players wch shall be our owne Company':

> And in regard of the Extraordinary Licence that hath bin lately used in things of this nature our pleasure is that there sall be noe more places of representacions or Companyes of actors or representacions of Scenes in the Citties of London or Westm[inste]ʳ … then the 2 Companyes now to be erected … and Wee doe by these presents declare all other Company or Companyes to be sylenced and surprest during our pleasure.

The '2 Companyes now to be erected' were to be managed by Thomas Killigrew and Sir William Davenant.

Davenant already had permission to build a playhouse and form a company. The patent had been granted to him by King Charles I in 1639, but events had conspired to prevent him from using it. Now it struck him as insufficient. The order for a royal warrant that Tom Killigrew had acquired established that Killigrew's would be the senior company: the King's Company, direct descendants – as it were – of Shakespeare's troupe, the King's Men. Sir William had ventured too much time, energy and money to risk being outdone by a crude jester who was six years his junior.

Within days of Killigrew receiving his order for a royal warrant, Davenant wrote up an order of his own. It was dated 19 July 1660 and addressed to the Attorney General, Sir Geoffrey Palmer:

> Our will and pleasure is that you prepare a Bill for our [the king's] signature to passe our Great Seale of England, containing a Grant unto our trusty and well beloved Thomas Killegrew Esquire, one of the Groomes of our Bed chamber and Sir William Davenant Knight, to give them full power and authoritie to erect Two Companys of Players consisting respectively of such persons as they shall chuse and apoint, and to purchase or build and erect at their charge as they shall thinke fitt Two Houses or Theaters with all convenient Roomes and other necessaries therto appertaining for the representations of Tragedys, Comedys, Playes, Operas, and all other entertainments of that nature

The two companies were 'to be under the jurisdiction, government and authoritie of them the sayed Thomas Killegrew and Sir William D'avenant'. All other 'places of Representations or Companys of Actors or Representers of sceanes in the Cittys of London or Westminster' were to be 'absolutely suppressed'.

At first the Attorney General wavered, unable to see the need for a royal warrant to establish a joint monopoly of stage plays in London. Davenant and Killigrew complained to the king, and the Attorney General was forced to back down. The warrant, for which Davenant had drafted the order, passed the privy signet on 21 August 1660. But Sir William was still not satisfied. He drafted another order, dated 20 August, which sought to quash all competition.

The new order noted that 'divers persons, and Companies have assembled, and doe dayly assemble themselves together' at various playhouses in London 'without the least Colour of Authority':

> and doe there act, performe and shew in publique, Comedies, Tragedies, and other Entertainments of the Stage, therein publishing much prophaneness, scurrility, obsceneness, and other abuses tending to the great Scandall of Religion, corruption of Manners, and ill example of our loving subjects.

Writing on the king's behalf, Sir William demanded that the City of London authorities force all such persons to 'desist and forbeare the performing, acting and shewing any Comedies, Tragedies, Operas by Recitative Musick, or any Representation by Dancing, or Scenes, or any Plays, or other Entertainments of the Stage whatsoever, uppon paine of our high displeasure'.

Davenant was overreaching himself. By resorting to the language of Puritanism he revealed his anxiety. Tom Killigrew had beaten him to pole position – and now an old adversary entered the fray.

Officially, Sir Henry Herbert had been appointed Master of the Revels in 1641, although he had been carrying out the functions of that role since 1623 as deputy to Sir John Ashley. The post required him to read, license and, where necessary, censor all forms of public entertainment. It could be a lucrative position: Sir Henry had been paid £150 a year by his predecessor for doing the actual work, and that stipend had come out of Ashley's fees for the post.

Herbert's misfortune had been to become Master of the Revels in his own right immediately before the theatres were closed at the outbreak of the Civil War. With the restoration of the monarchy in 1660 he fully expected the office to be revitalised and the fees to flow. He therefore came to an arrangement with Michael Mohun's company, based at the Red Bull in Clerkenwell, by which he would receive 40s for every new play performed, 20s for each old play revived, and no less than £4 a week, payable every Saturday.[1]

The warrant awarded to Killigrew and Davenant on 21 August authorised them to 'peruse all playes that have been formerly written, and to expunge all prophanenesse and scurrility from the same, before they be represented or acted.' The Master of the Revels protested in the strongest terms, referring to the relevant clause as an 'unjust surprize, and distructive to the powers graunted' to him as the official censor.

Sir Henry Herbert held a particular grudge against Davenant, going back to the 1630s. His animosity had been rekindled when Davenant started mounting theatrical productions under the Cromwellian regime without reference or benefit to Sir Henry.[2] Over the next few years Herbert would pursue every legal avenue against Davenant in an effort to suppress Sir William's company and to obtain the fees he believed to be his.

Meanwhile, Davenant and Killigrew pressed ahead with their plans. Tom Killigrew leaned on the king to suppress Major Mohun's Red Bull company. The two patentees then chose the best actors from the various companies in existence and brought them together under the banner of 'His Majesty's Comedians'. A list of these actors was prepared for the Lord Chamberlain and dated Saturday 6 October 1660.

That this united company got straight down to business is shown by a lawsuit, brought by Sir Henry Herbert on 16 October, in which Davenant and Killigrew were accused of conspiring to undermine the Office of the Revels and deprive Sir Henry of his fees, profits and advantages by presenting plays from 8 to 16 October at the Cockpit Theatre, Drury Lane, without submitting to Herbert's authority. The case was eventually tried on 3 February 1662. Davenant and Killigrew were acquitted by the jury and awarded costs.

The fifth of November had been declared a day of national celebration by an Act of Parliament in January 1606. Samuel Pepys noted in his diary that the festivities of 5 November 1660 were observed 'exceeding well in the City; and at night great bonfires and fireworks.'

That same day, the united company of His Majesty's Comedians split into two. Killigrew took the more experienced older actors associated with Michael Mohun to form the King's Company. They performed for three days at the Red Bull before moving to Gibbons's Tennis Court in Vere Street, just west of Lincoln's Inn Fields where Davenant was converting Lisle's Tennis Court into a theatre. Gibbons's Tennis Court opened as 'His Majesty's Theatre' on 8 November 1660 with a performance of Shakespeare's *Henry IV Part I*.

Davenant took the younger actors under his wing and formed the Duke's Company, named after the king's brother James, Duke of York. On 5 November articles were drawn up and agreed by three parties: Sir William himself; the leading members of the acting company, including the up-and-coming Thomas Betterton; and an additional actor, Henry Harris, who doubled as a scene painter.

Until Sir William provided them with a 'new theatre with scenes' the company would perform at Salisbury Court 'or elsewhere' and net profits would be divided into fourteen shares, of which Davenant was to have four. A band of musicians would be paid out of the gross receipts 'at not more than 30 [shillings] a day'.

Once the company had moved into its new theatre the profits would be divided into fifteen shares. Two would go to Davenant to cover the costs of rent, building and 'scene-frames' and another to pay for costumes, properties and scenery. The remaining shares were to be divided into seven for Sir William 'for maintaining the actresses of the company, and in consideration of his authority and "pains and expenses"' and five for the actors. Tom Killigrew was to have a 'free box holding six persons' at the theatre, and Davenant would be 'sole "Master and Superior," or governor, of the company.'

The new companies – the King's and the Duke's – might have gone their separate ways but the pressure was on to satisfy the king's desire for theatrical entertainments on a par with those he had seen during his European exile. So keen was King Charles to see Italian opera in England that he had already granted a licence to Giulio Gentileschi (whose father had served Charles I as a picture buyer) to build a theatre, import Italian musicians, and offer 'opere musicale, con machine mutationi di scene et alter apparenze'. This project never got off the ground, but the grant served as a reminder to Davenant and Killigrew of the king's impatience.

Finally, on the evening of Monday, 19 November, the first play to be performed for the Restoration Court was presented at Whitehall, in the Cockpit-in-Court – a round chamber, next to the Duke of York's apartments, which had been turned into an intimate theatre space by Inigo Jones. Killigrew's company was chosen to revive Ben Jonson's *Epicœne, or The Silent Woman*, the same cast having performed Davenant's *The Unfortunate Lovers* at their Vere Street venue that afternoon.

As poet laureate, Davenant had the honour of penning a special Prologue, addressed to the king:

> *Greatest of Monarchs, welcome to this place*
> *Which* Majesty *so oft was wont to grace*
> *Before our Exile, to divert the Court,*
> *And ballance weighty Cares with harmless sport.*

Sir William took the line that theatre and the monarchy were much the same – they had shared '*the same* Foes' and '*the same* Banishment' when the Civil War blurred the distinction between make-believe bloodshed and real-life violence:

Affrighted with the shadow of their Rage,
They broke the Mirror of the times, the Stage [...]
And silenc't us that they alone might act

But those angry amateurs paled beside the professional players on the world stage:

If feigned Vertue could such Wonders do,
What may we not expect from this that's true!

Six months had not yet passed since 'His Sacred Majestie's most happy Return' to England. The race to restore the stage to something like its pre-Civil War status had been won by Thomas Killigrew, whose company had a monopoly of almost all existing plays – including those written by Sir William Davenant.

Work was proceeding on the conversion of Lisle's tennis court, but the need to remove someone's garden wall was costing time and money and would soon land Davenant in legal difficulties. He was under near-constant attack from the Master of the Revels – 'molested by Sir Henry Harbert with severall prosecutions at Law', as he put it two years later in a 'humble Petition' to the king. Striking a low blow, Herbert brought up the matter of Davenant having published an 'Epithalamium in praise of Olivers daughter Ms. Rich; – as credibly informed.' In other words, the laureate had written a wedding poem to celebrate the marriage of one of Cromwell's daughters in 1657.

A parliamentary bill calling for Cromwell's remains to be disinterred from Westminster Abbey had been introduced on 6 November, the day after Davenant formed his company. In these febrile times, any hint of collaboration with the regicide could have ruined Sir William's reputation.

To cap it all, a hot-tempered actor-manager named George Jolly arrived in London that November and petitioned King Charles for a licence to act. The king had seen Jolly's company perform at Frankfurt Fair in September 1655; as soon as Charles's identity became known, Jolly's English players took to calling themselves 'The King's Servants'. Regardless of the monopoly he had granted to Davenant and Killigrew, King Charles awarded 'George Jolly Gentleman' the 'full power and authority to erect one company' and 'to purchase, build or hire ... One House or Theatre with all convenient Roomes'. Jolly gathered up a troupe of actors and began performing at the Cockpit, just off Drury Lane.[3] It would be another two years before Davenant and Killigrew dealt with the nuisance of George Jolly by renting his grant from him at the cost of £4 per week, leaving themselves with the theatrical monopoly in London and Jolly with a licence to tour the provinces.

For a moment, Davenant seems to have lost heart. His dreams of spearheading a dramatic renaissance in England were evaporating. So he turned his gaze towards Ireland. On 26 November, one week after the first performance at Court, he received a royal warrant whereby 'Sir William Davenant may be authorised to erect or provide a Theater in Our Citty of Dublyn':

And wheras We have lately authorised Two Howses or Theaters and noe more to be erected in Our Citty of London, soe in consideracion of the expences necessary to that work We doe enjoyne that noe more Theaters or Play Houses be permitted in Our Citty of Dublyn then that One Theater or Play house to be erected or provided by the said Sir William Davenant. And Our further Will and pleasure is That by the said Pattent the said Sir William Davenant shall enjoy the authority and office of Master of Revells of Ireland during his life with such priviledges annext unto it as you shall thinke fitt

Ireland already had a deputy Master of the Revels in the shape of John Ogilby, a Scottish cartographer who produced the first road map of Britain. Ogilby had established Ireland's first purpose-built playhouse in the 1630s. But, as he explained to the king, 'after his great preparations and disbursements in building a new theatre, stocking and bringing over a company of actors and musicians, and settling them in Dublin' the Werburgh Street Theatre had fallen 'to utter ruin by the calamities of those times'. Ogilby was hoping to open a new playhouse in Smock Alley and, 'notwithstanding Sir William Davenet's pretences', he petitioned King Charles for the grant of the office of Master of the Revels in Ireland.

If Davenant was seeking to displace John Ogilby there was little hostility in his actions. He had previously written a poem 'To my Friend Mr. Ogilby' in praise of the Scotsman's verse translations of Aesop's Fables (which almost certainly offered a subtle critique of the recent troubles). But whatever his intentions, Davenant lost out again. Having given the office of Master of the Revels in Ireland to Sir William, the king reversed his decision. In March 1661 he granted Ogilby the authority to set up a theatre in Dublin and included 'a Revocation of all Grants made to other under ye Signet or Sign Manual for representing anything of ye same or like nature.'

Davenant's failed gambit had probably been inspired, more than anything, by the need for money. The costs of preparing Lisle's Tennis Court for his lavish stage productions were spiralling. His only option was to sell off some of the shares which had been allocated to him in the agreement of 5 November 1660.

On 7 March 1661, Davenant sold a half-share to Richard Alchorne of Crowshurst in Sussex and a whole share for 'six hundred pounds of lawfull money' to Sir William Russell of Strensham, Worcestershire. A few days later he made over another half-share to Russell to be held in trust for the widow of Davenant's old friend, Endymion Porter.

Sir William Russell had been created 1st Baron of Wytley in 1627. He was a prominent Royalist and the former Governor of Worcester. Although he was a wealthy man, Russell had lost a considerable part of his estate in the Civil War and there was no firm guarantee of a return on his investment in Davenant's theatre. Accordingly, Davenant agreed to defray certain expenses, including the rent for the theatre, so that Russell would 'be quitt thereof'.

The Lincoln's Inn Fields theatre in 1821.

The baron got the better of the deal but, nevertheless, when Davenant urgently needed cash Sir William Russell had answered the call. There might have been an element of family loyalty involved. Russell's grandfather had married Elizabeth, the daughter of Ralph Sheldon of Beoley, Worcestershire. Ralph Sheldon had been one of the staunchest Catholics in England and was related by marriage to William Shakespeare. His son-in-law, Sir John Russell of Strensham, was the half-brother of Thomas Russell, whose manor of Alderminster lay 4 miles from Stratford-upon-Avon. Shakespeare was said to have spent much time in his retirement with Thomas Russell, whose stepson, Leonard Digges, wrote a prefatory poem for the First Folio of Shakespeare's works in 1623.

The investor who rescued Sir William Davenant with a timely injection of funds was descended from a kinsman of William Shakespeare. Indeed, Sir William Russell's great-uncle was so trusted by Davenant's 'godfather' that he had been named as one of just two overseers of Shakespeare's will ('ITEM *I gyve unto my wief my second best bed*') of 1616.

3

A Teeming Muse

hrough the second half of 1660 Davenant was eclipsed by Killigrew, who had a virtual monopoly of all existing stage plays. It was not until 12 December that Davenant persuaded the Lord Chamberlain's office to grant him the exclusive rights to a number of plays, including nine of Shakespeare's.

Killigrew's company had moved into their Gibbons's Tennis Court premises on Vere Street where, on 3 January 1661, Samuel Pepys 'saw Women come upon the stage' for the first time in Fletcher and Massinger's *The Beggar's Bush*. An actress had already played the part of Desdemona in Killigrew's production of *Othello*, which opened on 8 December 1660, an occasion for which the poet Thomas Jordan wrote a Prologue 'to introduce the first Woman that came to act on the stage'. This was a landmark moment in English theatre history – and Killigrew had beaten Davenant to it.[1]

Davenant's company comprised the younger actors around at the time: essentially, those who had acted with John Rhodes's company at the Drury Lane Cockpit and at Salisbury Court. Rhodes had been wardrobe-keeper at the Blackfriars before the closure of the theatres in 1642; he then became a 'stationer' selling books at the sign of the Bible in Charing Cross. When, in 1659, he secured a licence to set up a company of players at the Cockpit his troupe included two apprentices: Edward Kynaston, who specialised in female roles, and Thomas Betterton – 'the best actor in the world', in the opinion of Pepys and his wife, who would name her dog 'Betterton' after the star performer.

By 5 November 1660, Davenant had inherited most of John Rhodes's young players, with the exception of the pretty-boy Kynaston, who joined Killigrew's company. Their temporary home was to be the Salisbury Court Theatre, also known as the Whitefriars and Dorset Garden. Situated to the south of Fleet Street, Salisbury Court was the last playhouse built before the closure of the theatres. Pepys went there on Tuesday 29 January 1661 – '(the first time I ever was there since plays begun)' – and saw 'three acts of "The Mayd in ye Mill" acted to my great content', although he left before the end, 'it being late'.

A slow start, no doubt. But Davenant was at last able to give Killigrew a run for his money. On Saturday, 2 March Pepys went to the Vere Street theatre, only to find so few people in the audience that he left and went to Salisbury Court, 'where the house as full as could be' for Davenant's production of *Love's Mistress* by Thomas Heywood. Later that month Pepys celebrated the third anniversary of his life-threatening operation to remove a bladder stone by taking his wife and some friends to Salisbury Court, where they saw Massinger's *The Bondman* 'done to admiration.' On 6 April, the diarist paid his last visit to Salisbury Court. Sir William Davenant was shutting up shop to prepare for the grand opening of his new playhouse in Lincoln's Inn Fields.

The best show in town that April took place in none of the theatres. Early in the morning of 22 April, the king travelled by barge from his palace of Whitehall to the Tower of London to take part in a spectacular procession. The streets were gravelled and strewn with flowers. Carpets and tapestries were hung on the houses. The water conduits ran with wine. John Evelyn, watching from his vantage point near Temple Bar, described the 'splendid cavalcade'.

First came the Duke of York's Guards, with their plumes of black and white, and then royal messengers, sergeants and servants, all on 'prancing horses'. Sixty-eight Knights of the Bath 'in crimson robes, exceeding rich' were accompanied by trumpets. The peers of the realm rode two abreast between lines of volunteers in white doublets. The Duke of York came after the Lord Mayor and was soon followed by King Charles 'in royal robes and equipage' ('a most rich embroidered suit and cloak' wrote Samuel Pepys). The King's Guard sported plumes of red and white feathers. Somewhere towards the rear, presumably among the 'many other officers and gentlemen', was Sir William Davenant. Typically, Tom Killigrew, as a Groom of His Majesty's Bedchamber, took precedence.

'This magnificent train on horseback,' noted Evelyn, was 'as rich as embroidery, velvet, cloth of gold and silver, and jewels, could make them'. Pepys, ensconced in a house on Cornhill, found the 'show with gold and silver' a little overwhelming, but he admired the City ladies leaning out of their windows.

The procession passed through several ornate triumphal arches. One was surmounted by a woman representing Rebellion, her crimson robe crawling with snakes and a bloody sword in her hand. 'I am Hell's daughter,' she declaimed, 'Satan's eldest child'. She was challenged by the figure of Monarchy, who bade her to 'shrink from this glorious light' – meaning the king. The words were by John Ogilby, who brought 'The River *Thames*' to life, 'his Garment Loose and Flowing, Colour Blew and White', to greet Charles II.

Pepys was up at four the next morning to find a place in Westminster Abbey for the coronation. After a month of rain, the day dawned fine. Blue cloth lined the route from Westminster Stairs to the west door of the abbey, where the benches were swathed in scarlet. The 'glittering plenty of this Golden Age' was everywhere apparent, from the king's golden high-heeled sandals to the 12,000 borrowed gemstones sparkling on the stirrups of the Horse of State.

Only as the king was leaving Westminster Hall that evening was thunder heard. Some argued that the violent storm was a heavenly portent; others pointed out that the sun had shone brilliantly throughout the coronation. The medal struck for the occasion displayed a Royal Oak bursting into leaf and bore the motto *Iam Florescit* – 'Already it blossoms'.

Though he would eventually father more than a dozen children by various mistresses, the king lacked a legitimate heir. The scandalous marriage of his brother James, Duke of York, to the daughter of the stuffy Lord Chancellor, Edward Hyde, coupled with the death from smallpox of young Henry, Duke of Gloucester, the previous September, only increased the pressure on King Charles to find a suitable bride.

In May 1661, Parliament was informed that negotiations with the immature and unstable king of Portugal had been concluded. The contract was signed on 23 June; Charles would marry the 22-year-old Portuguese princess Catherine of Braganza. He was already writing to Catherine in Lisbon as 'The very faithful husband of Your Majesty', although faithfulness was never one of his stronger qualities.

A year would pass before Catherine set foot in England. Still, in honour of her homeland the causeways running either side of Davenant's new theatre in Lincoln's Inn Fields were named Portugal Street and Portugal Row.

The Duke's Playhouse finally opened on Friday, 28 June 1661 with a revival of Davenant's *The Siege of Rhodes*. The following Tuesday, Samuel Pepys went to 'Sir William Davenant's Opera; this being the fourth day that it hath begun, and the first that I have seen it.' The audience was obliged to wait 'a very great while' for the king to appear with his aunt Elizabeth, 'Queen of Bohemia', and Pepys cheerfully reported that 'by the breaking of a [floor]board over our heads, we had a great deal of dust fell into the ladies' neck and the men's hair, which made good sport.' At last, King Charles arrived and 'the scene opened; which is indeed very fine and magnificent,' wrote Pepys, 'and well acted, all but the Eunuch, who was so much out that he was hissed off the stage.'

The hapless 'Eunuch' was John Downes, so struck with stage-fright – not least of all because the 'Duke of York, and all the Nobility' were present, this being 'the first time the King was in a Publick Theatre' – that he gave up acting altogether and became Davenant's prompter and bookkeeper.

Thomas Betterton made his debut at the Duke's Playhouse, playing Solyman the Magnificent, with Henry Harris in the role of Alphonso. Hester Davenport and Mary Saunderson made such an impression as the wives of Solyman and Alphonso that Pepys insisted on referring to them thereafter as 'Roxolana' and 'Ianthe', no matter what parts they were playing.

John Downes later recalled that *The Siege of Rhodes* 'continu'd Acting 12 days without Interruption with great Applause.' The 'Enlarg'd' texts of both parts of *Rhodes* were published in 1663 with an 'Epistle Dedicatory' to Davenant's old friend Edward Hyde, Lord Chancellor and 1st Earl of Clarendon, which sounded a familiar note of paranoia:

Yet when I consider how many, and how violent they are who persecute Dramatick Poetry, I will then rather call this a *Dedication* than a *Present*; as not intending by it to pass any kind of obligation, but to receive a great benefit; since I cannot be safe unless I am shelter'd behind your Lordship.

Pepys came to think of *The Siege of Rhodes* as 'the best poem that ever was wrote'. He read it to his wife when she was in bed with a cold and wrote his own music for one of Solyman's songs – 'Beauty, retire! Thou dost my pity move!'

Davenant followed *The Siege of Rhodes* with a revival of *The Wits*, which he had written in 1633. The first performance on 15 August was again attended by royalty, the king being there with the Duke and Duchess of York. Pepys found it 'a most excellent play' with 'admirable scenes' and saw it twice more during its eight-day run.

Davenant's next production was Shakespeare's *Hamlet*. It opened on Saturday 24 August 1661 and made stars of its 26-year-old lead, Thomas Betterton, and Mary Saunderson, who played Ophelia to Betterton's Prince of Denmark.

'No succeeding Tragedy for several Years got more Reputation, or Money to the Company than this', remembered the prompter John Downes. Pepys saw it that first afternoon and declared that Betterton 'did the Prince's part beyond imagination.' Betterton's triumph owed much to Davenant's direction: Downes later remarked that 'Sir *William* (having seen Mr. *Taylor* of the *Black-Fryars* Company Act it, who being Instructed by the Author Mr. *Shaksepeur*) taught Mr. *Betterton* in every Particle of it; which by his exact Performance of it, gain'd him Esteem and Reputation, Superlative to all other Plays.' When his Hamlet saw the ghost of his father, Betterton's face reputedly turned as white as his neckcloth.

John Downes's recollections, published in 1708, are not always reliable. Joseph Taylor, a former child actor, joined the King's Men after the death of their lead actor, Richard Burbage, in 1619, and whilst he was remembered for having 'acted Hamlet incomparably well' it is unlikely that Taylor had been coached in the role by Shakespeare himself. Nevertheless, Davenant had seen Taylor as Hamlet, Taylor having succeeded Richard Burbage, and so Davenant was able to show Betterton how to play the part in the manner of the original.

Betterton was still playing Hamlet as 'a young man of great expectation, vivacity, and enterprize' when he was well into his seventies. In 1709, Nicholas Rowe wrote of 'the Advantage with which we have seen this Master-piece of *Shakespear* distinguish itself upon the Stage, by Mr *Betterton's* fine Performance of that Part.'

Davenant's revival of Shakespeare's *Twelfth Night* opened at the Duke's Playhouse on 11 September, John Downes fondly recalling that the play enjoyed 'mighty Success by its well Performance'. Then, on Monday, 21 October, Davenant revived his own *Love and Honour*, which had first been performed at the Blackfriars in 1634. Pepys, who missed the opening of *Twelfth Night* because he had promised his wife that he would not go to the theatre ever again without her, broke his promise and saw all three performances of *Love and Honour* in its first week. It was a sumptuous production ('Richly Cloath'd', wrote Downes). As Alvaro and Prospero, Betterton and Harris wore the resplendent coronation suits which had been donated by King Charles and James, Duke of York.

The success of Davenant's first six months at Lincoln's Inn Fields presented his rival with a problem. After seeing *The Siege of Rhodes* at the Duke's Playhouse on 2 July 1661, Samuel Pepys went to Vere Street two days later to see Killigrew's *Claricilla* – '(the first time I ever saw it), well acted':

> But strange to see this house, that used to be so thronged, now empty since the
> Opera begun; and so it will continue for a while, I believe.

Avid playgoer that he was, Pepys could tell that Killigrew's venue was not a patch on Davenant's.

From the outside, the passer-by might have noticed little out of the ordinary. The Duke's Playhouse extended for some 90ft (27.5m) along Portugal Street, with a couple of small shops tacked on to its southern wall and an inn, known as the Grange, situated almost opposite. An alleyway ran between Lord Brudenell's stables and the west side of the theatre, leading to Davenant's house at the rear. Immediately to the east of Davenant's lodgings was a larger extension: the scene house.

The main building was about 45ft (13.7m) wide and 30ft (9m) high. The ground floor was dominated by a 'pit' with rows of benches facing the stage. There were boxes along the side walls and 'front boxes' for privileged spectators at the back of the pit. Above was a middle gallery of boxes and raked '18 pence' seating, and an upper gallery where the cheapest seats could be found. In all, the house could hold about 500 people.

Even as they took their seats in the candlelit auditorium the first audiences would have been aware of one of Davenant's innovations – the proscenium, which formed a sort of picture frame. There were practical doors for entrances and exits on either side and a room for musicians above. Beyond the candelabra which lit up the forestage, twin rows of grooves in the floor allowed for shutters of increasing height and width to be slid in from the wings. These 'side scenes' drew the eye towards the painted backcloth, which could be moved in and out of position from the scene house. A system of ropes, pulleys and counterweights allowed properties, performers and scenery to be 'flown' in and out, while trapdoors made it possible for ghosts and demons to rise up from below.

Additional candles could be fixed in tin sconces to the backs of the side scenes. Coloured glass and dyed silks were used to create lighting effects appropriate for the 'new Scenes and Decorations' in *The Siege of Rhodes*. The theatregoing public had seen nothing like it before.

Tom Killigrew soon realised that his Vere Street theatre, having no scope for scenery, was inadequate. He needed a bigger and better equipped playhouse if his King's Company was to compete with Davenant's Duke's.

Killigrew found a plot, known as the 'Riding Yard', between Drury Lane and Bridges (now Catherine) Street. An indenture, signed on 20 December 1661, stated that Killigrew, his actors, and the playwright Sir Robert Howard would spend £1,500 in constructing a new theatre before Christmas 1662. In the event, the theatre cost £900 more than the initial estimate, some of that money going on a glassy dome over the pit – which let in light, but also rain – and on gilt leather for lining the boxes. Killigrew's new playhouse was not without its flaws. The musicians were housed below the stage, and in order to accommodate as many customers as possible the distance between the forestage and the farther boxes was made such that Pepys was confident the actors would not be heard.

The 'Theatre Royall' opened on 7 May 1663, the first of several Theatres Royal to stand on that site up to the present day. Until then the King's Company had to continue performing at Vere Street. An anonymous citizen wrote to a friend in the country, sometime in the summer of 1662, with an update on the London theatre scene:

> First then to speake of his Majestys Theatre
> Where one would imagine Playes should be better
> Love att the first sight did lead the dance
> But att second sight it had the mischance
> To be so dash't out of Countenance as
> It never after durst shew itts face

Killigrew's revival of his own tragicomedy, *The Princess, or Love at First Sight*, played to a packed house on 29 November 1661 but ran for just two performances. Things looked a lot better at Lisle's Tennis Court, where Sir William Davenant managed the junior company:

> To come to the other Theatre now
> Where the Knight with his Scenes doth keep much adoe
> For the Siege of Rhodes all say
> It is an everlasting play.

Until Killigrew also had 'Scenes', his productions simply could not match those at the Duke's Playhouse.

Davenant's run of theatrical luck seemed to falter in February 1662. *The Law against Lovers* was an adaptation of Shakespeare's *Measure for Measure*, to which Davenant made some major changes: out went Mistress Overdone, the brothel-keeper; in came Beatrice and Benedick from *Much Ado About Nothing*.

The play is set in Turin, where the Duke of Savoy affects to leave the city in disguise so that he may 'compare the Customs, prudent Laws, / And managements of foreign States with ours.' As in Shakespeare's original, the duke secretly remains, posing as a friar, to observe the effects of his deputy's policies. Angelo, the deputy, is one 'who never feels / The wanton motions of the sense':

> but does
> Rebate and blunt his natural edge,
> With Morals, Lady. He studies much,
> And fasts.

Angelo's brother Benedick returns victorious from the wars and resumes his 'kind of merry war' with Beatrice, an heiress who is also Angelo's ward. Lord Angelo, meanwhile, revives 'an old Law, / Which condemns any man to death, who gets, / Being unmarry'd, a Woman with Child.' This 'dreadful act' snares Julietta, Beatrice's cousin, who is arrested because Claudio, her betrothed, has got her pregnant. Though Claudio protests that Julietta is his 'Wife by sacred vows, and by / A contract seal'd with form of witnesses', the proper ceremony having been deferred 'Only for the assurance of a Dowry', he is imprisoned.

Shakespeare's *Measure for Measure* was written in 1604, one year into the reign of Charles II's grandfather, King James I. The references to the law revived by Angelo then harked back to earlier laws proscribing Jesuit priests. Updated by Sir William Davenant, the 'nineteen years' preceding Angelo's reinstatement of the 'strict Statutes, and chastising Laws' glanced back at the closure of the theatres and the start of the Civil War. The duke admits, 'I have ever lik'd a life retir'd, / And still have weary of Assemblies been' and so, like King Charles I, 'It was my fault to give the People scope'. Where Shakespeare's Jacobean duke had delegated to a zealous secretary, Davenant's Caroline duke transfers his authority to a puritanical Cromwell figure and, like King Charles, enters a kind of self-imposed exile, 'very strangely gone from hence'.

Newly written tragedies were almost entirely absent from the Restoration stage, the execution of Charles I in 1649 having proved so traumatic that it negated tragedy. Instead, the playwrights turned to tragicomedy. It was comforting for Royalists like Davenant to think that the '*God-like-Father*' had come back as 'the *Royal Martyr's* Son', the tragedy of the king's execution thereby resolving into the happy ending of the king's return.[2]

The Law against Lovers helped to cement the vogue for tragicomedy. The hidden regicide-to-restoration theme plays out as a meditation on natural behaviour and its perversion. Angelo governs 'With a Rod in's hand instead of a Scepter, / Like a Country School-Master in a Church'. His 'Carthusian gravity' causes him to enforce the letter of the law whilst ignoring its spirit. Benedick, his brother, is equally guilty of extremism by bickering with Beatrice in order to avoid marriage:

> My Brother, Sir, and I, walk several ways.
> He takes care to destroy unlawful Lovers;

And I'll endeavour to prevent th' increase
Of lawful Cuckolds.

Claudio and Julietta are therefore to be punished simply for doing what comes naturally. But by professing against the bonds of marriage and 'restraining / The liberty of Lovers', Benedick and Angelo are starving the roots of life, so that 'if the Duke stay too long, he may chance find / A Dominion without Subjects.'

Davenant modernised Shakespeare's language ('privily' became 'privately'; 'accompt' became 'account') and rewrote some of Shakespeare's spicier expressions, turning 'Lechery' into 'that which the precise[3] call Incontinence', for example. In doing so, he was merely reflecting the sensibilities of the age and the contemporary view, recorded by Richard Flecknoe in 1664, that Shakespeare's writing was 'a fine garden, but it wanted weeding'.

Similar sensitivity is evident in his treatment of Angelo, who in Shakespeare's original is irredeemable. The law revived by Davenant's Angelo echoed the *Act for suppressing the detestable sins of Incest, Adultery and Fornication*, passed by Parliament in May 1650, and when Isabella, pleading for her brother's life, remarks:

Perhaps, in some hot season of your life,
Even you, Sir, would have err'd in that,
For which you censure [Claudio]

she may be hinting at Oliver Cromwell's alleged adultery with the wife of General John Lambert. But Davenant's Angelo is not the reptile of *Measure for Measure*. Shakespeare's Angelo offers to sleep with Isabella in return for her brother's life, a deal he has no intention of honouring. Davenant's Angelo amazingly reveals that he never intended to take Claudio's life; he staged the whole scenario as a trial of Isabella's virtue:

But since you fully have endur'd the test,
And are not only good, but prove the best
Of all your Sex, submissively I woo
To be your Lover, and your Husband too.

Unaware that Angelo has sealed Claudio's pardon, Benedick leads a 'Body of Disbanded Officers' in an assault on the prison. The Provost waves a severed head over the battlements, leading Benedick to believe that Claudio has been put to death. Benedick's renewed attack is halted when 'suddenly our Sov'raign Duke breaks forth, / From the dark Cloud of that disguise, in which, / It seems, he hath remain'd conceal'd'.

Like the Restoration itself, Benedick's revolution is relatively bloodless. The head that was displayed above the battlements was not Claudio's, neither was it that of the convict Bernadine, as it was in Shakespeare's original. One of the characters suspected 'that 'twas not *Bernadine*'s by / A small Wart upon his left eye-lid.' This suggests that the head was in fact Cromwell's – 'one, who of / A natural sickness dy'd i'th' Prison' – which, like those of his fellow regicides, had been disinterred and mounted on the roof of Westminster Hall. Cromwell's famously warty visage had already been alluded to:

> But *Angelo* in his short Government,
> Disfigur'd and disgrac'd that fair
> Resemblance which he wore of me,
> By many blemishes.

In keeping with the tragicomic genre, the duke returns in the form of the heirless Charles II – ('since I have no / Successors of my own'). Isabella and Angelo are paired off, as are Benedick and Beatrice, whose 'Cousin *Juliet*' has been 'advis'd by a bauld Dramatick Poet … to end her Tragy-Comedy / With Hymen the old way.' The Cromwellian dictatorship is over: 'The persecutions of your loves are past.'

Pepys saw *The Law against Lovers* on 18 February 1662 and thought it 'a good play and well performed'. He was particularly struck by 'the little girl's (whom I never saw act before) dancing and singing'. This was the character of Viola, introduced by Davenant as a pubescent sister to Beatrice and probably played by Mary ('Moll') Davis, a future mistress of King Charles II.

The Law against Lovers was performed for the king on 17 December and then dropped from the repertory. No play of the time could afford to divide its audience. One satirist branded it 'the worst that ever you sawe'. But the brittle banter of Beatrice and Benedick anticipated the 'gay couple' made popular by the comedic double act of Nell Gwyn and Charles Hart: the two first appeared as verbal sparring partners in *All Mistaken, or The Mad Couple*, written by James Howard (who married the daughter of King Charles and Tom Killigrew's sister) and performed at the Theatre Royal in May 1665.

After the disappointment of *The Law against Lovers* Davenant hastily mounted a production of Shakespeare's *Romeo and Juliet*, starring Henry Harris and Mary Saunderson as the star-crossed lovers and Betterton as Mercutio. Pepys saw it on 1 March 1662 and dismissed it as 'the worst that ever I heard in my life, and the worst acted that ever I saw these people do'. The cast was under-rehearsed. An actress named Mrs Holden ran onstage after the deaths of Tybalt and Mercutio, crying 'O my Dear *Count*!' According to John Downes, Mrs Holden 'Inadvertently left out, O, in the pronuntiation of the Word *Count*! giving it a Vehement Accent, [which] put the House into such a Laughter, that *London* Bridge at low-water was silence to it.'

Later in the year Davenant honoured an old friendship by putting on *The Villain*, a loose adaptation of Shakespeare's *Othello*, by Thomas Porter, the son of Sir William's late patron, Endymion Porter, for which Davenant supplied an Epilogue.

Somewhat to the company's surprise, *The Villain* enjoyed a successful run, playing to full houses for ten days, and was given a command performance at Court on 1 January 1667.

Thomas Betterton married Mary Saunderson on Christmas Eve 1662. This must have relieved some of the pressure on the Davenant household. The bride had been one of four actresses who had lodged with the Davenants since the opening of the Duke's Playhouse – another, Hester Davenport, was tricked into a sham marriage by the Earl of Oxford, who then abandoned her with his child; Pepys deeply regretted the loss of the 'first Roxolana' while Davenant coached her replacement, Mary Norton.

Lady Mary Davenant bore Sir William nine sons between 1656 and 1668, in addition to which the Davenants took in a future star of the stage, Elizabeth Barry (*b.* 1658), when her family lost all its wealth. There would have been servants, too. The house beside the theatre must have been bedlam at times.

And there were problems with the company: Henry Harris, one of Davenant's leading actors, was creating difficulties. Pepys heard about this from a shoemaker in Fleet Street. Harris had grown 'very proud of late'. He demanded an extra £20 – 'more than Betterton or any body else' – for every new play and £10 for revivals. Davenant refused, and Harris 'swore he would never act there more'. Harris was almost certainly hoping to join Killigrew's company, their new Theatre Royal having opened in May 1663. But Davenant appealed to the king, who forbade Harris from defecting to the rival theatre.

Pepys was back at the shoemaker's on 24 October, where he heard that the Duke of York had brokered a truce: 'Harris is come again to Sir W. Davenant upon his terms that he demanded, which will make him very high and proud.'

Shortly after Henry Harris walked out on him, Davenant staged one of his most technically ambitious productions. The gentry usually left London for the summer vacation, leaving the citizens in search of entertainment. Davenant provided it in August 1663 in the form of a variety piece, *The Play-House to be Let*.

The Prologue set out to tease:

> *A teeming Muse big with imagination,*
> *Conceiv'd a Monster of so new a fashion*
> *That of the hasty birth, b'ing brought to Bed,*
> *We found it neither had a Tail or Head.*

The first act consisted of a player and housekeeper interviewing a succession of characters eager to hire the empty theatre. A 'Monsieur' wishes to put on a French farce. Two 'very hot Fencers' want to rent the space 'to teach the Art of Duel'. A musician, who hopes to hire the venue for a 'Heroique story / In *Stile Recitativo*', is told 'There is another Play-house to let in *Vere-Street*' – Tom Killigrew's old theatre then being dark.

A dancing-master wants to present 'Historical dancing'. John of Leiden, the Anabaptist of Münster, wishes to hire the turban, sceptre and throne of Solyman the Magnificent so that he might 'reign / This long Vacation over all the dominions / In *Portugall-Row*' (the player refuses to hear him: 'He was an Enemy / To the exil'd Comicks'). Finally, a poet offers 'Romances travesti … In Verse Burlesque.'

This opening act was probably performed on the forestage, in front of the curtain which now opened to reveal an interior setting: the house of Sganarelle, the self-deceived husband of Molière's *Le Cocu imaginaire*. The farce had been loosely translated by Davenant – possibly with the help of his French wife – and, in a jibe at the Comédiens de Mademoiselle d'Orléans who had recently performed at the Drury Lane Cockpit, was delivered in ludicrous accents:

Sganarelle: Vat does see consider vit so muche attention.
   Dis Picture speake no good ting to min honeur;
   I feel de little horne on mi bro.

The farce ended with a song and dance. The player and the housekeeper returned to the forestage to introduce the next item, a revamped version of Davenant's *The History of Sir Francis Drake*, sung in operatic recitative.

The curtain opened again to reveal a busy harbour in Peru, the whole prospect seen 'through a Wood, differing from those of European Climats, by representing of Coco-Trees, Pines, and Palmitos. And on the Boughs of other Trees are seen Munkies, Apes, and Parrots.' There were several scene changes, each accompanied by music, in this act alone. The spectacular settings ranged from 'a Rockie Country' peopled by slaves to 'the rising of the Sun through a thick Wood, and *Venta-Cruz* at a great distance on the South side.' The latter 'suddenly changed into the former prospect of the rising of the Morning … but about the Middle, it is vary'd with the discovery of a Beautiful Lady ty'd to a Tree, adorn'd with the Ornaments of a Bride, with her hair dishevel'd, and complaining, with her hands towards Heaven'. Just as suddenly, the scene changed again, 'where the Lady is vanisht, and nothing appears but that Prospect which was in the beginning'.

The next act was another Davenant revival – *The Cruelty of the Spaniards in Peru*. A Priest of the Sun, 'cloth'd in a garment of Feathers', described the history of the Incas, their conquest by the Spaniards and rescue by the English, with songs and dances. The eye-popping scenery included 'a dark Prison at great distance' in which 'the *Spaniards* are tormenting the Natives and *English* Mariners'. Two Spaniards were discovered, 'the one turning a Spit, whilst the other is basting an *Indian* Prince, which is rosted at an artificial fire.'

For the final act, the scene shifted to Egypt for a burlesque rendition of the Antony and Cleopatra story in mock-heroic couplets:

Ptolomy:	Most puissant Plund'rer! know the short and long is,
	That all who know thee, find thy breath so strong is,
	As meerly with a word it quells the mighty,
	And stuns them past the cure of *Aqua-vitae.*

The Play-House to be Let was an oddity, a theatrical 'Monster' designed to thrill the holiday crowd with its blend of farce and opera, high action and low comedy. It also gave Davenant a chance to show off the scenic possibilities of his theatre and inspire the novice playwrights. *The Play-House* certainly prompted the Duke of Buckingham to start work on his own burlesque, satirising Davenant and his pretensions – but as *The Rehearsal* did not reach the stage until 1671 it was Davenant's successor, John Dryden, who caught the sting of Buckingham's mockery.

Sir William's next production was a grandiose revival of Shakespeare and Fletcher's *Henry the Eighth*. Davenant spared no expense, the prompter Downes remarking that the play 'by Order of Sir *William Davenant*, was all new Cloath'd in proper Habits':

The part of the King was so right and justly done by Mr. *Betterton*, he being Instructed in it by Sir *William*, who had it from Old Mr. *Lowen*, that had his Instructions from Mr. *Shakespear* himself.

It is doubtful that Shakespeare had been much involved with the original production of *Henry VIII* at the Globe, which took place two years into his retirement. But it is telling that, once again, Davenant had taken pains to preserve the traditions established by his godfather.

The Rivals – Davenant's adaptation of *The Two Noble Kinsmen*, another play attributed jointly to Shakespeare and John Fletcher – ran for nine days in September 1664. John Downes later remembered that 'all the Womens Parts [were] admirably Acted', perhaps none more so than that of Celania, 'a Sheperdess being Mad for Love; especially in Singing several Wild and Mad Songs. *My Lodging it is on the Cold Ground*, &c.' The lovely Moll Davis played the part 'so Charmingly, that not long after, it Rais'd her from Bed on the Cold Ground, to a Bed Royal.' It also earned her a ring worth several hundreds of pounds and a fully-furnished house in Suffolk Street, courtesy of the enamoured king.

On Saturday, 5 November 1664 Samuel Pepys saw Davenant's production of *Macbeth*, 'a pretty good play, but admirably acted.' The three witches entered flying, their cave and cauldron 'sinking' into the Underworld, and a 'Machine' descended to pick up Hecate. Sir William made substantial alterations to his godfather's text to bring it closer to the neoclassical ideal. The parts of Lord and Lady Macduff – played by Henry Harris and Jane Long – were expanded to provide a Royalist counterpart to the regicidal Macbeths (Thomas and Mary Betterton). The plot was streamlined, the dialogue simplified, to focus the tragedy on the pertinent topic of '*Ambition*':

La. Macd: Ambition urg'd him to that bloudy deed:

May you be never by Ambition led:

Forbid it Heav'n, that in revenge you shou'd

Follow a Copy that is writ in bloud.

It would have been difficult not to see Macbeth's 'bloudy deed', his murderous usurpation of the throne, as a reflection of the parliamentary rebellion against King Charles I.

Davenant's 'alter'd' *Macbeth* was a huge success, 'it being all Excellently perform'd', wrote John Downes, 'it Recompenc'd double the Expence'. Pepys saw it at least nine times – once when King Charles and the Duke of York were there, the king with his beautiful mistress, Lady Castlemaine, but still making eyes at Moll Davis in one of the upper boxes – and thought it 'one of the best plays for a stage, and variety of dancing and music, that ever I saw'. Even in 1708 it proved 'still a lasting Play' and would remain the standard until David Garrick returned to something approaching Shakespeare's original in 1744.

Sir William meddled a lot less with *King Lear*, which was '*Acted* exactly as Mr. *Shakespear* Wrote it' and would have to wait for Nahun Tate's notoriously happy ending to be added in 1681.

Meanwhile, disaster loomed.

War had been simmering with the Dutch, leading Davenant's witches to toss 'a fat *Dutchman*'s Chawdron [entrails]' into their cauldron. James, Duke of York, sent forces to seize Dutch assets in West Africa and America, including the settlement of New Amsterdam, which the English renamed after the duke. But trade with the 'Hollanders' continued. Cotton bales were still being brought to London in ships from old Amsterdam, where the bubonic plague had claimed more than 50,000 lives.

Through the early months of 1665 the number of burials in the parishes of St Giles in the Fields, St Andrew Holborn, St Clement Danes and others steadily mounted. Red painted crosses began to appear on locked and guarded doors, along with the words 'Lord have mercy upon us'.

On Monday, 5 June 1665, the theatres were closed by order of the Crown.

4

His Exit

The theatres were closed whenever the weekly number of plague deaths exceeded forty. Two days after the Lord Chamberlain ordered the closure, Samuel Pepys noticed 'two or three houses marked with a red cross upon the doors' in Drury Lane.

By the end of June the Lord Mayor and aldermen of the City of London had published a series of orders 'concerning the Infection of the Plague'. The 'master of every house, as soon as any one in his house complaineth, either of blotch or purple, or swelling in any part of his body' was required to inform the local examiner of health within two hours. If the plague was confirmed, the entire household would be locked in together for a month. The dead, collected in carts, were buried at night.

'In August, how dreadful is the increase!' wrote Thomas Vincent, Puritan author of *God's Terrible Voice in the City*, who lost seven members of his household to the contagion. The epidemic peaked in the week of 17 September, when 7,000 deaths were recorded. The streets were so quiet by then that grass grew in the main thoroughfare of Whitehall.

It is not known whether Davenant and his family remained in London or escaped, following the Court, perhaps, to Oxford, where the tavern in which Sir William had grown up was now in the hands of one William Morrell.[1] The Court had moved to Oxford in July. The king's beautiful mistress, Lady Castlemaine, presented Charles II with yet another bastard, born in Oxford, on 28 December. But the king was obsessed with the long-legged and defiantly virtuous Frances Stewart, who resisted his advances. King Charles commissioned a medal, commemorating victories in the Dutch War, with 'La Belle Stewart' as a helmeted, trident-wielding Britannia on the reverse. Her image would grace British coins for more than 300 years.

The cold weather brought a respite from the plague. The king returned to Whitehall on 1 February 1666, but the theatres were still closed, and they remained so for Sir William Davenant's 60th birthday later that month.

Tom Killigrew made the most of the extended closure. After dinner on 19 March, Pepys walked 'to the King's play-house, all in dirt, they being altering of the stage to make it wider.' This would give the Theatre Royal an advantage over Davenant's narrow stage – although, as Pepys exclaimed, 'God knows when they will begin to act again.' The diarist wanted to inspect 'the inside of the stage and all the tiring-rooms and machines':

> and what a mixture of things there was; here a wooden-leg, there a ruff, here a hobbyhorse, there a crown, would make a man split himself to see with laughing [...] But then again, to think how fine they show on the stage by candle-light, and how poor things they are to look now too near hand, is not pleasant at all.

Killigrew's new stage machinery was 'fine', the scene paintings 'very pretty'. Pepys declared himself 'mightily satisfied in my curiosity'.

There were more plague-related deaths in 1666, though nothing on the scale of the previous year's outbreak. And then, early in the morning of Sunday, 2 September, a baker's shop caught fire in Pudding Lane. The easterly wind fanned the flames.

As recently as April, King Charles had written to the City authorities, expressing his fears about the fire hazard posed by London's crowded tenements. Wooden 'jetties' projected from the upper storeys, so that opposing structures almost met above the dismal passageways, increasing the risk that fire could spread between the buildings. The Great Fire of 1666 leapt greater distances than these. On Tuesday, 4 September, Ludgate Hill became a torrent of flame. Even Westminster and Whitehall were threatened. St Paul's Cathedral went up, the great sheet of lead on its roof completely melting.

John Dryden would picture the fire as a Cromwellian 'Usurper':

> Such was the rise of this prodigious fire,
>   Which in mean buildings first obscurely bred,
> From thence did soon to open streets aspire,
>   And straight to Palaces and Temples spread.

As with the earlier rebellion, the king and the Duke of York battled with the chaos. The royal brothers spent the Tuesday directing the firefighting efforts, carrying water and encouraging labourers to pull down vulnerable buildings, until the king's face was black with soot. The Great Fire came to an end the next day. More than 13,000 houses had been destroyed. London was a charred and smoking ruin.

Rumours spread as quickly as the flames. The Privy Council concluded that the inferno was caused by nothing other than 'the hand of God, a great wind and a very dry season' and King Charles assured a crowd of homeless Londoners on 6 September that there had been no conspiracy. But decades of propaganda had made Catholics the natural suspects in any disaster. When, in the 1670s, a 202ft column of Portland stone was erected to commemorate the Great Fire, a Latin inscription on its north side explained that the conflagration had consumed 89 churches and 400 streets. In 1681, new words were added: 'But Popish frenzy, which wrought such horrors, is not yet quenched.' This slur was not removed until 1830.

The theatres reopened in November, eighteen months after their precautionary closure, and then only after large donations to charity had been promised. The mood was alarmist. Pepys saw none of the traditional bonfires on 5 November, 'which is strange, and speaks the melancholy disposition of the City at present, while never more was said of, and feared of, and done against the Papists than just at this time.' He had unnerved himself by reading Francis Potter's *Interpretation of the Number 666*, an excitable thesis – published in 1642 – which ignited the scare that Catholics would commit widespread slaughter on or around 10 November 1666.

Things calmed down, and by April 1667 Sir William was presenting a 'corrected and enlarged' version of *The Wits*, which Pepys felt 'had much wit in it'. *The Wits* was performed at Court in May, followed by a command performance of *The Siege of Rhodes* at Davenant's theatre.

Theatrical production stopped again in June. For the third time in two years the capital was thrown into a panic. A fog bank blew away on 6 June[2] to reveal Dutch warships sailing into the mouth of the River Thames. A fort on the Isle of Sheppey was attacked. On 12 June a Dutch squadron advanced up the Medway and captured several ships, including the *Royal Charles* which had brought the king over from Holland in 1660. The English scuttled thirty of their own ships to prevent them falling into enemy hands. Wealthy Londoners fled yet again as the Dutch taskforce laid waste to the Chatham dockyards. The Hollanders then withdrew but continued to harass the coastal ports. They seemed to be everywhere: 'By God, I think the Devil shits Dutchmen', cried Pepys's colleague, Sir William Batten.

The raid brought an end to the second Anglo-Dutch War. It also marked the end of the king's honeymoon period.

The licentiousness of the Court – and King Charles in particular – had provoked comment, although criticism of the bed-hopping monarch was also prompted by concerns about the place of women in society. Like those actresses who appeared on the public stage, the king's 'whores' were emblematic of a new era: sensual, extravagant and acquisitive. Women such as Aphra Behn, Katherine Philips and Margaret Cavendish, Duchess of Newcastle, were expressing themselves.

Actresses were routinely exploited, onstage and off. The popularity of 'breeches roles' owed much to the snug fit of male clothing and the inevitable revelation of the wearer's sex. In *The Rival Ladies*, John Dryden had two actresses, disguised as boys, undressing for bed and discovering that they each have 'Two swelling Breasts!' *The Rival Ladies* was performed by the King's Company in August 1664, shortly before Killigrew staged an all-female production of his bawdy comedy, *The Parson's Wedding*.

The Restoration actress challenged conventions. Dryden's *Secret Love*, in which the king took a proprietary interest, was performed early in 1667 at the Theatre Royal. The part of Florinell was written for Nell Gwyn, who bantered her way to a refreshingly equitable pre-nuptial agreement with Charles Hart's Celadon. It was played for laughs, but Nell's Florinell easily proved herself a match for her man.

Griping about the king's adulteries – with Nell, amongst others – was another way of complaining that women were being both seen *and* heard.

When King Charles declared war on 4 March 1665, he caught up with the popular anti-Dutch sentiment. But after the devastations of plague, fire and the raid on the Medway, the public mood turned against the king.

There would have to be a sacrifice.

Davenant had a tenuous connection to his successor as poet laureate. Sir William's great-grandfather had a brother whose granddaughter, Judith, married twice, the second time to Dr Thomas Fuller, Rector of Aldwinkle St Peter's in Northamptonshire. Judith Fuller died in 1632, a year after John Dryden was born in the rectory of the sister parish of Aldwinkle All Saints.

Dryden was mostly associated with the King's Company, his marriage to the sister of Sir Robert Howard bringing him into Killigrew's extended family. 15 August 1667, however, saw the premiere of Dryden's *Sir Martin Mar-all* at the Duke's Playhouse. The theatre was packed; Samuel Pepys could not get a seat. Three months later, on 7 November, Pepys attended the opening of another play – 'the most innocent play that ever I saw' – at the Duke's. Again, the house was full, with the king in attendance. The play was a new adaptation of Shakespeare's *The Tempest*.

'*The Tempest, or The Enchanted Island. A Comedy*' was published in 1670, with a Preface by John Dryden, who wrote that it had been Davenant's idea to add a 'Counterpart to *Shakespear*'s Plot, namely, that of a Man who had never seen a Woman … This excellent contrivance he was pleas'd to communicate to me, and to desire my assistance in it. I confess that from the very first moment it so pleas'd me, that I never writ anything with more delight.'

Dryden penned the main plot of the adaptation. Prospero, the rightful Duke of Milan, had been cast away fifteen years earlier with his young daughters and a boy – Hippolito, the heir to the dukedom of Mantua – whom Prospero has raised in seclusion. Hippolito is the 'Man who had never seen a Woman', and because Prospero's daughter Miranda is destined to fall in love with Ferdinand, heir to the dukedom of Savoy, another daughter was provided: Dorinda, who has never seen a man.

The naivety of the marooned youngsters offered ample scope for comedy:

Miranda:	But, Sister, I have stranger news to tell you;
	[…] shortly we may chance to see that thing,
	Which you have heard my Father call, a Man.
Dorinda:	But what is that? for yet he never told me.
Miranda:	I know no more than you: but I have heard
	My Father say we Women were made for him.
Dorinda:	What, that he should eat us Sister?
Miranda:	No sure, you see my Father is a man, and yet
	He does us good. I would he were not old.
	[…]

Dorinda:	But pray how does it come that we two […] have not Beards like him?
Miranda:	Now I confess you pose me.
Dorinda:	How did he come to be our Father too?
Miranda:	I think he found us when we both were little, and grew within the ground.

According to Dryden, it was Davenant who supplied the subplot: 'The Comical parts of the Saylors were also his invention, and for the most part his writing, as you will easily discover by the style.' This included the flurry of nautical expressions in the opening scene, which were meant to impress King Charles and his brother James, who loved to race their yachts against each other.

The shipwrecked mariners bicker over which of them shall be 'duke' of the desert isle. Mustacho and Ventuso quarrel when the ship's master, Stephano, offers to make them both his viceroy (*Stephano*: 'Hold, loving Subjects: we will have no Civil war during our Reign'). Trincalo enters half-drunk and takes umbrage at the fact that Stephano has been elected duke 'in a full Assembly':

Mustacho:	Art thou mad *Trincalo*, wilt thou disturb a settled Government? […]
Trincalo:	I'll have no Laws.
Ventuso:	Then Civil War begins.

Trincalo is declared a rebel. He then encounters Prospero's indigenous slave, Caliban, and vows to marry Caliban's monstrous sister, so that he can 'lay claim to this Island by Alliance'.

The absurd 'civil war' between the sailors and the natives, led by a drunkard, allowed Davenant to satirise the anarchy which ensued when Parliament rebelled against Charles I. At a time when support for Charles II was on the wane, Sir William reminded the audience that 'proud Ambition' dwelt in 'the lowest Rooms of Hell', supported by 'Grim Deaths and Scarlet Murthers'.

John Dryden's admirers have often sought to distance him from 'this perversion of Shakespeare', preferring to blame Davenant, whom Dryden admitted had acted as script editor:

It had perhaps been easie enough for me to have arrogated more to my self than was my due in the writing of this Play, and to have pass'd by his name with silence in the publication of it, with the same ingratitude which others have us'd to him, whose Writings he hath not only corrected […] but has had a greater inspection over them, and sometimes added whole Scenes together, which may as easily be distinguish'd from the rest, as true Gold from counterfeit.

Sir Walter Scott, editing *The Works of John Dryden* in 1808, observed that Davenant's 'ludicrous contest betwixt the sailors, for the dukedom and viceroyship of a barren island, gave much amusement at the time, and some of the expressions were long after proverbial.'

There was more than just a scenic backdrop to *The Tempest*. Storms had been brewing in the state. A faction, spearheaded by the king's mistress, Lady Castlemaine, and championed by such courtier playwrights as Sir Robert Howard and the Duke of Buckingham, worked tirelessly to undermine the Lord Chancellor, Davenant's old friend and sometime roommate, Edward Hyde, 1st Earl of Clarendon. The king, reeling from the disasters of the Great Fire and the Dutch Raid, and embittered by the elopement of his beloved Frances Stewart, connived in making Clarendon a scapegoat.

On the morning of 26 August the recently widowed Lord Chancellor was summarily dismissed. Samuel Pepys described how Lady Castlemaine rose from her bed in Whitehall and ran in her nightdress to her aviary, 'joying herself at the old man's going away'. Passing through the garden, Clarendon turned and said, 'O madam, is it you? Pray remember that if you live, you will grow old' – a theatrical moment.

On the night of 30 November, three weeks after *The Tempest* premiered, Lord Clarendon took ship for France, becoming an exiled Prospero in his own right.

An era was ending. London was being rebuilt under the supervision of His Majesty's Surveyor of Works, Sir Christopher Wren. Henry Jermyn was creating his exclusive St James's Square development, the model for the West End, on forty-five acres north of Pall Mall, while Davenant and Killigrew had established the pattern for West End theatre, their patents eventually founding the Royal Opera House and Theatre Royal. But the Civil War heroes were fading away, displaced by a cynical, insatiable generation.

On Thursday, 26 March 1668 King Charles attended a performance of Davenant's latest play, *The Man's the Master*.

Davenant had taken a French comedy – Paul Scarron's *Jodelet, ou le Maître valet* – and turned it into a Restoration tragicomedy. Don John and his manservant, Jodelet, arrive in Madrid to woo Isabella, the daughter of Don Ferdinand, who instead of receiving a portrait of Don John has been mistakenly sent one of Jodelet. The sight of a man leaping from Isabella's balcony causes Don John to swap places with his servant in order to test Isabella's virtue. Meanwhile, Don John's sister has come to Don Ferdinand's house, seeking the man who promised her marriage but then killed her brother. That man is Don Ferdinand's nephew, Don Lewis, who is also in love with Isabella.

There was plentiful comedy in Davenant's production, with Jodelet crudely acting the part of his master to the dismay of Don Ferdinand's household, but the shadow of tragedy hovered over the piece – at least until Don John revealed that his brother was not killed by Don Lewis but was secretly restored to life by a surgeon. This theme of death-and-resurrection was a recurring motif in Davenant's later work. In *The Tempest*, Ferdinand slays Hippolito in a duel; Prospero swears to execute justice on Ferdinand, only for Ariel to announce that Hippolito has been miraculously cured. Likewise, in *The Law against Lovers*, Claudio – believed to have been beheaded – is then shown to be alive. It is impossible to detach this motif from the anguish of the king's execution and the subsequent relief of the king's restoration.

The notion that the father could be revived as the son appealed to Davenant. What might look like Royalist propaganda was also a personal testament, for if there was a prevailing myth in Davenant's life it was that a martyred father had been resurrected. The Restoration struck such a deep chord because it reflected his self-image. Like Charles II, Davenant was his own genetic father, reborn.

It seems fitting, then, that a command performance of *The Man's the Master* was given at Davenant's theatre on Shakespeare's birthday, 23 April 1668, although Davenant was not around to see it. Pepys had attended the first performance on 26 March and 'found the King and his company did think meanly of it, though there was here and there something pretty'. The diarist saw 'the latter part' of the play again on Friday, 3 April.

On 7 April Pepys went to Drury Lane to see *The English Mounsieur* by James Howard. He nipped backstage afterwards to flirt with the actress Elizabeth Knepp. It was then that he heard 'Sir W. Davenant is just now dead'.

The next day, Pepys saw *The Unfortunate Lovers* at Davenant's playhouse ('no extraordinary play, methinks'), and the day after he watched as the hackney coaches gathered in Portugal Street. Sir William's body was transported to Westminster Abbey, the 'whole Company attending his Funerall' – as John Downes remembered – but no laureate's wreath on his coffin.

An anonymous poem 'Upon the Death of Sr WILLIAM DAVENANT' soon appeared in print:

> If those Great *Heroes* of the Stage, whose Wit
> Swells to a wonder here, shall think it fit,
> When *Poet Lawreat*'s dead, that he should ly
> Twelve days, or more, without an *Elegie*:
> I that am less presume to undertake,
> A short Memorial for their Credits sake

The poet imagined Davenant 'encircled in a Sphere / Of those Great Souls who once admir'd him here':

> First, *Johnson* doth demand a share in him,
> For both their Muses w[hip']d the Vice of time:
> Then *Shakespear* next a brothers part doth claim,
> Because their quick inventions were the same.

The 'Experience'd *Davenant*' was irreplaceable: 'Now thou (Great Soul) art gone, who shall maintain / The Learned Issue of thy pregnant Brain?'

> Such were his virtues that they could command
> A General Applause from every hand
> His *Exit* then this on Record shall have,
> A *Clap* did usher *Davenant* to his Grave

Leslie Hotson, who reproduced this elegy in *The Commonwealth and Restoration Stage* (1928), considered the 'low jest in the last line … an egregious example of Restoration bad taste.' But Hotson might have missed something. Davenant's '*Exit*' was sudden: he dropped dead without warning.

Syphilitic aortitis is the commonest complication of cardiovascular syphilis. The main artery from the heart becomes enlarged, its walls growing weaker, until eventually a rupture occurs. The resulting internal haemorrhage sends the body into shock. Death quickly follows.

John Aubrey would report that Davenant 'got a terrible clap … which cost him his nose' in 1630. Thirty-eight years later, in its tertiary stage, the disease perhaps caused a fatal aortic aneurysm – in which case it was indeed a '*Clap*' that ushered Davenant to his Poets' Corner grave.

But this does not explain the reticence of his fellow poets. The anonymous author of the 'Elegy' stated that Davenant was 'Admir'd by all, envied alone by those / Who for his Glories made themselves his foes'. John Dryden would mention the 'ingratitude' of those whose scripts Davenant had improved, for which he received no credit – '*(there being nothing so base as to rob the dead of his reputation)*'. And then there is Pepys's remark that 'the King and his company did think meanly' of *The Man's the Master* when they saw it less than two weeks before Davenant died. Pepys later decided that it was 'a very good play', but the first performance seems to have gone sour, as if a powerful faction had turned against the poet laureate.

The 62-year-old Davenant was closely associated with the old order represented by the disgraced Earl of Clarendon. King Charles – nudging 40 and still no legitimate heir – was happy with his compliant mistresses and his dreams of building a new Rome in the ashes of old London: he no longer wished to be reminded of the past.

Sir William's widow contrived to keep his estate out of the hands of his creditors. Lady Mary named John Alway as the 'principal creditor' but Davenant's stepson, Thomas Cross, dismissed Alway as 'an absurd person of no residence'. As late as 1684, Cross – who served as the company's accountant until he was replaced by Davenant's son, Alexander, in 1675 – was complaining that 'all things were so secretly transacted' between John Alway, Lady Mary and her eldest son that he 'could not discover what personal Estate' of Sir William came into the hands of his widow. By making the elusive Alway the 'principal creditor' Lady Mary had ensured that her husband's estate remained intact.

Charles, the eldest son of Sir William and Lady Mary, was no more than 12 when his father died. While Lady Mary managed the company as Charles's guardian, artistic direction was entrusted to Thomas Betterton and Henry Harris. Before long, plans were afoot to build a new playhouse, larger and more luxurious than the converted tennis court in Lincoln's Inn Fields.

Davenant had probably been planning a better home for his company; perhaps it was he who had chosen the 'Garden Plot behind Salisbury House in the Strand' as a suitable site. Led by Betterton, the company settled on a part of Dorset Garden overlooking the River Thames. The sharers in the company agreed to raise £3,000 (the final cost was nearer £9,000) and a 39-year lease of the site was made over to Davenant's brother Nicholas and stepson, Thomas Cross, to be held in trust for Lady Mary, the principal shareholder.

The new Duke's Theatre was to be the most magnificent playhouse yet built in Britain. Twice the size of the old Duke's Playhouse, it boasted a deep porch at the front and columns supporting two upper stories, in one of which Betterton had his own apartment. Inside, a central pit formed an amphitheatre surrounded by two

The Duke's Theatre,
Dorset Garden.

tiers of seven boxes and an upper gallery to which servants were sometimes admitted for free. Behind the wide forestage and the proscenium, with its ornate carvings by Grinling Gibbons, the scenic stage was 50ft (15m) deep and 30ft (9m) high.

The new theatre opened on 9 November 1671 with a revival of Dryden's comedy *Sir Martin Mar-all*. Soon afterwards, on 25 January 1672, a fire started under the stairs at the back of the Theatre Royal, destroying half of the building and several other properties on Drury Lane. The King's Company moved into Davenant's old playhouse in Lincoln's Inn Fields while Tom Killigrew tried to raise funds. He appealed to the company's patron for a subsidy. King Charles ordered a collection from all the parish churches in England in 1673 to pay for the rebuilding of the Theatre Royal.

Also in 1673, Lady Mary published *The Works of Sr William D'avenant Kt* with her own dedicatory epistle to 'His Royal Highness' James, Duke of York. Lady Mary humbly begged the duke to 'Protect the Works of her Deceased Husband from the Envy and Malice of this Censorious Age':

> *I have often heard (and I have some reason to believe) that your Royal Father, of Ever Blessed Memory, was not displeased with his Writings; That your most Excellent Mother did Graciously take him into her Family; That she was often diverted by him, and as often smil'd upon his Endeavours; I am sure he made it the whole Study and Labor of the latter part of his Life, to entertain His Majesty, and your Royal Highness, and I hope he did it successfully.*

The book was sold by Henry Herringman from his shop in the New Exchange. Herringman had entered a collection of Davenant's 'Maskes, Playes and Poems' at Stationers' Hall in August 1667, when Sir William was still very much alive.[3] He now added his own foreword, explaining that Davenant 'was *Poet Laureat* to two Great Kings' and had often expressed his 'great Desire' to see his works in '*One Volume*'. Accordingly, Herringman had brought together many of Davenant's poems along with '*Sixteen Plays*, whereof *Six* were never before Printed.'

Not included were Davenant's adaptations of Shakespeare, other than *The Law against Lovers*. One text that would have been interesting to see was a version of Shakespeare's *Cardenio*. Lewis Theobald, who produced his own adaptation of *Cardenio*, entitled *Double Falshood; Or, The Distrest Lovers*, at Drury Lane in 1727, claimed to have a sixty-year-old copy of the original 'in the Handwriting of Mr. *Downes*, the famous Old Prompter' and that this was 'early in the Possession of the celebrated Mr. *Betterton*, and by Him design'd to have been usher'd into the World.'

Lewis Theobald had also received a manuscript copy from a 'Noble Person' who informed him that Shakespeare wrote *Cardenio* during his retirement as a 'Present of Value' for a 'Natural Daughter of his'. This raises the possibility that Davenant, who liked to be thought of as Shakespeare's son, had planned to produce a 'lost' play written by Shakespeare for the financial benefit of another love child.

Lady Mary handed nominal control of the theatre company over to her eldest son, Charles Davenant, in 1673. In May 1677 the company performed his version of *Circe*, 'an Opera', with its spectacular last act showing a city on fire and 'thunder and lightning here'. That same year, Charles inherited his father's patent and shares in the company. He found a marriage partner in the form of Frances, of the famous Molins family of surgeons, whose father lived close by the Duke's Theatre in Salisbury Court. Before he married her, though, he purchased a lucrative post as Commissioner of the Excise, which he held until 1689.

Charles Davenant had gone up to Balliol College, Oxford, but left without taking his degree. He was later awarded an LL.D. ('Doctor of Laws') and sat as MP for St Ives in Cornwall in James II's first parliament; he was also made Master of the Revels by King James – formerly the Duke of York – a post he again held until 1689, when the Catholic James had been deposed in favour of William of Orange. Thereafter, Charles's chief interest lay in political economy. He published a series of influential papers between 1694 and 1712 and is credited with being the first to recognise the importance of balance of trade.

Doctor Davenant died intestate, like his father, on 7 November 1714. Of Sir William's other surviving sons from his third marriage: William studied at Magdalen Hall, Oxford, where he translated François de La Mothe Le Vayer's *Jugement sur les anciens et principaux historiens grecs et latins*[4] and gained his master's degree in 1680; he drowned while swimming in the River Seine in 1681. Alexander absconded to the Canary Islands in 1693, having taken over from Thomas Cross as treasurer to Davenant's company and defrauded several shareholders. Thomas Davenant was appointed manager of the theatre company by Alexander in 1688 and died in Hertfordshire ten years later. Richard served as page to the Duke of Monmouth (an illegitimate son of King Charles II) and then fought under King William before dying in June 1745, aged 78. George was buried at St Martin-in-the-Fields on 19 March 1710. Their mother, Lady Mary Davenant, was laid to rest in the old vault of St Bride's, Fleet Street, on 24 February 1691.

It was Thomas Betterton who really inherited Sir William's mantle. He ran the Duke's Company with Charles Davenant, and when the mismanaged King's Company collapsed under the weight of its debts in 1682 Betterton took a lead role in the United Company, formed by merging the two companies.

Betterton had bought a portrait of Shakespeare which was sold after Davenant's death. The actor told Robert Keck, a lawyer, that the portrait 'was painted by John Taylor' – possibly a confused recollection of Joseph Taylor, the actor who joined Shakespeare's company after the death of Richard Burbage in 1619 – '& this John Taylor in his will left it Sir William Davenant' (this was reported by George Vertue, a reliable witness, in 1719). A copy of the portrait was made by Sir Godfrey Kneller for John Dryden, who hung it in his study:

Shakspeare, thy gift I place before my sight;
With awe I ask his blessing as I write

When Betterton died, intestate, on 28 April 1710 the portrait was bought by Robert Keck, from whom it descended to James Brydges, 3rd Duke of Chandos. Now known as the 'Chandos' portrait, the painting was sold in 1848 to the Earl of Ellesmere, who presented it to the National Portrait Gallery on its opening in 1856.

Davenant had therefore owned one of the best-known portraits of William Shakespeare. He might also have commissioned a lesser-known image of the Bard.

The King's Company, under Tom Killigrew, made use of Davenant's old Lincoln's Inn Fields theatre when their playhouse burned down, returning to the rebuilt 'Theatre Royal in Drury Lane' in 1674. The former Duke's Playhouse was then converted back into a tennis court, until the United Company split and Betterton acquired a licence to form a separate company. Lisle's Tennis Court was renovated, opening as a theatre again in April 1695. In 1714 it was demolished to make way for a new playhouse, and it was here that John Gay's hit, *The Beggar's Opera*, was first performed in January 1728 – Lewis Theobald's adaptation of Shakespeare's *Cardenio* having opened at the Theatre Royal five weeks earlier. The success of *The Beggar's Opera* paid for a grand new theatre to be built in Covent Garden. The Lincoln's Inn Theatre finally closed in December 1732.

Davenant's old playhouse then became a barracks, an auction room and a warehouse for Spode china before it was pulled down in 1848.

William Clift was the 'conservator' of the collection of scientific papers and specimens belonging to the Scottish surgeon John Hunter, which were kept at the Royal College of Surgeons in Lincoln's Inn Fields. By 1834, Clift was arguing that more space was needed to house the collection. A couple of neighbouring properties were duly purchased, one of them having belonged to a Mr Dennett.

The Dennett property had previously belonged to Charles Fleetwood, who went on to manage the Theatre Royal in 1733. Like Davenant before him, Fleetwood had lodged next door to the Lincoln's Inn Theatre. It was whilst inspecting this property that William Clift noticed two busts placed high up in the wall of the house. He wrote to the owner, Mr Dennett, asking permission to remove the busts.

One of them did not survive – Clift blamed this on the workmen. The other was covered with layers of paint, which Clift stripped away. He had recognised the subjects straightaway. The bust which was destroyed had depicted Ben Jonson. The other, which Clift exhibited at Kensington Palace on 10 May 1834, was of William Shakespeare.

Clift bequeathed the terracotta bust to his son-in-law, Professor Richard Owen of the British Museum. Owen sold it to the Duke of Devonshire, who presented it to the Garrick Club. It is known as the Davenant Bust. The Garrick Club attributes it to the French sculptor Louis-François Roubiliac, who created a full-length marble statue of Shakespeare for the actor-manager David Garrick in 1758. But while Roubiliac almost certainly restored the bust after he moved to London in 1730, he had no connection to Davenant, who died thirty-five years before Roubiliac was born.

Shortly before the Duke's Theatre opened at Dorset Garden in 1671, Thomas Betterton made a trip to France. When it opened to the public the Duke's Theatre was adorned with busts of the major dramatists – they were mentioned by Thomas d'Urfey in *Collin's Walk Through London and Westminster* (1690):

> Collin saw each box with beauty crown'd,
> And pictures deck the structure round;
> Ben, Shakespear, and the learned rout,
> With noses some, and some without.

John Dryden also referred to these likenesses in a piece he wrote for the opening of the rebuilt Theatre Royal in 1674:

> Though in their House the Poets' Heads appear,
> We hope we may presume their Wits are here.

The Dorset Garden theatre seen from the River Thames.

What became of these 'Heads' is not known. Maybe Betterton took some of them with him in 1695 when he refurbished the Lincoln's Inn Fields theatre.[5] They might even explain his trip to France before the theatre opened in 1671.

Stylistically, the Davenant Bust is reminiscent of the baroque flamboyance of Gian Lorenzo Bernini, who had previously sculpted busts of King Charles I and his queen, Henrietta Maria. More likely, the bust was crafted by Michel Anguier, who had worked with Bernini in Rome and Paris. Anguier was the favourite sculptor of Henrietta Maria's sister-in-law, Anne of Austria, whose apartments in the Louvre he decorated between 1655 and 1657.

If Sir William Davenant had desired a set of 'Poets' Heads' for his company's new theatre, Michel Anguier was the ideal candidate for the job. In 1671, when Thomas Betterton visited France, Anguier became director of the Academie Française and gave a lecture on the relationship between sculpture and architecture. Betterton's French jaunt might have been to collect the busts of Shakespeare, Jonson and others which had been commissioned by Davenant to grace the Duke's Theatre, then under construction.

'Almost all the personal anecdotes about Shakespeare have come down to us from Sir William Davenant,' wrote the Victorian scholar Charles Isaac Elton. One was recorded by Nicholas Rowe in his 1709 edition of *The Works of William Shakespear*. Relating that the Earl of Southampton once made Shakespeare a gift of £1,000 'to enable him to go through with a Purchase which he heard he had a mind to', Rowe admitted that he would have dismissed the tale 'if I had not been assur'd that the Story was handed down by *Sir William D'Avenant*, who was probably very well acquainted with his [Shakespeare's] affairs'.

The advertisement to Bernard Lintott's edition of Shakespeare's *Poems*, also published in 1709, remarked:

> That most learn'd Prince, and great Patron of Learning, King *James* the First was pleas'd with his own Hand to write an amicable letter to Mr. *Shakespeare*; which Letter, tho now lost, remain'd long in the Hands of Sir William D'Avenant, as a credible person now living can testify.

William Oldys, the antiquarian, made a note in his copy of Fuller's *Worthies* that the 'credible person now living' was that great admirer of Shakespeare, John Sheffield (1648–1721), Lord Privy Seal and 1st Duke of Buckingham and Normanby, who was probably the 'Noble Person' who told Lewis Theobald that Shakespeare wrote *Cardenio* as a pecuniary gift for his 'Natural Daughter' – a story he perhaps heard from Davenant.

Thomas Fuller's *History of the Worthies of England* was published in 1662. It incorporated Fuller's description of Ben Jonson and Shakespeare as 'like a Spanish great galleon and an English man-of-war', Jonson being 'built far higher in learning' while Shakespeare was 'lesser in bulk but lighter in sailing'.

Born in the rectory at Aldwinkle St Peter's, Northamptonshire, in 1608, Thomas Fuller never knew Shakespeare and probably never met Jonson. But he might have been informed by a man who had known them both: his third cousin, Sir William Davenant.

Not for nothing did the American scholar, Arthur H. Nethercot, describe Davenant in 1938 as the 'acknowledged custodian of the Shakespeare tradition'.

The trial of King Charles I, Westminster Hall, January 1649.

PART TWO

Revolution

1639 — 1659

5

Davenant the Poet

Discord a malicious Fury, appeares in a storme, and by the Invocation of malignant spirits, proper to her evill use, having already put most of the world into disorder, endeavours to disturbe these parts, envying the blessings and Tranquillity we have long enjoyed.

So began the Subject of the Masque of *Salmacida Spolia*. Performed at the palace of Whitehall on Tuesday, 21 January 1640, it was the last masque Davenant wrote for the Court of King Charles I and Queen Henrietta Maria.

His star had been rising. He had become a 'Servant of the Queen' in 1635 and, three years later, England's second poet laureate.[1] On 26 March 1639 he was awarded a royal patent granting him 'full Power Licence and Authority' to 'erect, new-build and set up … a Theatre or Playhouse … containing in the whole forty yards square at the most, wherein plays, musical entertainments, scenes or other like present-ments, may be presented'. This patent was the basis for his later bid to form a company and open his playhouse in Lincoln's Inn Fields, in competition with Tom Killigrew. For now, though, the intended site was a parcel of ground 'lying near unto or behind the Three Kings Ordinary [diner] in Fleet Street', close to the church where his third wife would one day be buried.

The dimensions specified that, at around 33.5 square metres, Davenant's theatre was to have been the largest in town. The proposed scale of the venue, coupled with the reference in the patent to 'scenes', suggests that he was planning to introduce stage scenery of the sort designed by Inigo Jones for masques at Court – and with which Davenant would delight theatregoers more than two decades later – to the public.

But before he could build his playhouse, Davenant went to war.

King James VI of Scotland became King James I of England on the death of Elizabeth I in 1603. For the first time, 'Great Britain' was ruled by a single sovereign.

James's arrival in London was marred by the number of indigent Scots who followed the Stuart king down from Edinburgh, eager for advancement. After cen-turies of intermittent warfare with the Scots, the English bridled at the sight of so many former enemies receiving perquisites and honours from the newly installed monarch. Worse was that James's queen, Anne of Denmark, had converted to Catholicism, offending both her husband (who preferred the company of male favourites) and the Protestant zealots who dominated the City of London and the Westminster parliaments. The Protestants grew fond of James's eldest son, Henry, who was tall, athletic and puritanically inclined; they were less impressed by the king's second son, Charles, who was small, weak and had difficulty speaking.

Born on 19 November 1600, Charles had a lonely childhood. He suffered from rickets and was considered too sickly to make the journey to London in 1603, so he remained for a year in Dunfermline, learning to walk and 'beginning to speak some words'. King James cared little for his second son, who was also bullied by his elder brother. At the age of 9, Charles wrote to his 'Sweet, sweet brother', Prince Henry, bribing and begging his 'Good brother' to 'love me'. It was a vain hope.

Little by little, Charles learnt to mask his feelings. Years of watching his words gave him a stammer.

A wave of grief burst over the 'godly' – as the Puritans liked to think of themselves – when Prince Henry died of typhoid fever, at the age of 18, on 6 November 1612. The stuttering, stunted, 12-year-old Charles, who would grow to be just over 5ft tall, suddenly became the heir apparent to his father's thrones.

The Stuarts had reigned in Scotland, by and large successfully, since 1371. After 1603, though, they spent as little time as possible in Scotland. Charles was the last of the Stuart monarchs born north of the border. He left his country halfway through his fourth year and did not return until his coronation at Holyroodhouse on 18 June 1633 – more than eight years after he had become King Charles I of England, his father having died on 27 March 1625.

Charles craved order. His father's court had been unruly, pleasure-seeking and corrupt. With his French wife, Henrietta Maria, who was even shorter than he was, King Charles restored decorum to the Court and set a dignified example for the country.

His reforms extended to the Church. In 1633, following the death of the puritanical George Abbott, Charles appointed as Archbishop of Canterbury the scholarly William Laud, a repressed homosexual who saw the altar as 'the greatest place of God's residence on earth' and insisted on it being separated from the rest of the church by railings. The Puritans, who preferred plain communion tables, were appalled.

The Reformation in Scotland had led to the creation of a national Church that was more extreme in its Calvinist principles than its English counterpart. The Scottish Kirk rejected bishops in favour of local elders or 'presbyters'. King Charles demanded an Anglican ceremony for his Scottish coronation. Five days later, at Edinburgh's St Giles Kirk, his chaplains read from the English *Book of Common Prayer* while the Bishop of Moray preached in his episcopal robes – a clear signal that the king supported the Episcopalian hierarchy. In an attempt to impose uniformity of worship Charles then introduced a new version of *The Book of Common Prayer*, written by Scottish bishops with Archbishop Laud's approval, to Scotland. But when the Dean of Edinburgh began to read from the book in St Giles's Cathedral on

Sunday, 23 July 1637, a market trader named Jenny Geddes threw a stool at his head, and riots erupted.

At the end of February the following year a large crowd gathered at Edinburgh's Greyfriars Kirk to sign the National Covenant, committing themselves to upholding the doctrine of Presbyterianism and opposing 'superstitious and papistical rites'. By December, the General Assembly of the Church of Scotland, meeting in Glasgow, had resolved that all bishops should be deposed and the king's prayer book abolished. Scottish soldiers serving overseas came home to join the Covenanters' army under its 'lord general in command', Alexander Leslie, 1st Earl of Leven. A military showdown was looming.

On 27 March 1639, the day after he granted Davenant his patent to set up a playhouse, King Charles marched north. He had mustered an irregular force of some 20,000 men. The elegant poet Sir John Suckling had raised a troop of horse at his own expense. John Aubrey, who probably got his information from Suckling's 'intimate friend' William Davenant, would report that Sir John's 'troop of a hundred very handsome young proper men' was 'clad in white doublets, and scarlet breeches, and scarlet coats, hats and feathers, well hosed and armed' – all of which cost Sucking £12,000 but made little impact on the Scottish militants.

Davenant was also on the march, serving under the king's Master of Ordnance, Mountjoy Blount, 1st Earl of Newport. Blount's wife Anne was the sister of Olivia Porter, whose husband – Davenant's patron, Endymion Porter – was also in the king's train. Four years earlier Anne, Countess of Newport, had performed with her husband in the first of Davenant's elaborate masques for the Court. They would soon appear together in his last.

After a month spent gathering his forces at York the king proceeded via Newcastle to Alnwick in Northumberland. Morale was low: 'our army is but weak', wrote Sir Edmund Verney to his eldest son. 'Our purse is weaker ... Truly here are many brave gentlemen that for point of honour must run such a hazard as truly would grieve any heart but his that does it purposely to ruin them.' Verney blamed the Catholics who, at the queen's behest, had made financial contributions to the king's campaign.

Heavy rain accompanied the troops to the long-disputed border town of Berwick-upon-Tweed. The army made camp to the south of Berwick. About 400 horses were pastured in fields belonging to James Fawcett at Goswick, near Lindisfarne. Fawcett would complain that he had not received the $12d$ per day he was promised for each horse and that 'William Davenant, the pay-master' had accused him of hurting some of the horses when he turned them off his land. A suit was filed against Fawcett for his 'insolent speeches'; he had called Davenant and Lord Newport 'Knaves'.

To the king's dismay, a huge army of Scots appeared across the River Tweed in early June. Urgent peace talks began, with Davenant keeping an anxious Queen Henrietta informed by pigeon post. Sir John Suckling explained to a friend that he could not send regular updates 'unless I had one of Mr Davenants Barbary pigeons (and he now employs them all, he says, himself for the queens use)'.

The First Bishops' War, as it came to be known, ended when the Pacification of Berwick was signed on 18 June.

Back in London, Davenant encountered a problem with his proposed Fleet Street theatre. The king issued an 'Indenture' on 2 October, declaring that the site behind the Three Kings eating-house was 'inconvenient and unfit' and that Davenant 'shall not nor will not' erect a playhouse there or on 'any other parcel of ground lying in or near' the cities and suburbs of London and Westminster without the approval of Thomas Howard, Earl of Arundel.

It is not clear what had gone wrong – although there are grounds for assuming that Davenant's nemesis Sir Henry Herbert, acting Master of the Revels, was behind it all. Davenant vented his annoyance in a poem addressed '*To the Duke of Richmond, in the Year* 1639':

My Lord,
> The Court does seem a Ship, where all are still,
> Busie by office, or imploy'd for skill;
> And active grow through stirring hope or fear:
> For Courts breed stormes, and stormes are lasting there.

He had thought his 'little venture … safely stow'd', only to see it shipwrecked, the 'sheets all rumpled and the Cordage slack', thanks – he implied – to 'Informers':

> On whose distastful mischiefs Pow'r must wink,
> And still endure them active though they stink.

It was against this disgruntled background that *Salmacida Spolia* was presented in the 'King's Masking-House' at Whitehall. Designed by Inigo Jones, with songs and speeches by 'her Majesties Servant', William Davenant, it was reckoned 'the noblest and most ingenuous that hath been done heere in that kinde.'

The title referred to the 'Salmacian spoils, [gained] without bloodshed, without sweat'. The curtain flew up to reveal 'a horrid Sceane … of storme and tempest'. The Earth, transformed into a Fury – 'her hayre upright, mixt with snakes, her body leane wrinkled and of a swarthy colour' – regaled the audience:

> *How am I griev'd, the world should every where*
> *Be vext into a storme, save only here*

She summoned evil spirits to turn the rich greedy and the poor '*apt to obey / The False*':

> *And make Religion to become their vice,*
> *Nam'd, to disguise ambitious Avarice.*

The 'good Genius of Great *Britaine*' then descended with 'Concord' in a silver chariot, lamenting the fate of the wise king Philogenes ('Lover-of-the-Nation') to '*rule in adverse times, / When wisedome must awhile give place to crimes.*'

The 'Peoples folly' was personified by an alchemist who promised to 'cure the defects of nature, and diseases of the mind'. The quack's panaceas encouraged false hopes by offering to right all wrongs, real or imagined, and drew on the latest news-sheets, those precursors to revolution.

A 'Chorus of the beloved people' sang to the Queen Mother, Marie de Médicis, praising her as the sacred source of '*the faire Partner of our Monarchs Throne*' (no mention made of the fact that Marie's enormous retinue was costing the king's purse £3,000 a month), and then King Charles was discovered sitting in the golden Throne of Honour, 'adorned with Palme trees, betweene which stood statues of the ancient Heroes'. The chorus intoned:

> *If it be Kingly patience to out last*
> > *Those stormes the peoples giddy fury rayse,*
> *Till like, fantastick windes themselves they waste,*
> > *The wisedome of that patience is thy prayse.*

A 'huge cloud of various colours' descended, in which were seated Queen Henrietta, 'representing the chiefe Heroin', and her ladies 'in Amazonian habits of carnation, embroidered with silver'. Again, the chorus sang:

> *All that are good, she did inspire!*
> *Lovers are chaste, because they know*
> *It is her will, they should be so;*
> > *The valiant take from her their Fire!*

The Lilliputian king and queen then danced. When the 10-year-old Charles had performed in a masque other children crowded round him to hide his feeble legs. Now, he was surrounded by lords and ladies and lauded by Davenant's theatrical 'Deities':

> *All that are harsh, all that are rude,*
> *Are by your harmony subdu'd;*
> *Yet so, into obedience wrought,*
> *As if not forc'd to it, but taught.*

So reassuring was the message of *Salmacida Spolia* that it was repeated on Shrove Tuesday, the last dance of a glittering Court before that '*malicious Fury*', Discord, turned their world upside down.

King Charles had recalled the Lord Deputy of Ireland, Thomas Wentworth, to help him deal with the Scottish rebels. Created Earl of Strafford in January 1640,

The Banqueting House and Whitehall Palace, 1669.

Wentworth persuaded Charles to call Parliament on 13 April in the hope of financing the war effort.

This 'Short Parliament' – the first to sit in eleven years – was dissolved on 5 May. No funds had been voted through. Instead, the MPs presented a list of their own grievances, summed up in a long speech by John Pym, who was in touch with the Scottish Covenanters.

Also in May, an unlicensed play performed by William Beeston's company at the Cockpit in Drury Lane referred disrespectfully to 'the King's journey into the North'. Beeston was arrested and replaced as manager of the King's and Queen's Servants by 'William Davenant. Gent' who, on 27 June, received a warrant to 'take into his government and care the said company of players'. Davenant would return to the Cockpit in later years. But although he had written a new play, *The Spanish Lovers*, his entrepreneurial dreams were again put on hold when the Second Bishops' War broke out. Once more, Davenant headed north.

On 17 July 1640 the Earl of Conway wrote to the Secretary of State, Sir Francis Windebank, decrying the army's chronic shortage of cash:

> There are 400. draught horses comme hither 800. more will be here within fowre dayes, there is noe order taken for theire payment or any man that knows what to doe with them, there is only one sent downe a deputy to Mr Davenant, if another man should doe soe he would put it into a play

Davenant was equally exasperated, writing from Newcastle to Lord Conway on 24 August:

> May it please your lordship I find a command sent hither to despatch from hence three hundred and 50 horse for draught of the artillery towards Hull, and with

all possible hast; but unlesse your Lo[rdshi]p send money (according to your owne computation) for theire charges thither, and mony for more iron to shoe them, and a warrant for theire weekly pay who attend them, it is impossible to sett them forward.

Four days later, Conway was beaten at the Battle of Newburn on the River Tyne. Charles Porter, a son of Davenant's friend Endymion, was killed. The king agreed to a truce with the Covenanters. It would cost him dear.

Under the terms of the truce Scottish soldiers would remain in the north at English expense. The bankrupt king had no choice but to call Parliament on 3 November. In contrast to its short-lived predecessor, this 'Long Parliament' would sit for thirteen years.

Traditionally, parliaments had been summoned and suspended at the sovereign's pleasure, their main purpose being to debate finance bills and pass subsidies. The 'godly' faction, however, had made them troublesome. For eleven years, Charles had governed without Parliament. The fiasco of the Bishops' Wars and the collapse of his Ship Money initiative meant that he needed Parliament to pass new funding measures.

Parliament had other ideas. Archbishop Laud's determination to introduce a ceremonial element to the Anglican Church – bringing back altar rails and stained glass windows, raising set prayers above pulpit sermonising – had alarmed the Puritans. On the one hand, Laud's measures were seen as an infringement of liberty: the freedom, that is, for the 'godly' to worship as they saw fit. Worse, though, was the suspicion that Laud was pursuing a 'popish' agenda.

On 18 December, Parliament voted to impeach William Laud, Archbishop of Canterbury, for the crime of high treason.

John Pym, MP for Tavistock in Devon, had been a small boy when the Great Armada sailed along the southern coast in 1588. He was a young gentleman at the Middle Temple when, in 1605, the Gunpowder Plot was exposed. Though the attempted Spanish invasion was unlucky, and the 'powder treason' unlikely, they proved to Pym's developing mind that the Roman Catholic 'Antichrist' was hell-bent on world domination.

The Armada, in the reign of Elizabeth I, and the Gunpowder Plot, in the reign of James I, became iconic moments in the forging of English identity. To be English, Pym and his followers felt, was to be engaged in a spiritual war with Rome and its diabolical emissaries. The fact that King Charles had married a devout 'papist', whose chapel at Somerset House attracted Catholics to Mass, implied that the whole kingdom was in peril. Laud's 'popish' Church reforms merely confirmed those suspicions and gave John Pym common cause with the Scottish Covenanters.

Nothing would help Pym so much as the explosive growth of cheaply printed pamphlets. England's first weekly newspaper appeared in 1641, but the standard had been set by crude newssheets with titles like *The truest relation of the discoverie of a damnable plot in Scotland* and *Gods Late Mercy to England, in discovering of three damnable plots by the treacherous Papists.* The Puritans and the press fuelled each other's paranoia. The Long Parliament discussed five imaginary 'popish' plots in its first few months and set up a committee to suppress the perceived increase in 'popery'. On 25 October 1641, a newssheet gleefully reported a (non-existent) 'devilish plot against the parliament' in the form of 'a contagious plaster of a plague-sore, wrapped up in a letter and sent to Mr. Pym'.

At the same time as Parliament ordered the arrest of Archbishop Laud, Pym moved to have Thomas Wentworth, Earl of Strafford, impeached. As Lord Deputy of Ireland, Strafford had ruled with an iron fist. Since his return to England he had become the king's chief minister. In March 1640, Strafford secured a vote in the Irish Parliament for an army to be levied for use against the Scottish rebels. Pym was intent on portraying this as an act of treason.

Charles had given Strafford his word that 'you shall not suffer in life, honour, or fortune' when the Lord Deputy came to London. After confronting his accusers in Parliament, however, Strafford was promptly sent to the Tower.

There were no masques at Court that Christmas. Charles and Henrietta Maria had just lost their 3-year-old daughter Anne. The Secretary of State, Sir Francis Windebank, and Sir John Finch, Lord Keeper of the Great Seal and Speaker of the House of Commons, had fled overseas to escape the wrath of Pym's fanatics.

Davenant addressed a poetic missive '*To the* QUEEN' at around this time. Henrietta's task, he wrote, was to persuade the king '(in the Peoples cause) / Not to esteeme his Judges more then Laws' and to test his 'extreame obdurateness' with her diamond-like resolve:

> You are become (which doth augment your state)
> The Judges Judge, and Peoples Advocate:
> These are your Triumphs which (perhaps) may be
> (Yet Triumphs have been tax'd for Cruelty)
> Esteem'd both just and mercifully good:
> Though what you gain with Tears, cost others Blood.

Parliament presented its detailed accusations against the Earl of Strafford on 31 January 1641. His trial, attended daily by the king and queen, began on Monday, 22 March and quickly ran into difficulties. The prosecution case began to crumble in the face of Strafford's smart, sarcastic responses. Meanwhile, a plan was taking shape.

So obsessed were Pym and his agitators with attacking their own bugbears that neither the Scottish Covenanters nor the English army in the north had been paid. The English troops were on the point of mutiny. Captain James Chudleigh travelled south to beg Parliament urgently to address the issue. Somehow, he made contact with William Davenant, who hinted that Pym and his friends were 'so well affected' to the Covenanters that they would pay the Scottish army first. Davenant then introduced Captain Chudleigh to Henry Jermyn, who took him to see the queen.

The plot was hatched in Henrietta Maria's chamber. The English soldiers would be brought south to Nottinghamshire under the command of William Cavendish, Earl of Newcastle and governor to the 10-year-old Prince Charles, with Lord Goring as his deputy. If the Earl of Strafford were convicted, the army would seize the Tower of London and forcibly dissolve Parliament.

Captain Chudleigh returned to the army in the north with a letter requesting that George Goring be appointed lieutenant-general. Only a handful of officers signed the letter which Chudleigh, back in London, took to Sir John Suckling, another of the plotters. The army, it seemed, could not be relied upon.

The final summing-up in Strafford's trial was scheduled for Saturday, 10 April. Pym and his party had failed to prove their case against him. Another 'godly' MP, Arthur Haselrig, proposed that the impeachment process be halted in favour of a Bill of Attainder, which would condemn Strafford to death on the basis of a major-ity vote. Nearly half of the MPs did not attend the Bill's third reading on 13 April, such was their fear of Pym's faction in Parliament and on the streets. The remaining MPs voted 204 in favour, 59 against. The dissenters' names were posted outside the House of Commons with the incendiary words, 'These are the Straffordians, the Betrayers of their Country'.

It was not until late on Sunday, 9 May that King Charles, after much wrestling with his conscience, finally signed Strafford's death warrant – a decision which would haunt him the rest of his days. The previous Wednesday, John Pym had informed MPs of the 'secret practices' he had discovered 'to discontent the army with the proceedings of Parliament'. Details of the plot to bring the army south had been leaked, probably by George Goring. An inquiry was set up and a Bill imme-diately passed to prevent 'this present Parliament from adjourning, proroguing, or dissolving without the consent of both Houses'. The alleged conspirators were summoned on 6 May to answer questions 'concerning Designs of great Danger to the State'. But the suspects had flown.

With typical exaggeration, the Army Plot was described as 'the greatest treason … that was in England since the [Gun]powder plot'. The ringleaders were named as 'Mr Jermyn, Mr Percy, Sir John Suckling, Davenant the poet, and such youths (unsworn counsellors) … as my lord of Essex called them in the House, the new Juntillio.' Henry Percy had been part of a parallel scheme to influence the army against Parliament; he escaped using a passport acquired for him by the queen. Henry Jermyn received a warning note from Henrietta Maria and hastily left for France. Sir John Suckling had also fled to Paris.[2] 'It is strangely thought on, this their so sudden flight, and they are esteemed much more culpable than I hope they are', wrote Sir Henry Vane.

Parliament already had some of the lesser conspirators in Percy's plot – Henry Wilmot, John Ashburnham and Hugh Pollard – whose distaste for the courtier-poets implicated in the Army Plot was expressed by Captain Pollard: 'Wee did not very well like the men, for *Suckling*, Jermaine and Davenant were in it.' But while

Jermyn and Suckling made it to safety on the Continent, 'Wm. Davenant the poet' did not get so far. He was apprehended with his servant, Elias Wallen, on the road to Dover.

Davenant's nose betrayed him. A contemporary jingle noted:

> Soon as in *Kent* they saw the Bard,
> (As to say truth, it is not hard,
> For *Will.* has in his face, the flawes
> Of wounds receiv'd in Countreys Cause:)
> They flew on him, like Lions passant,
> And tore his Nose, as much was on't;
> They call'd him Superstitious Groom,
> And Popish dog, and Curre of *Rome*;
> But this I'm sure, was the first time,
> That *Wills* Religion was a crime.

On the morning of Wednesday, 12 May a crowd of 200,000 citizens gathered on Tower Hill to witness the execution of the Earl of Strafford. On 15 May, Davenant and his servant were summoned as 'Delinquents' to Parliament.

After gruelling examination, Davenant was committed to the custody of the sergeant-at-arms. His fate seemed sealed. Admiral Sir John Penington heard on 29 June that 'Wilmot, Ashburnham, and Pollard were committed to several prisons. 'Tis thought Jermyn, Suckling, and Davenant will be judged guilty of death.'

The ballad-mongers had a field day:

> But *Davenant* shakes and Buttons makes
> As strongly with his breech-a
> As hee ere long did with his tongue
> Make many a bombast speech-a.

A balladeer hoped he'd '[e]scape the rope', and that's precisely what he did. Preferring to submit a written statement than to appear before them again, Davenant composed a 'humble Remonstrance' to 'The Honourable KNIGHTS, CITIZENS And Burgesses Of The House of Commons, assembled in Parliament'. He confessed, 'I may be guilty of some mis-becoming words' and had 'perhaps committed errours' in writing, 'but never irreverently or maliciously against Parliamentary government.' As for his fellow accused, 'Master *Iarmin* and Sir *Iohn Suckling* … they were strangely altered, and in a very short time, if it were possible they could design any thing against [Parliament's] happy and glorious proceedings'. He pointed out that he had recently praised 'the Queenes Majesty' as 'the Peoples advocate' on the grounds that she was pleading Parliament's cause to the king on the people's behalf – which doesn't seem to be quite what Davenant meant in his poem '*To the* QUEEN'.

Since Parliament had issued its warrant for him, Davenant complained, 'men did avoid me, even my old friends, like one stricken with an infectious kinde of death, so terrible already is every marke of your displeasure growne'. He prayed that the MPs would 'leave me to posterity as a marke of your compassion, and let not my flight or other indiscretions be my ruine'.

On 8 July, upon reading his petition, Parliament resolved 'That Mr. Wm. Davenant be bailed upon such Bail as this House shall allow of.' Bail was set at £4,000,[3] half to be offered by Davenant and the balance by two of the king's servants. A month later, on 12 August, Parliament voted Jermyn, Suckling and Henry Percy guilty of high treason, 'and then falling out about Mr. Davenant there was great debate, but broke off till further consideration of the evidence against him.'

The MPs soon had graver matters to concern them. A violent rebellion erupted in Ireland in October as the Catholic gentry sought to seize control of the English administration. The uprising rapidly degenerated into an ethnic war between Irish Catholics and Protestant settlers from England and Scotland. Refugees swarmed into the western counties of England and Wales, bringing overblown tales of Catholic atrocities (one of these, curiously, concerned a 'Mr Davenant and his Wife', supposedly bound to their chairs while 'their 2 Eldest Children of 7 years old' were roasted on spits 'before their Parents faces').

The perennial fear of 'papists' convinced Puritans, parliamentarians and pamphleteers that the Irish rebellion was the start of a general Catholic backlash. John Pym declared, 'the papists here [in England] are acted by the same principle as those in Ireland'. Lack of evidence did not prevent him from claiming that 'many of the most active [English Catholics] have lately been there; which argues an intercourse and communication of counsels.' As the rumours flew, panic gripped the nation: 'the poor people ... were ready either to run to arms,' wrote Richard Baxter, a Puritan, 'or hide themselves thinking that the Papists were ready to rise and cut their throats'.

Had Davenant's trial taken place a few weeks later than it did, the outcome might have been different. A poet-playwright accused of conspiring with the Catholic queen to raise an army against Parliament would have received no mercy after the Irish rebellion got underway. But his hopes that 'if I were layed aside awhile, my Cause would be forgotten' were realised because, in addition to the Irish problem, Parliament got bogged down in debating another 'Remonstrance' – the Grand Remonstrance put forward by John Pym.

As ever, Pym blamed everything that was wrong on an illusory Catholic conspiracy. Influenced by the Scottish radicals, he set out a raft of objections to the king's rule and demanded the expulsion of bishops from Parliament, a purge of Crown-appointed officials and a General Synod of 'the most grave, pious, learned and judicious divines of this island, assisted with some from foreign parts professing the same religion with us' to 'consider all things necessary for the peace and good government of the Church.'

Pym's Grand Remonstrance divided Parliament, driving some who had been critical of the king's policies – such as Davenant's friend Edward Hyde – firmly into the Royalist camp. They felt that Pym and his supporters were inciting the 'godly' extremists and 'telling stories to the people' about the king. A fiery debate on 22 November ended with the Grand Remonstrance being passed by just eleven votes. Delivered to King Charles on 1 December, it was swiftly followed by a petition signed by 15,000 Londoners demanding 'Root and Branch' reform of the Church.

Until then, the king had been wavering and indecisive, stunned by the vehemence of Pym's opposition. The Grand Remonstrance provoked him into action. On Tuesday 4 January 1642 – a week before Davenant's daughter Mary was baptised at St Martin-in-the-Fields – King Charles marched to Parliament with a 200-strong armed guard and demanded the arrest of five MPs together with that of the peer Edward Montagu, Viscount Mandeville. Charles looked around the Commons for the five members: John Pym, John Hampden, Arthur Haselrig, Denzil Holles and William Strode. They were nowhere to be seen. The king then addressed the House, explaining that the men he sought had encouraged the Scots to invade England – an act of treason. Parliament was unimpressed.

The five members had slipped away moments before the king arrived.[4] The MPs escaped by boat to the City of London, where they were protected. The king went to the Guildhall the next morning and was met with cries of 'Parliament! Privileges of Parliament!' to which Charles replied that 'no privileges can protect a traitor from legal trial.' Crowds menaced the king as he made his way in his coach back to Whitehall.

Parliament declared the king's attempted arrest of the five MPs 'unjust and illegal'; his entering the Commons with 'soldiers, papists, and others' was 'a traitorous design'. The Puritans were raising the militia. Some houses were stockpiled with '20 to 40 muskets with ammunition'.

On Sunday, 9 January the king learned that Parliament was preparing to 'accuse Her Majesty of high treason'. The following day a procession of 20,000 armed citizens, supported by artillery and headed by the five fugitive MPs and Viscount Mandeville, was called to defend Parliament. That evening, the king and queen left Whitehall with 'thirty or forty' bodyguards and three of the royal children: Charles, Mary and James.

It was decided that Henrietta Maria should leave the country, taking the couple's jewellery with her to raise much-needed money. Her servant, William Davenant, probably sailed with her on the *Lion*: he was in Amsterdam by July, acting as the queen's agent in pawning her jewels. His friend Sir John Suckling had committed suicide in Paris, aged 32. 'What is become of Davenant, who alone / And onely he, is able to bemone / So great a losse?' asked another poet:

Speake, learned Davenant, speake what was the reason?
To praise thy friend, I hope, will not prove treason!

77

'The Cruelties of the Cavaliers', woodcut from a 1644 Puritan pamphlet.

The king, meanwhile, set off for the north. Parliament had already secured Hull, with its royal arsenal, but Charles hoped to find 'a safe place' in York where he could muster support. On 22 August 1642 the king came 'weary ... to Nottingham' and 'commanded the Standard to be brought forth'. Carried by the young princes, Charles and James, with diverse 'Lords and Gentlemen accompanying the same', the royal standard was raised in the pouring rain, only to be blown down that night by the wind.

The English Civil War had begun.

6

Davenet the Poet (Now Knighted)

The last play Davenant wrote before the Civil War was *The Spanish Lovers*,[1] licensed on 30 November 1639. There is no evidence that it was performed. It shows signs of having been written in haste – so much so that Davenant let slip his own reflections on the drift towards revolution. Nearing the end of the play, when two rivals are revealed to be long-lost brothers, Catholic deference is contrasted with the surly obstinacy of the mercantile Protestants:

> You had best produce a trick
> Of disobedience at first sight? That I
> May think my Spanish Off spring, chang'd for some
> Dull Dutch Burghers Issue, that sold
> Stockfish and Pickled Herring.

Dullness is also associated with a puritanically-inclined servant:

> I thought she would have catechiz'd my Man [...]
> And the dull Slave began to listen too:
> For let me tell you, he's a very great
> Misleader of Weavers,
> And may in time make a Rebellion.

Partisan sentiments, yes – but they suggest that Davenant was alert to the underlying causes of the struggle between king and Parliament. The mood of disobedience apparent in the more extreme Protestants, who saw themselves as allied with the Dutch in a holy war against Rome, combined with their habit of interpreting events as signs of God's judgement or proofs of diabolical conspiracy, created a kind of insanity. Religious fervour boiled over into mob rule.

Barely had the king raised his standard at Nottingham than Parliament issued an 'Order for Stage-plays to cease'. The order advocated 'Fasting and Prayer' – rather than 'lascivious Mirth and Levity' – as the proper 'Means to avert the Wrath of God':

It is therefore thought fit, and Ordained [...] That, while these sad causes and set Times of Humiliation do continue, Public Stage Plays shall cease, and be forborn, instead of which are recommended to the People of this Land the profitable and seasonable considerations of Repentance, Reconciliation, and Peace with God, which probably may produce outward Peace and Prosperity, and bring again Times of Joy and Gladness to these Nations.

Truly an ordinance against pleasure and a shutting down of alternative voices.

By then, Davenant was shuttling between Henrietta Maria, hurriedly raising money on the Continent, and Newcastle-upon-Tyne, where William Cavendish, Earl of Newcastle, was gathering a Royalist army. The queen wrote to 'my cousin, the Earl of Newcastle' in early October – 'I have received your requests by Davenant and Cooke, whom I sent back to you' – and again, on 11 October:

Cousin,

Having written to you yesterday, these few words are sufficient to tell you that I beg you not to make any promise in the army that you are raising, for the place of master of the artillery, for I have it in my thoughts to propose you one whom I think very fit for it, and with whom you will be satisfied

Newcastle took the queen's hint, Sir Philip Warwick later noting that the earl 'had a tincture of a Romantick spirit, and had the misfortune to have somewhat of the Poet in him; so as he chose Sir William Davenant, an eminent good Poet, and loyall Gentleman, to be Lieutenant-generall of his Ordinance.'

Davenant served under Newcastle for nine months, until August 1643. John Aubrey wrote a brief account of Davenant's time in the north: 'In the civil wars in England he was in the army of William, Marquess of Newcastle (since duke), where he was general of the ordinance. I have heard his brother Robert say, for that service there was owing to him by King Charles the First £10,000.' This was followed by an anecdote:

During that war, it was his hap to have two aldermen of York his prisoners, who were something stubborn, and would not give the ransom ordered by the council of war. Sir William used them civilly, and treated them in his tent, and sat them at the upper end of his table *à la mode de France* and having done so a good while to his charge, told them (privately and friendly) that he was not able to keep such expensive guests and bade them take an opportunity to escape, which they did

This certainly sounds like Davenant, the amiable gentleman at war. According to Aubrey, the aldermen had gone some distance before they agreed that 'they ought to go back and give Sir William their thanks' – which must have surprised Davenant – before making their getaway.

Being stationed in the north, Davenant missed the first full-scale engagement of the Civil War. King Charles had been marching from Shrewsbury to London. The Earl of Essex, commanding a Parliamentary army, went to Worcester, where his vanguard clashed with the cavalry led by the king's nephew, Prince Rupert of the Rhine, and then backtracked to Warwick, where he heard that the king's army was threatening the Puritan enclave at Banbury. Late in the frosty evening of 22 October 1642 the Royalists discovered that the enemy was close by. The king drew up his forces on the long escarpment of Edge Hill, with Prince Rupert commanding the horse and dragoons on the right wing and Sir Henry Wilmot on the left. The two young princes, Charles and James, were also there, under the less-than-watchful eye of William Harvey, the physician who first described the systemic circulation of the blood.

The Battle of Edgehill came as a shock to all parties. The revolution had divided the nation, pitting cousin against cousin, father against son. Sir Edmund Verney, who had written so despairingly of the First Bishops' War, sacrificed himself by refusing to wear armour that day, his eldest son having come out on Parliament's side. For weeks afterwards there were reports of 'portentious apparitions of two jarring and contrary armies where the battle was strucken':

> Pell mell to it they went, where the corporeal armies had shed so much blood, the clattering of armes, noise of cannons, cries of soldiers, sounds of petronels [firearms], and the alarum was struck up, creating great terror and amazement.

The fact that neither side gained total victory meant that the war would drag on for four weary years. For Davenant, the first major battle would have had an added poignancy, fought as it was 10 miles south-east of Stratford-upon-Avon, on the road that his godfather had frequently taken to Oxford.

King Charles entered Oxford on 29 October. The Royalists 'came in their full march into the towne, with about 60 or 70 cullours borne before them which they had taken at the saide battell of Edgehill from the parlament's forces', wrote Anthony Wood. The queen was still in the Netherlands, where Parliament's ambassador, Walter Strickland, was keeping Pym informed. Henrietta was anxious to join her husband, 'but it is thought she will not until she has heard from England by Davenant, Percy, Philpot or Sir Thomas Dorvill'. Strickland understood that 'the Queen intends to take over horses and ammunition. Great endeavours are made to raise money by borrowing and pawning jewels.' In all, she amassed about £180,000.

Finally, in late February, Henrietta landed at Bridlington, Lord Newcastle accompanying her thence to York. On or around 25 March – the old New Year's Day – Davenant presented 'A New-years-Gift to the Queen, in the year 1643':

Madam, 'tis fit I now make even
   My numerous accompts with Heaven,
Least all my old years crimes, if unforgiven,
     Should still stand charg'd upon the new:
And, since Confession makes them less,
My greater Crimes I will confess,
   Which are, my Praises writ of you.

He deplored his past attempts at acclaiming her 'The Poets dull and common way' and begged forgiveness for 'the course injustice I have done / By either dull or false comparison':

   For when I liken or Commend
   Each single vertue with the rest
   That strive for higher place within your Breast,
     I find your Mercy does transcend.

Summer brought better travelling conditions. Henrietta Maria made her way south with a large escort and was met by Prince Rupert at Stratford-upon-Avon, where she stayed for three days as a houseguest of Shakespeare's daughter, Susanna. On 14 July she was reunited with King Charles at his Oxford headquarters.

A month later, on 13 August, the queen wrote from Oxford to the Earl of Newcastle: 'Davenant has arrived; I have not yet spoken to him. On his return, he will inform you of many things which cannot be written, but I will not fear to write'. But Davenant did not return to the northern army. Against Henrietta's advice, Charles had laid siege to the Parliamentary garrison in Gloucester. Davenant hastened to join the king. It was at Gloucester, just before the siege was broken in September 1643, that Davenant, 'in great renown for his loyalty and poetry' (as Anthony Wood put it), received the honour of knighthood from King Charles I.

The king passed the winter in filthy, overcrowded Oxford. Sir William probably stayed at his family's tavern on Cornmarket, which was then run by his elder sister, Jane.

Parliamentarian propagandists made much of the courtly hedonism at Oxford. The *Mercurius Britanicus* newssheet proclaimed:

in time they will go neere to put downe all *preaching* and *praying*, and have some *religious Masque* or play instead of Morning and Evening Prayer, it has been an old fashion at Court, amongst the Protestants there, to shut up the *Sabbath* with some wholesome Piece of *Ben Johnson* or *Davenant*, a kinde of *Comicall Divinity*

The 'godly' faction was seeking to ban Christmas, along with other festivals. Another Puritan sneered in October 1643: 'the Queen will not have so many Masks at

Christmas and Shrovetide this yeare as she was wont to have other yeeres hereto-fore, because *Inigo Jones* cannot conveniently make such Heavens and Paradises at *Oxford* as he did at White-hall, & because the Poets are dead, beggered, or run away'.

Beggared or not, Davenant had neither perished nor bolted. That winter, he addressed a poem '*To the* QUEEN; *Entertain'd at Night. In the Year* 1644':

> Unhappy Excellence, What make you here?
> Had you had sin enough to be afraid,
> Or we the vertue not to cause that feare,
> You had not hither come to be betray'd.

The poet laureate hopefully bestowed Queen Henrietta's qualities on the people:

> Your patience, now our Drums are silent grown;
> We give to Souldiers, who in fury are
> To find the profit of their Trade is gone,
> And Lawyers still grow rich by Civil Warr.

This was possibly the occasion of another Davenant poem, recited by Lord Goring 'In the Person of a Spy', when the queen entertained the king at Merton College, which had been cleared of its Parliamentarian sympathisers. Davenant observed:

> the Owner of this Building knowes
> That to your influence, he intirely owes
> His preservation, instant breath, and all
> We Fortunes gifts, or Natures bounty call

But his 1644 poem '*To the* QUEEN' lacked the unctuous assurance of his '*New-years-Gift*' of 1643. Sir William was becoming disenchanted.

Marooned in Oxford, the Court split into factions. The hot-blooded warriors constellated around the dashing, impetuous Prince Rupert – at 23, the very defini-tion of a 'Cavalier'. They were opposed by the cautious courtiers: men like Edward Hyde, a reluctant convert to the Royalist cause, who favoured negotiations with Parliament.

Sir Henry Wilmot was very much in the Rupert mould. Hyde would describe him as 'proud and ambitious … He drank hard, and had a great power over all who did so, which was a great people'. Wilmot had been party to Henry Percy's plot, planned in tandem (or in competition) with the Army Plot hatched by Davenant, Jermyn and Suckling. He probably shared Hugh Pollard's supercilious view of the courtier-poets.

Wounded in action near Worcester on 23 September 1642, Wilmot recovered to lead half of the king's cavalry at Edgehill. He was appointed lieutenant-general of the horse, under Prince Rupert's command, in April 1643. When Rupert left Oxford in February 1644 to lead a Royalist army in northwest England, Sir Henry – now Baron Wilmot – assumed overall command of the cavalry. He was agitating to get the king's principal advisers, Lord Digby and Sir John Colepeper, dismissed.

Years later, in 1664, Davenant would produce Lord Digby's adaptation of a Spanish comedy at his Lincoln's Inn Theatre. He also offended Edward Hyde by aligning himself with Hyde's rival, Sir John Colepeper. The reckless Lord Wilmot would have had reason to see Davenant as an obstacle to his ambitions.

It was in this context that, as Victor Hugo claimed in 1864, 'Sir William Davenant, created knight by Charles I, wrote to Rochester: "Know this, which does honour to my mother, I am the son of Shakespeare".' Sir Henry Wilmot was created Earl of Rochester in 1652. In 1644, when Sir William supposedly wrote to him, he was conspiring against Davenant's allies.

Coming from a wealthy Oxfordshire family, Lord Wilmot surely looked down on the poet who was born and raised in the town. Defending his new knightly status, Davenant played his trump card. His mother might have been the mistress of a tavern, but she was fascinating and witty enough to be Shakespeare's lover.

Not all of his time was spent in his hometown. Davenant was also sourcing and 'conveying Arms and Ammunition' from Europe. *The True Informer* – a pro-Parliament newsbook – revealed in January 1644 that '*Davenet* the Poet (now Knighted)' was the chief Royalist agent to have visited Rotterdam. In March, Parliament ordered that articles be drawn up for his impeachment of high treason.

With Parliament's forces closing in, the king and queen rode out of Oxford on 17 April, two days after Shakespeare's Globe Theatre in London was pulled down to make way for housing, and parted tearfully at Abingdon. Henrietta was heavily pregnant. She would never see her husband again.

Davenant stayed with the king. On 13 June he was in Shropshire, where he wrote from Halford to Prince Rupert, who was wavering between relieving Lord Newcastle – forced by a Scottish invasion to retreat to York – and reinforcing the king's dwindling army. Davenant argued that the king could not afford to lose the north; Rupert would be better employed supporting Newcastle.

Two weeks later, King Charles inflicted a heavy defeat on the Parliamentarians near Banbury. But Royalist joy at the successful defence of Cropredy Bridge was short lived. On 2 July, at Marston Moor, the combined forces of Parliament and the Scots smashed the army commanded by Newcastle and Prince Rupert. *The Parliament Scout* reported that among the 4,000 Royalist dead was '*Davnant* the Poet', which says something about contemporary journalism.

The Parliamentarian triumph at Marston Moor owed much to the lieutenant-general of the horse, Oliver Cromwell, who described it as an 'absolute victory obtained by God's blessing', even though his nephew was killed. The Royalists had lost what Davenant knew they could not afford to lose – the north of England.

Henrietta Maria sailed to France on 14 July, accompanied by her favourite, Henry Jermyn. King Charles then marched into Cornwall, with Davenant in his train.

On 16 August, Lord Digby sent a letter from Boconnoc, near Lostwithiel, to Edward Seymour, commander of the port of Dartmouth, by 'this bearer, Sir William Davenant, my very good friend'. Three days later, Sir Hugh Pollard also wrote to Colonel Seymour:

> I join with Sir William Davenant in desiring you to let him know whether you have any ship or bark in your harbour that will transport him into France; that secrecy and speedy answer is likewise desired, and I am sure when you consider whose business he carries with him, you will need no quickening to afford him all the accommodation you possibly can

Davenant had a new role: gun-runner. Over the next 18 months he would repeatedly break the Parliamentarian blockade, bringing £13,000 worth of weaponry from Henrietta in France to the king's army in the west, along with £1,000 worth of ammunition (which he apparently paid for himself). In December 1645, a spy wrote from Paris to Cromwell's cousin, Oliver St John, referring to 'Sir William Davenant, the poet – *now the great pirott* – and that he was the agent in projecting and bring[ing] up the northerne army three years since [sh]ould be putt into the exceptions for life' – meaning that there would be no amnesty if Davenant was captured.

Another letter was read to Parliament in November 1645. It had been written in May by Henry Jermyn to Lord Digby and disclosed what Davenant knew, and didn't know, about the queen's hopes to secure military support from the Dutch in return for a marriage contract between her son and the Princess of Orange:

> This bearer, Sir William Davenant, is infinitely faithful to the King's cause; he hath been lately in Holland, so that he met there with the knowledge of our treaty so that it was neither possible nor needful to conceal it from him. The treaty of the marriage and the proposition he knows, but the design of the Duke of Lorraine he does not; of the other two he will speak to you, but charge him with secrecy, for the Queen does still desire the business of the marriage may not be divulged, and the other is destroyed if it yet take wind. Pray if Davenant have need of your favor in anything else use him very kindly for my sake, and let him know [who] conjured you to do so.

Davenant was tireless in his efforts. 'No man hath don you more hurt,' wrote Oliver St John's contact in Paris, 'and hath been a greater enemy to the parliament'.

Parliamentarian troops were reluctant to fight on unfamiliar soil. As Davenant pointed out to Prince Rupert in June 1644, if the king marched north he would 'hardly be follow'd by those Armys which consist of Londoners; for it was never heard that any force or inclination could leade them so farre from home'.

Parliament's solution was to require all MPs to choose between their parliamentary seats and their officers' commissions. With military operations removed from Parliament's control the way was cleared for the creation of a more disciplined radical army.

Exempted from the Self-Denying Ordinance, Cromwell and his son-in-law, Henry Ireton, retained their seats in Parliament and their commissions in the 'New Modelled Army'. On 14 June 1645, the New Model, commanded by Cromwell and Sir Thomas Fairfax, annihilated the Royalist army near the Northamptonshire village of Naseby.

Leicester, Bridgewater, Bath, Sherborne and Bristol quickly surrendered. Cromwell captured Winchester and then joined the siege of Basing House, a 'nest of Romanists' where such artists as Davenant's colleague, the architect and designer Inigo Jones, the engravers Wenceslaus Hollar and William Faithorne (who would later engrave Davenant's portrait), and Davenant's cousin Thomas Fuller had taken refuge. The fortified mansion was stormed on 14 October. The 72-year-old Inigo Jones was carried out of the house naked in a blanket. Captain William Robbins, formerly a comic actor with the Queen's Company and the King's Men, was summarily shot in the head.[2]

Lord Goring, who had replaced Lord Wilmot as lieutenant-general of the Royalist cavalry after the rout at Marston Moor, became a drunken wreck. In December he sailed for France, Davenant conducting him to Le Havre, and thence to Rouen and Paris. Straightaway, Davenant received orders from Queen Henrietta to convey 5,000 French troops to Dartmouth, to be commanded by Goring once he was 'passed his cure'. Davenant, who felt that the 15-year-old Prince Charles would make a better commander, was then working on a scheme to make the port of Dartmouth impregnable, as a 'famous Engineer, and servant to Sir William Davenant' admitted when he was seized and interrogated by Parliamentarians.

Wenceslaus Hollar's depiction of the Siege of Basing House.

The French troops never materialised. As the New Model Army advanced on Oxford in April, the king fled, disguised as a serving man. He made his way to Newark, where a Scottish army was encamped. At Southwell, on 5 May 1646, King Charles surrendered himself to David Leslie, acting commander of the Covenanters' army.

Davenant took up residence with the exiled Henrietta at the Château de St Germain-en-Laye, near Paris. His friend and patron, Endymion Porter, was also there, desperately impoverished and, for a while, dangerously ill. Davenant wrote to a friend in Paris on 1 September, stating that he had hoped to enjoy his good company but was 'void of that happiness by reason of Mr. Porters indisposition of body'.

He was soon able to celebrate with a poem, '*To all Poets upon the recovery* of Endimion Porter *from a long Sickness*':

Arise! bring out your Wealth! perhaps some Twiggs
Of Bay, and a few Mirtle Sprigs
Is all you have: but these ought to suffice,
Where spacious hearts make up the Sacrifice.
Be these your Off'ring as your utmost Wealth,
To shew your joy for lov'd *Endimions* Health.

It was during this time that Davenant is said to have 'changed his religion to that of Rome' – if he hadn't already done so under the influence of Henrietta Maria, whose sumptuous chapel at Somerset House was vandalised in 1643 by John Pym's brother-in-law. Davenant had been branded a 'Popish dog' when he was caught trying to leave the country in 1641. He may then have been guilty of nothing more than papistry-by-association. But the fact that Davenant did convert to Catholicism only added to Parliament's indignation, as well as that of later critics who, like the Kentish militia, seemed to think that '*Wills* Religion was a crime.'

A letter survives, sent from St Germain to the English ambassador, Sir Richard Browne, and dated 14 August 1646:

Sir,

I understand that I have 2 Children newly arrived at Paris, which a servant of my wives hath stolne from an obscure Country education in which they have continued during this Parliament neere London: And I shall desire you will be pleased to contribute a little of your care toward the provision of such necesserie things as shall refine their Bodys, and for their mindes, I will provide a Magiciene of mine owne. Mm Porter tells me Mistresse Sayers will upon your intreaty take this paynes: and I will intreat you to give her mony to furnish them cheap and handsomely which upon sight of your hand shall be returnd you by

Your most humble and affectionate servant

Will: Davenant

The '2 Children newly arrived at Paris' were not Davenant's offspring. Sir William was referring obliquely to the 16-year-old Prince Charles and the 18-year-old Duke of Buckingham, who were both received by the prince's cousin, Louis XIV, on 14 August – the date of Davenant's letter to His Majesty's Resident at the Court of France. Davenant had taken it upon himself to arrange for the care of the noble youths, providing a 'Magiciene' – Thomas Hobbes – to teach them mathematics and a 'Mistresse Sayers' to feed them.[3]

The king, meanwhile, was being held by the Scots at Newcastle-upon-Tyne. Henrietta believed that his best hope lay in joining forces with the Scottish Presbyterians against the 'Independents' of Cromwell's New Model, even if it meant abolishing episcopacy. Davenant was sent as a special envoy in October 1646 to put the queen's case to the king.

An account of the interview was written up, many years later, by Edward Hyde. Davenant was 'an honest man and a witty,' wrote Hyde, 'but in all respects inferior to such a trust':

> Sir William had, by the countenance of the French ambassador, easy admission to the King; who heard him patiently all he had to say, and answered him in that manner that made it evident he was not pleased with the advice. [...] Davenant then offering some reasons of his own, in which he mentioned the church slightingly, as if it were not of importance enough to weigh down the benefit that would attend the concession, his majesty was transported with so much passion and indignation that he gave him more reproachful terms, and a sharper reprehension, than he did ever towards any other man; and forbade him to presume to come again into his presence.

Hyde was not there at the time; he was in Jersey, writing his *History of the Rebellion and Civil Wars in England*. In a letter to Jermyn, Ashburnham and Colepeper, King Charles explained that he 'found Davenant's instructions to be such both for matter and circumstance, that my just griefe for them had been unsupportable, but that the extraordinary and severall kynde expressions of my wife ... abated the sharpness of my sorrow.' He was especially pained to have been 'threatned' by Davenant with the information that Henrietta was considering 'retyring from all business into a monostary. This if it fall out,' wrote the king, 'is so destructife to all my affairs – I say no more of it; my hart is too bigg'.

To Henrietta, Charles declared that 'the absolute establishing of Presbiteriall governement would make me but a titular King', adding that Davenant had acknowledged this. The queen wrote back in November:

> My dear heart,
>   Davenant hath given me a large account of the business where you are, upon which I must conclude with more fear than hope. Yet I may believe, that if the

Scots could find security for performing their duty, they will not consent to desert you, much less basely to deliver you up to them at Westminster. That which they have proposed concerning the coming of persons from me to you […] may be of great use to your affairs, in many respects

Charles replied on 5 December: 'I have, as thou desired me, done my part concerning Davenants Proposition for the sending of persons from thee to me, with fitt asseurances for theire safty'. Evidently, Davenant had not offended the king as much as Edward Hyde liked to imagine.

Davenant's 'Proposition' involved an attempted rescue. A Dutch ship moored on the River Tyne on Christmas Eve. William Murray, who had attended Davenant's interview with the king, paid the captain £100 and then prepared to bring Charles to the boat 'in the habit of a sailor'. But Murray somehow managed to arouse suspicion. The king's guards were doubled.

On 3 January 1647, thirty-six wagonloads of 'good gold and silver coins' trundled into York – the first instalment of the £400,000 promised by the English Parliament to the Scottish army in back pay, and in return for handing over the king.

At Naseby in 1645, Cromwell's New Model soldiers captured the king's baggage, including his private correspondence. This became a public relations disaster for the Royalists when Charles's letters were published as *The King's Cabinet opened*.

The book argued that King Charles's correspondence proved what Parliament had suspected all along: 'the Kings Counsels are wholly managed by the Queen; though she be of the weaker sexe, borne an Alien, bred up in a contrary Religion, yet nothing great or small is transacted without her privity & consent'. A deep vein of misogyny ran through Puritan thinking. Women were not expected to meddle in men's affairs. Queen Henrietta was not just a woman; she was French, and a Catholic to boot!

Previously, in January 1644, a ship sailing from Dunkirk to Spain had run aground on the Sussex coast. Its cargo was impounded. Among the 'Popish pictures and superstitious Imagery' found by Parliamentarian troops was a large painting which, it was alleged, depicted the English king offering his sceptre to Queen Henrietta, who 'declines it and offers it to the Pope'. The message was clear: '*Pope and Queene* share the *Sceptre of England* between them'.

A more sober view was taken by the churchman Daniel Featley. In a pamphlet entitled *The Sea-Gull*, he explained that the 'Popish' picture was painted in Antwerp; the 'Pope' in the picture was an ordinary bishop, and the crooked spire visible in the background identified the setting as Cologne. The subject of the painting was obviously St Ursula. It had nothing whatever to do with King Charles and Henrietta Maria.

The 'godly' faction was obsessed with images. Those they could not despoil, they misconstrued. And though John Pym had died of stomach cancer in 1643 his followers remained determined to portray the king as utterly dominated by his 'popish' queen. As usual, everything could be traced back to an imaginary Catholic conspiracy.

King Charles was now their prisoner. However, the Long Parliament was not yet ready to put him on trial. A new power struggle was underway, this time between the Presbyterians in Parliament and the non-conformists of the New Model. In June 1647 a party of soldiers seized the king, taking him to their headquarters at Newmarket, and then to Hampton Court, where the army started its own negotiations with the monarch. On 11 November, Charles escaped. He was soon recaptured and imprisoned on the Isle of Wight.

The exiles were trying to keep their spirits up. That December, the Parliamentarian newsbook *Perfect Occurrences* reported, 'From *France* little of newes; but that the Queen of Great *Brittaine* hath provided for two Playes this *Christmasse* (as they call it).'

Davenant was lodging with Henry Jermyn in the Louvre. In the winter of 1647–48 the two men went to Calais to confer on Prince Charles's behalf with some British ships which had broken away from the Parliamentarian navy. A captain named Griffin attacked Jermyn, whom Davenant defended, and then followed the pair back to Paris, loudly broadcasting his intention to 'cause Davenant to be pistolled and Lord Jermin to be gelt'.

It was inevitable that those who were closest to the queen would attract the criticism of frustrated rivals. Sir Balthazar Gerbier complained that a 'secret cabale' had instigated an assault on him between Rouen and Dieppe and then ridiculed Gerbier's story as 'a fixion' – 'who should be the authour of this abominable falsehood, but William [Crofts] and Davenant the poet, who reported it frequently at the Louvre, and up and down Paris.' Davenant responded to the slurs by announcing that those who advised Prince Charles did so 'by virtue of my Lord Jarmins pleasure, who might, if he pleas'd, as well have appointed him for one'. Lord Digby went so far as to challenge Jermyn to a duel in the summer of 1648. Jermyn chose Davenant as his second; Digby nominated his brother, Sir Kenelm Digby, who had been Ben Jonson's literary executor. In the end, the duel was called off. Sir Kenelm left Paris in disgust at his failure to slay Sir William Davenant.

The Second Civil War broke out in 1648. English Presbyterians, in collusion with the Scots and the remaining Royalists, rose up against Cromwell's New Model Army. Revolts occurred across the country. Prince Charles commanded a rebel fleet in the Channel. But the uprisings were crushed by the New Model, the death blow dealt in August by Cromwell's defeat of the Scottish army at Preston.

On Wednesday, 6 December, Colonel Thomas Pride marched his Regiment of Foot to the House of Commons. As the MPs arrived, their names were checked against a list. Those who were not approved of by the New Model were denied entrance or arrested.

Pride's Purge was a military coup. It reduced the Long Parliament to a 'rump' of 200 members, of whom 86 then chose to absent themselves. Soldiers remained to terrorise even those MPs who supported the New Model. A republic was now a *fait accompli*.

The execution of King Charles I outside the Banqueting House.

On 15 December the army ordered the king to be removed to Windsor Castle, ready for his trial.

King Charles was brought to Westminster Hall on 20 January 1649. One hundred and thirty-five commissioners had been appointed to try him; sixty-eight actually turned up.

The prosecutor, John Cook, read out the indictment. Charles Stuart had 'traitorously and maliciously levied war against the present Parliament' and 'caused and procured many thousands of the free people of this nation to be slain'. He was a 'tyrant, traitor, murderer, and public enemy of the commonwealth'.

Wearing black, his treasured Garter star glistering on his cloak, the king refused to plead guilty or not guilty, demanding to know 'By what lawful authority I am seated here?' For once, his stammer had left him.

Cook asserted that the charges were brought against the king in the name of 'the Commons and Parliament assembled and all the good people of England'. A masked woman cried out, 'It's a lie, not half nor a quarter of the people!' This was Lady Anne, the wife of Sir Thomas Fairfax, commander-in-chief of the New Model Army. Oliver Cromwell was a traitor, she exclaimed, and her husband too sane and sensible to attend this travesty.

The soldiers trained their muskets on her. Colonel Axtell shouted, 'Down with the whores!'

The verdict, delivered a week later, was a foregone conclusion. Just as English Protestants had beheaded his grandmother, Mary Queen of Scots, so English Puritans would execute King Charles I.

Shortly after two in the afternoon of Tuesday, 30 January, Charles emerged from the first floor of the Banqueting House at his palace of Whitehall, accompanied by William Juxon, Bishop of London. A small block lay before him, draped in black.

Troops kept the spectators at bay. Those who had gathered – including the 15-year-old Samuel Pepys, playing truant – were unable to hear the king's scaffold speech and so missed his admission that the unjust sentence he had allowed to be passed on the Earl of Strafford 'is punished now by an unjust sentence on me'.

Charles knelt, placing his neck on the low block, and stretched out his hands. A terrific groan was heard from the crowd as his head was severed by an axe.

It fell to Henry Jermyn to break the news, on Friday, 9 February, to Henrietta Maria in Paris. The little queen sat 'quite overwhelmed' at her dinner table – 'without words, without action, without motion, like a statue'.

7

Gondibert

Charles I is often portrayed as the architect of his own ruin – a weak, detached ruler trapped in an archaic concept of monarchy. Those who spent time with him, however, tended to become fiercely loyal to the undersized sovereign.

James Harrington, political theorist and proto-republican, was appointed to serve the captive king in 1647–48. His attendance was terminated at the start of 1649 because he had grown too fond of Charles, whose death upset Harrington so much that 'he contracted a disease by it; that never anything did go so neer to him'. James Butler, 1st Duke of Ormonde and close friend of the Earl of Strafford, would later admit that the death of his son had affected him deeply, 'but since I could bear the death of my great and good master King Charles the First I can bear anything else.'

It was Davenant who best captured Charles's predicament, observing in *Salmacida Spolia* that it was the king's misfortune 'to rule in adverse times'. Those who did not know his Majesty were content to vilify him:

Murmur's *a sicknesse epidemicall;*
   'Tis catching, and infects weake common eares;
For through those crooked, narrow Alleys, all
   Invaded are, and kil'd by Whisperers.

Calumny and rumour, as much as his own intransigence, doomed King Charles. The same maniacal prejudices which had ignited the Civil War would bring about the 'Glorious Revolution' of 1688, when Charles's second son, James II, was deposed by a small clutch of MPs to make way for the Dutch Protestant William of Orange. Less bloody but farther reaching than the revolution of the 1640s, the Glorious Revolution saw the political triumph of the Whig party.[1] Since then, British history has essentially been Whig history, written by supporters of the Protestant powerbrokers.

Defenders of the Whig point of view sought to justify the killing of one Stuart king and the deposition of another (not forgetting the execution of Mary, Queen of Scots) by slandering the entire dynasty. The denigration of Sir William Davenant, and the dismissal of his claim to be Shakespeare's son, was part of the collateral damage. Like Charles I, he became the victim of Whiggish revisionism.

On the other side of the politico-religious chasm, the beheading of King Charles was devastating. The Royalist cause was broken. The new king, Charles II, was an impoverished 18-year-old in exile; his mother, Henrietta Maria, was at 39 'much disfigured by the greatness of her illness and misfortunes' and 'so pierced with her sorrows, that she wept almost all the time'.

Initially, revenge came in two forms. Royalist death squads hunted down Isaac Dorislaus, an Anglo-Dutch lawyer who helped to prepare the charge of high treason against Charles, in The Hague, and Anthony Ascham, Parliament's appointed tutor to the princes James and Henry, in Madrid. But retribution for the fifty-seven commissioners who had signed the king's death warrant would have to wait until the Restoration of 1660.

More effective at the time was *Eikon Basilike* – 'The King's Image' – which was published ten days after the king was decapitated at Whitehall. Purporting to be the king's spiritual autobiography, the book presented Charles as a Christ-like martyr.

The frontispiece to *Eikon Basilike*.

It went through thirty-five English editions, and twenty-five foreign ones, in 1649 alone and proved so popular that Parliament commissioned John Milton to produce a counterblast, *Eikonoklastes* ('Image-breaker').

Milton was in many ways the anti-Davenant: a Republican, while Sir William was a Royalist; arrogant, where Davenant was affable. They were roughly the same age. Both had written poems in praise of Shakespeare, and both served their respective rulers, Milton becoming Cromwell's secretary of foreign languages. Milton's greatest work, *Paradise Lost*, was published in 1667, a year before Davenant's death. The apocalyptic epic depicted the Fall of Mankind as a consequence of Satan's civil war against 'Heav'n's awful Monarch'. 'Better to reign in Hell, than serve in Heav'n', argues Satan, an arch-republican. Like that other Puritan classic, Bunyan's *Pilgrim's Progress*, Milton's *Paradise Lost* presented a cosmic struggle in luridly paranoid terms.

By way of contrast, the Royalist response to the tragedy of the king's execution was to retreat into literary escapism. Izaak Walton's *The Compleat Angler*, published in 1653, extolled the virtues of fishing and closed with a quotation from the First Epistle to the Thessalonians: '*Study to be quiet*'. Lost in his riverside idyll, Walton's *Piscator* could blot out the turmoil and the agony.

Walton also quoted a song:

> *Musick! miraculous Rhetoric, that speak'st sense*
> *Without a tongue, exceeding eloquence;*
> *With what ease might thy errors be excus'd,*
> *Wert thou as truly lov'd as th' art abus'd?*
> *But though dull souls neglect, & some reprove thee,*
> *I cannot hate thee, 'cause the Angels love thee.*

This same song appeared, with slight variations, in a 1653 collection entitled *Select musical ayres and dialogues*. It was credited to '*W.D.* Knight' – Sir William Davenant, no doubt, whose distrust of those puritanical 'dull souls' who disliked music would reappear in *The Law against Lovers* (1662), and who had written his own 'Heroick Poem' in response to the tearful times.

Davenant's old friend and patron, Endymion Porter, had been one of the fifty-nine 'Betrayers of their Country' who voted against the Earl of Strafford's attainder in 1641. He campaigned with King Charles in the two Bishops' Wars and was implicated in the Army Plot which almost cost Davenant his life.

Porter left England late in 1645, returning after the king's execution to discover that most of his property had been confiscated or wrecked. He was buried at St Martin-in-the-Fields on 10 August 1649. His Catholic widow lived on until the Restoration, when Davenant arranged for a part of his share in the Duke's Playhouse to be held in trust for Olivia Porter.

George Porter, the eldest son of Endymion and Olivia, had been a major-general in Newcastle's army. He was wounded at Marston Moor. George married the sister of Lord Goring and made his peace with Parliament in 1645. This inspired Davenant to write a poem 'To Mr. George Porter', which he entitled 'The DREAME'. Royalist turncoats, Davenant suggested, were like bereaved lovers; such 'Lovers of this Land' believed themselves 'quit from Loves command' but soon 'ceast to boast / Of freedome found, and wept for thought / Of their delightful bondage lost'. George Porter's reconciliation with Parliament merely exchanged 'safety in Monarchal Reign' for 'proud strutting in a Chaine'. The poem was prescient: Porter would plot to restore the monarchy in 1659, but the Royalists no longer trusted him.

The death of Endymion Porter in 1649 prompted Davenant to write a loving tribute, in the form of a duet, to Endymion and his widow:

ENDIMION: *Olivia* 'tis no fault of Love
To loose our selves in death, but O, I fear,
When Life and Knowledge is above
Restor'd to us, I shall not know thee there [...]

OLIVIA: When at the Bowers in the Elizian shade
I first arrive, I shall examine where
They dwel, who love the highest Vertue made?
For I am sure to find *Endimion* there.

Soon after the sad news of Endymion's death reached him, an exciting new prospect opened up for the poet laureate. William Claiborne, the puritanical Treasurer of Virginia, was 'affected to the Parliam[en]t'. In September 1649, King Charles II appointed Davenant to replace him. Sir William duly sailed to the island of Jersey in January 1650, taking with him a French manservant, Jean Bernard, and his future stepson Thomas Cross, who would serve as his secretary.[2]

Before he left France, Davenant hastened to complete the first two parts of the 'Heroick Poem' which had provided him with a release from the day-to-day reality of life in exile. He condemned 'all those hastie digestions of thought which were published in my Youth; a sentence not pronounc'd out of melancholly rigour, but from a cheerfull obedience to the just authoritie of experience'. The execution of the king had altered everything. All that had gone before no longer mattered. *Gondibert* would be his masterpiece.

On 2 January 1650 Davenant addressed a lengthy Preface '*From the* Louvre' to '*his much honour'd Friend* Mr HOBS.' Thomas Hobbes had been in Paris since 1640, having fled from England when the rebellious Long Parliament was called. Davenant arranged for Hobbes to teach mathematics to Prince Charles and the Duke of Buckingham. He also relied on the philosopher for a 'daily examination' of his work on *Gondibert*.

Hobbes returned the compliment, remarking: 'I have used your Judgement no less in many things of mine, which coming to light will thereby appear the better.' Thomas Hobbes published *Leviathan* the following year, having presumably received Davenant's help in drafting his classic of political philosophy.

Davenant had completed the first two books of *Gondibert* and 'a little time would make way for the Third'. He intended to delay publication 'of any part of the Poem' until he could send it to Hobbes from America, 'whither I now speedily prepare'. In the 'Authour's Preface' he explained his plan for the whole work.

There would be five books, corresponding to the five 'Acts' of the 'Drama'. The first introduced 'the chiefest characters … ending with something that looks like an obscure promise of design.' The second brought in 'new persons'. The third would establish subplots – 'the under-walks (or lesser intrigues) of persons' – and end with a major plot twist. The fourth act, '(ever having occasion to be the longest)', would bring unexpected developments in the subplots and 'a counter-turn to that main design which chang'd in the third'. The fifth would send main plot and subplots off in new directions before 'an easie untying of those particular knots, which made a contexture of the whole'. In short, the ideal dramatic structure.

Davenant used the Preface to set out his philosophical stall. He confessed that 'the desire of Fame made me a Writer':

Fame is to our Sons a solid Inheritance, and not [un]usefull to remote Posterity; and to our Reason, 'tis the first, though but a little taste of Eternity.

Thus wrote the poet who claimed to be Shakespeare's son.

He then took a swipe at those 'who are provok'd to become Authours, meerly out of Conscience', but whose 'Conscience' was often 'so unskilfull and timorous, that it seldom gives a wise and steddy account of God; but grows jealous of him as of an Adversary' – 'like a fearfull Scout, after he hath ill survey'd the Enemy, who then makes incongruous, long, and terrible Tales.' Better the painstaking 'wise Poet' than the godly demagogue who evinced 'extemporary fury, or rather *inspiration*, a dangerous word; which many have of late succesfully us'd'.

The upheavals triggered by intolerance and bigotry had made Davenant wary of religious dogmatism: 'The good (who are but few) need not the power of *Religion* to make them better, the power of *Religion* proceeding from her threatnings'. Consequently, he had evolved his own spiritual philosophy, in which poetry 'is the best Expositor of Nature' and:

Nature is the best Interpreter of God; and more cannot be said of Religion. And when the Judges of Religion (which are the Chiefs of the Church) neglect the help of Moralists in reforming the people, (and Poets are of all Moralists the most usefull) they give a sentence against the Law of Nature: For Nature performs all things by correspondent aids and harmony.

It followed that 'all affronts to Nature are offences to God, as insolencies to all subordinate officers of the Crown are rudenesses to the King.'

Thomas Hobbes wrote his answer to Davenant on 10 January 1650. Professing that he was 'corrupted with the Honour done me by your Preface' the 61-year-old philosopher admitted 'that I never yet saw Poem, that had so much shape of Art, health of Morality, and vigour and beauty of Expression, as this of yours.' It deserved to 'last as long as either the *Æneid*, or *Iliad*'.

Particular praise was reserved for *Gondibert*'s set pieces – '*The Hunting, The Battel, The Citie Mourning, The Funeral, The House of Astragon, The Library and the Temple*' – which were, Hobbes felt, equal to the Roman poet Virgil or '*Homer* whom he imitated.' He added his own thoughts on godly extremism:

> Unskilfull Divines do oftentimes [raise 'spirits' they cannot control]; For when they call unseasonably for *Zeal*, there appears a spirit of *Cruelty*; and by the like errour instead of *Truth*, they raise *Discord*; instead of *Wisdom, Fraud*; instead of *Reformation, Tumult*; and *Controversie* instead of *Religion*.

The philosopher and the poet were of one mind.

Hobbes concluded with a gracious statement: 'The virtues you distribute there amongst so many noble persons, represent (in the reading) the image but of one mans virtue to my fancy, which is your own; and that so deeply imprinted, as to stay for ever there, and govern all the rest of my thoughts and affections, in the way of honouring and serving you, to the utmost of my power'.

'Two Colleagues' had also read *Gondibert* in its early stages. These were probably Edmund Waller and Abraham Cowley, who both contributed prefatory poems. Waller's 'To Sr WILL. D'AVENANT, Upon his two first Books of GONDIBERT, *Finish'd before his Voyage to* AMERICA' observed that Davenant's countrymen had '*impov'rished themselves, not you*', since '*To banish those who with such art can sing, / Is a rude crime which its own Curse does bring*'. Cowley, meanwhile, saw *Gondibert* as a natural prelude to Davenant's American adventure:

> Sure 'twas this noble boldness of the Muse
> Did thy desire, to seek new Worlds, infuse;
> And ne'r did Heaven so much a Voyage bless,
> If thou canst Plant but there with like success.

A few stanzas of *Gondibert* were published, with Davenant's Preface and Hobbes's Answer, in Paris in 1650. Two editions were printed in London in 1651, and the following year the first two books, plus part of the third, were published with the poems by Waller and Cowley. Midway through the third book, the poem broke off. A 'POST-SCRIPT', signed 'WILL. D'AVENANT' and dated '*Cowes-Castle in the Isle of Wight, October 22.* 1650', explained that Davenant had:

intended in this *POEM* to strip Nature naked, and clothe her again in the perfect shape of Virtue, yet even in so worthy a Design I shall ask leave to desist, when I am interrupted by so great an experiment as Dying

On 16 February 1650, shortly after his arrival in Jersey, Davenant received another royal commission; this time, it was to take over as Governor of Maryland from Cecil Calvert, 2nd Baron Baltimore, who 'doth visibly adhere to the Rebells of England'. The Royalist bailiff of Jersey, Sir George Carteret, had his own interests in America – it was he who changed the name of New Netherlands to New Jersey. Carteret provided a ship and, in early May, Davenant set sail for Maryland.

On 10 May an anxious Abraham Cowley wrote to Henry Bennet, who was with the exiled royals at Breda: 'We have not heard one word from Sir W. Davenant since he left us; be pleas'd to give me some account of him and his Voyage.' No news had yet reached the Court-in-exile, which issued a new commission on 3 June 1650 making Davenant one of the sixteen members of the Council of Virginia appointed to fortify the colony 'for the better suppressing of such of Our subjects as shall at any time rebel against Us or Our Royal Governor there'.

Cowley wrote to Bennet again, later in May:

> I should write to Sir G. Carteret but have not now time, be pleased to let him know the Misfortune that is befallen Sir Will Davenant (in which I believe he has a share) it is he is taken, and now Prisoner with all his Men

Davenant's ship had been intercepted off Falmouth by the *Fortune*, an English frigate, on 4 May and his company stripped of all possessions, including Sir William's clothes. Cowley was distraught: 'We are strangely pursu'd in all things, and all places, by our evil Fortune, even our retreats to the other World (except by death) are cutt off.'

Edward Hyde wrote from Madrid to Abraham Cowley on 12 July, adding in a postscript: 'I am exceedingly afflicted for the misfortune of poore Will Davenant. I beseech you lett me know w[ha]t is become of him, for I heare no more then yt he was taken prisoner and carried to ye Isle of Wight.' Davenant was indeed a prisoner. The joint-governor of the Isle of Wight had been instructed by the Council of State on 17 May to keep Davenant incarcerated in Cowes Castle until Parliament had decided his fate, 'he having been an active enemy to the Commonwealth.'

Davenant had chosen a dreadful time to fall into Parliament's hands. The year before, Sir Isaac Dorislaus had been butchered by vengeful Royalists. A month after Davenant was captured, Anthony Ascham was stabbed to death in Madrid. On top of which, King Charles II sailed to Scotland, early in June, with the aim of leading a Presbyterian army into England. Parliament reacted with fury, determined to 'pitch upon' six Royalist prisoners for exemplary punishment.

Four 'Malignants' were selected on 28 June. On 3 July six more names were put to Parliament, one of them being '*Davenant*, called *Sir William Davenant*'. A fifth victim was chosen. Then the House came to vote on Davenant.

The vote was evenly split, twenty-seven each way.

The Speaker had the casting vote. He 'declared himself to be a No'. The commentators were bitterly amused. *Mercurius Politicus* smirked that 'some *Gentlemen*, out of pitty, were pleased to let him have the *Noes* of the House, because he had [no nose] of his own'. Parliament voted again the next day, and Davenant's name became the sixth on the list.

An Act was ordered to be printed on 9 July, naming '*William Davenant*, otherwise called *Sir William Davenant*' and five others who would stand trial for 'all Treasons, Murthers, felonies, Crimes and offences done and committed', the trial to be followed by their 'Condemnation and Execution'. The MPs were resolved on making a 'publique Manifestation of their just Resentment'.

Not everyone was eager to see Davenant hanged – a newssheet hoped that '*Will. D'Avenant* may not dy, till he hath finished his own *Monument*'. But when Davenant wrote his 'POST-SCRIPT' to *Gondibert* on 2 October he was genuinely 'threatened with Death; who, though he can visit us but once, seems troublesom; and even in the Innocent may beget such a gravitie, as diverts the Musick of Verse.' His monument remained unfinished, interrupted as it was by 'so great an experiment as Dying:

and 'tis an experiment to the most experience'd; for no Man (though his Mortifications may be much greater than mine) can say, *He has alreadie Dy'd*.

The inspiration for *Gondibert* came in part from the ancient history of Lombardy. The sixteenth-century Italian writer Matteo Bandello had borrowed from the *Historia Langobardorum*, written by Paul the Deacon, an eighth-century monk, for his *Novelli*, which were then translated into French by François de Belleforest, whose *Histoires tragiques* provided material for Shakespeare's *Romeo and Juliet*, *Twelfth Night*, *Much Ado about Nothing* and *Hamlet*. It may be that Davenant was introduced to Belleforest's fables by his famous godfather.

The aged Aribert[3] is king of the Lombards of northern Italy, the incomparable Rhodalind his only child. Prince Oswald seeks Rhodalind's hand in marriage, and with her the throne. But both Aribert and Rhodalind secretly favour Duke Gondibert.

Gondibert, encamped near Bergamo, leads a stag-hunt:

The Hunts-men (Busily concern'd in show
    As if the world were by this Beast undone,
And they against him hir'd as Nature's Foe)
    In haste uncouple, and their Hounds out-run.

Now wind they a Recheat, the rows'd Deers knell;
    And through the Forrest all the Beasts are aw'd;
Alarmd by Eccho, Natures Sentinel,
    Which shews that murdrous Man is come abroad.

The 'Royal Stag' is killed. Gondibert and his youthful warriors are then ambushed by 'fierce *Oswald*' and his men. Gondibert and his seconds agree to fight with Oswald and his. Oswald is killed, and a free-for-all ensues.

Gondibert is so severely wounded that he is 'reckon'd with the slain.' The timely arrival of 'old *Ulfin*' and his squadron saves the duke. Ulfin gives Gondibert a refreshing cordial and carries him to the palace of '*Astragon* the wise and wealthy', a 'fam'd Philosopher'.

The second book opens with day breaking over Verona. The city comes to life:

From wider Gates Oppressours sally there;
    Here creeps th'afflicted through a narrow Door;
Groans under wrongs he has not strength to bear,
    Yet seeks for wealth to injure others more […]

Here through a secret Postern issues out
    The skar'd Adult'rer, who out-slept his time;
Day, and the Husbands Spie alike does doubt,
    And with a half hid face would hide his crime.

Funerals are held for those killed in the battle. Rhodalind, 'Truth's Altar', hears a rumour that Gondibert is among the dead. Oswald's sister, '*Gartha* the renown'd', is informed of her brother's death. Cursing Rhodalind, Gartha sets out in her chariot for the camp at Brescia, where she fires up Oswald's warriors into swearing revenge. Their eagerness to attack King Aribert's city of Verona is calmed by Hermegild, who treacherously offers to secure Aribert's throne – and Rhodalind – for Oswald's brother, in return for Gartha's hand. Hermegild returns with Gartha to Verona to further their plotting.

Davenant resumes Gondibert's story. The 'House of *Astragon*' is described – not so much a palace as a cloistered university, replete with alchemists, botanists and stargazers. In '𝕲reat 𝕹atures 𝕺ffice' old 'busie Men' study fish and fowl, entering the details in their registers of Natural History; in '𝕹ature's 𝕹urserie' every herb and berry is grown. A 'dismall Gall'ry' known as '𝕿he 𝕮abinet of 𝕯eath' houses Astragon's collection of '*Skelitons*' and '𝕿he 𝕸onument of baniſh'd 𝕸inds' forms a library of every text 'Which long-liv'd Authors writ ere *Noah's Showr*.' By contrasting Aesop's parables with the work of 'grave dull *Moralists*' Davenant reveals why he wrote a poem in praise of John Ogilby's verse translation of Aesop's fables at around this time: '*Æsop* with these stands high, and they below; / His pleasant wisdom mocks their gravitie':

> High skill their *Ethicks* seems, whilst he stoops down
>   To make the People wise; their learned pride
> Makes all obscure [...]
>   With ease he teaches, what with pain they hide.

The inner sanctum of Astragon's palace is a triangular temple of black marble dedicated to Praise, Penitence and Prayer. The 'House of *Praise*' contains an elaborate mural showing 'great Creation by bold Pencils drawn'. Biblical history is graphically depicted, from the first appearance of 'the Sun's Parent, Light', via Adam and Eve, to the Crucifixion:

> And know, lost Nature, this resemblance was
>   Thy frank Redeemer, in Ascension shown;
> When Hell he conquer'd in thy desp'rate cause;
>   Hell, which before Man's common Grave was grown.

It is to this 'House of *Praise*' that Gondibert is brought. His battle-wounds are healed, but fresh wounds occur when he is nursed by Astragon's only child, the bashful and unworldly Birtha, who falls helplessly in love with him.

Astragon tests Gondibert's devotion to Birtha and his lack of ambition to win Aribert's crown and, with it, Princess Rhodalind: 'Man still is sick for pow'r, yet that disease / Nature (whose Law is Temp'rance) ne'r inspires':

> And as in persons, so in publick States,
>   The lust of Pow'r provokes to cruel war;
> For wisest Senates it intoxicates,
>   And makes them vain, as single persons are.

Satisfied, Astragon gives his blessing to Gondibert, who is unaware that two of his companions are also in love with Birtha.

The published text states that the third book was '*Written by the Authour during his Imprisonment.*' Davenant seemed conscious that *Gondibert* was his legacy:

> Thus when by knowing me, thou know'st to whom
>   Love ows his Eyes, who has too long been blind;
> Then in the Temple leave my Bodies Tomb,
>   To seek this Book, the Mon'ment of my Mind.

Gondibert's courtship of Birtha is interrupted by the sudden arrival of King Aribert, who proclaims Gondibert his heir and successor, meaning that he must wed Rhodalind. Gondibert assures Astragon that 'Rhodalind I never sought, / Nor now would with her love her greatness take.' He presents Birtha with a 'chearfull' emerald, known as the Bridal Stone, which 'will, when worn by the neglected wife, / Shew when her absent Lord disloyal proves, / By faintness, and a pale decay of life'. Gondibert then leaves with Aribert.

Birtha grows jealous. Her father advises her to go to Verona 'and there serve Rhodalind', giving Gondibert the chance to discover which of the two women he prefers. Meanwhile, two lords who also love Birtha – Goltho and Ulfinore – arrive in Verona, where they attract the attention of a 'fatal beautie', the black-eyed Dalga. Goltho is smitten, though Ulfinore is wary:

> But, *Goltho*, flie from Lust's experiments,
>   Whose heat we quench much sooner than asswage,
> To quench the Fornace-lust stop all the vents,
>   For give it any Air the Flames will rage.

And there the poem ends. Davenant confided in his postscript that 'I was now by degrees to present you (as I promised in the *Preface*) the several Keys of the main Building; which should convey you through such short Walks as give an easie view of the whole Frame.' But like his journey to America, *Gondibert* would never be completed. Sure, there were some who objected that 'I beget a *POEM* in an unseasonable time' and 'I may very possibly not live to enjoy' the fame which inspired him to write it:

> But I will gravely tell thee (*Reader*) he who writes an *Heroick POEM*, leaves an Estate entayl'd; and he gives a greater Gift to Posteritie, than to the present Age; for a publick benefit is best measured in the number of Receivers; and our Contemporaries are but few, when reckon'd with those who shall succeed.

Gondibert drew ecstatic praise from the Welsh poet Henry Vaughan – a Royalist who, like Davenant, converted to Catholicism. In 'To Sir William D'avenant, upon his *Gondibert*', Vaughan remarked that, previously, heroic poems were 'Made up of spirits, prodigies, and fear', but – 'Well, we are rescued!' – Davenant had chased these hobgoblins away:

> This made thy fire
> Break through the ashes of thy aged sire,
> To lend the world such a convincing light
> As shows his fancy darker than his sight.

Shakespeare ('thy aged *Sire*') had happily brought ghosts and witches, prophecies and nightmares onto the stage. Davenant eschewed such fantastic elements, opting for a naturalistic setting with decidedly human characters. Nature and Love were constants, to which Art and Ambition were mankind's responses. In a world lacking gods and giants, men were equal ('Souls are alike, of rich and ancient Race; / Though Bodies claim distinctions by descent'). Vaughan was especially impressed that Davenant had crafted his unfinished masterpiece in the 'forlorn restraint' of a prison cell. He considered the 'matchless Gondibert' no more than a mirror of Davenant himself – the 'Prince of *Poets*, and of *Lovers* too.'

Margaret Cavendish, the wife of Lord Newcastle, Davenant's former commander in the wars, declared that 'of all the Heroick Poems' she had read 'I like Sir *W.D.s.* as being Most, and Nearest to the Natures, Humours, Actions, Practice, Designs, Effects, Faculties, and Natural Powers, and Abilities of Men or Human Life'. There were dissenters, of course. Davenant's future rival, Thomas Killigrew, listed himself, Will Murray, John Denham and William Crofts among 'all Gondibert's dire foes'. But the influence of Davenant's poem cannot be denied. Even the verse form – four lines of pentameter, rhyming *abab* – was borrowed by Edmund Waller for his 'Panegyrick to my Lord Protector' (1655), John Dryden likewise using the 'Gondibert stanza' in his 'Poetic Stanzas on the Death of Oliver Cromwell' (1658) and his 'Annus Mirabilis' of 1666.

Davenant's postscript to *Gondibert*, dated 22 October 1650, was written when he was about to be transferred from the Isle of Wight to the Tower of London. His trial was underway by December. John Aubrey was surely correct when he wrote that Sir William 'expected no mercy from the parliament, and had no hopes of escaping with his life.'

A cute legend, reported by Aubrey, has John Milton personally intervening to save Davenant, who returned the favour when Milton was threatened with arrest and trial at the Restoration. Quite possibly, Milton was anxious to know how *Gondibert* would end. He had long intended to compose an epic poem of his own but was unable to settle on a subject. Davenant's description of Astragon's decorated temple included a reference to the creation of Man and 'the Worlds first Maid':

> Deep into shades the Painter leads them now;
> > To hide their future deeds; then storms does raise
> Ore Heav'n's smooth face, because their life does grow
> > Too black a storie for the House of *Praise*.

The extraordinary frieze displaying biblical history, as Davenant presented it in the sixth canto of *Gondibert*'s second book, might have been the spur which goaded Milton into commencing his epic of 'Mans First Disobedience'. Just as the Puritan poet had responded to *Eikon Basilike* with his counterblast, *Eikonoklastes*, so work on *Paradise Lost* was possibly Milton's reaction to *Gondibert*. If so, then Davenant has received no credit for this. Whig historians demoted Davenant's achievements whilst Whig critics lauded Milton's sonorously godly epic, effectively ignoring Davenant's more varied, humanistic poem. But that John Milton began writing *Paradise Lost* in about 1652 – dictating it after he went blind – and *Gondibert* was published in its fullest form that year, cannot be wholly coincidental.

Whether Milton had sufficient influence to protect Davenant, whose politics he would have abhorred, is another matter. John Aubrey also claimed that Davenant was defended by the 'two aldermen of York' whom he had treated in a gentlemanly manner when they were his prisoners:

> hearing that he was taken and brought to London to be tried for his life, which they understood was in extreme danger, they were touched with so much generosity and goodness, as, upon their own accounts and mere notion, to try what they could to save Sir William's life who had been so civil to them and a means to save theirs, to come to London: and acquainting the parliament with it, upon their petition etc, Sir William's life was saved.

In a margin note, however, Aubrey explained that it was the regicide Henry Marten who spoke up for Davenant. Marten was a Puritan who liked 'pretty girls, to whom he was so liberal that he spent the greatest part of his estate'. When Parliament was debating whether or not to sacrifice Davenant, Henry Marten allegedly argued that 'in sacrifices they always offered pure and without blemish: now yee talke of making a sacrifice of an old rotten rascall'. Aubrey scuppered the anecdote by adding that Marten was himself saved at the Restoration 'by this *very jest*'. And yet there may be some veracity in the story. Davenant would write from the Tower to Henry Marten on 8 July 1652:

> I would it were worthy of you to know how often I have profess'd that I had rather owe my libertie to you than to any man, and that the obligation you lay upon me shall be for ever acknowledg'd.

In the event, Davenant was reprieved, although he would spend more than two and a half years in the Tower of London. It seems likely that he was held prisoner because Charles II was still at war with Parliament.

Charles spent his 21st birthday, 29 May 1651, in Scotland. The previous September, Cromwell – fresh from his brutal suppression of the Irish rebels – had led the New Model Army to a surprise victory over the Scots at Dunbar. Exactly one year later, on 3 September 1651, Charles's invasion of England with an army of Scottish Presbyterians came to a bloody end at Worcester. The king escaped, wandering across the country and enduring perils and privations, the recital of which would bring tears to the eyes of Samuel Pepys when he sailed back to England with King Charles in 1660.

A report on Davenant was presented to Parliament in May 1651. His French serv-ant was set free from the Gatehouse prison in June, but Davenant was presumably deemed too likely to join his royal master, then preparing to invade England, to warrant release. He was still in the Tower when his 'beautifull and ingeniose' eldest son William died, aged 27, at the family's tavern in Oxford.

On 9 October 1652, Davenant wrote to Bulstrode Whitelocke, Lord Keeper of the Great Seal, to thank Whitelocke for procuring him the liberty of the Tower:

> But whilst I endeavour to excuse this Present of Thankfulness, I should rather ask your Pardon for going about to make a Present to you of Myself, for it may argue me to be incorrigible, that after so many Afflictions, I have yet so much Ambition as to desire to be at liberty, that I may have more opportunity to obey your Lordship's commands, and show the World how much I am, My Lord,
>> Your Lordship's most obliged, most humble and obedient Servant,
>>> Will Davenant.

Grateful as he was to have been granted some limited freedom of movement, the obsequiousness of Davenant's letter speaks of his desperation. Bulstrode Whitelocke must have taken pity on the poet because, within a few weeks, Davenant was given permission to leave the Tower, though not London.

He was on bail, heavily in debt, and – at the age of 46 – a widower.

8

How Daphne Pays His Debts

avenant's first wife vanished from the records after the baptism of their daughter Mary on 11 January 1642. By the time Sir William was released from the Tower of London, his wife was dead. Even his published works leave no clue as to when she died.

His song *The Philosopher and the Lover; to a Mistress dying*, calmly considered the possibility that the beloved would be 'chang'd at least into a Starr' on her death:

> But ask not Bodies doom'd to die
>   To what abode they go;
> Since Knowledge is but sorrows Spy,
>   It is not safe to know.

The simple fact is that we know next to nothing about the first Mrs Davenant. She left him with just one surviving child – young Mary, who would marry an uncle of Jonathan Swift, the author of *Gulliver's Travels*.

Davenant remarried almost as soon as he was out of prison. Anne Cademan was the widow of Sir Thomas Cademan, the royal physician who had treated Davenant for the dose of syphilis which cost him his nose. Dame Anne's first husband had been an apothecary; he left her an estate worth £800 and three sons, the eldest being Thomas Cross, whom Davenant was to have taken to America as his secretary. Part of Anne's fortune had been used to rescue Sir Thomas Cademan when he lost his possessions in a shipwreck, early in the Civil War. Sir Thomas then married Anne. He died in 1651.

There was little romance in Davenant's hasty marriage to Anne Cademan. One of Sir William's more persistent critics, Sir John Denham, described the bride as 'so-so':

Her beauty, though 'twas not exceeding,
Yet what in Face and shape was needing,
She made it up in Parts and Breeding.

Looks were unimportant – what Davenant needed was money. Dame Anne seemed happy to devote herself and her resources to aiding ruined Royalists. The marriage also brought Davenant four stepsons: Thomas Cross, aged 22; his brothers Paul (16) and John (11), and their half-brother Philip Cademan, who was 9.

Thomas Cross, recently returned from a stint as secretary to the governor of Barbados, was distressed to find himself scuttling between an apothecary in Warwick Lane, who handled Dame Anne's finances, and Sir William Davenant, who was spending the boys' inheritance. When her cash reserves were exhausted, Dame Anne raised another £600 for her impecunious husband by selling her jewellery. That, too, was quickly spent.

Davenant was arrested for debt soon after he gained his freedom from the Tower. A story was told that when he was being marched back to prison through London's Lombard district a crowd of beggars suddenly appeared and snatched him from the bailiffs' clutches – an occasion recalled by Sir John Denham as when the indigents freed 'the Knight who late did marry / The daughter of our 'pothecary.'[1] But Davenant was back in jail and complaining that he was 'made double prisoner', being confined to London and hounded by debt collectors. In an attempt to keep his property out of his creditors' hands he made the family's home in Tothill Street, Westminster, over to Thomas Cross, which kept the roof over their heads but would lead to legal wrangling between Davenant's widow and his eldest stepson after his death. The situation was hopeless, and early in 1654 Davenant appealed directly to Oliver Cromwell.

On 23 April 1653, Cromwell – with the assistance of forty musketeers – forcibly dissolved the 'Rump' Parliament, which was all that remained of the 'Long' Parliament elected in 1640. A replacement Parliament was convened, its members chosen for the godliness of their beliefs. This 'Barebones' Parliament[2] lasted only until December 1653, when it abolished itself out of fear that the radical Fifth Monarchists – who believed in and welcomed an imminent Apocalypse – might take over the assembly. Within four days of the dissolution of Parliament, Cromwell was sworn in as Lord Protector for life on a salary of £100,000.

Davenant addressed his appeal to the Lord Protector. Among the papers annexed to his petition for consideration by the Council of State was a letter, dated 1 February 1654, from Colonel John Bingham, Governor of Guernsey, who had previously agreed to exchange Davenant for another prisoner. Bingham wrote of the 'blemish' that he and Robert Blake, General at Sea, had received 'by the breach of conditions with Sir William Davenant.' Because Davenant remained 'a prisoner on bail to the Court of Articles, to return to the Tower when demanded' he was unable to 'stir out of town to recover his debt.' Bingham hoped that 'in lieu of his two years imprisonment after exchange, the Court will allow him some further time to follow his occasions, as his sufferings, contrary to the articles of war, have been great.'

Sir William himself begged that 'his Highnesse would please to set me at full liberty'; that the Lord Protector 'would please to stop all further proceedings of Two Writts' which had led to his arrest for debt; that the six weeks of freedom from 'all molestations and Arrests' which he had been allowed after his release from the Tower be extended for 'the better prosecution of my affaires'; and that he might 'have his Highnesse generall pardon whereby I may live in the capacity of a Subject freely and faithfully.'

A committee of the Council recommended on 27 June that Davenant's 'restraint as to any matter that concrnes ye state be forthwth taken off and he as to any such act pardond'. This was approved on 22 July. Warrants were issued on 1 August by the Lord Protector and the Council of State to 'discharge Wm. Davenant, prisoner in the Tower.' On 4 August 1654, Davenant finally secured his freedom.

Seven months later, on 5 March 1655, Anne 'wife of Sr William Davenant, Knt' was buried at the Church of St Andrew, Holborn. Davenant lost no time in applying to John Thurloe, Cromwell's spymaster and secretary to the Council of State, for permission to travel out of the country. When Thurloe failed to respond, Davenant wrote to him again on 15 June:

Sir,

I humbly desire to make a proposition to you, which will inferr my going into France; and consequently give occasion to dedicate my service to you during my short abode there. This doth continue that request, which I made to you not long since, by this way of address, to receive an appointment, when you have leisure to heare, Sir

Your most humble and most faythful servant [...]

What Davenant's proposition consisted of can only be guessed at. He was given a pass on 10 August, allowing him to cross the Channel, and promptly married his third wife, whom he had probably met during his Parisian exile.

Henrietta-Maria du Tremblay was described as being 'of an ancient family in St Germain Beaupré' in the Anjou region of France. Known in England as Lady Mary Davenant, she would bear her husband nine sons and support his theatrical ventures up till and beyond his death in 1668.

Marriage to the widowed Henrietta-Maria du Tremblay went some way towards resolving Davenant's chaotic finances – although the £100 he had undertaken to give to each of his stepsons by 7 February 1655 went unpaid. The family moved into a palatial dwelling in Charterhouse Yard, near today's Barbican underground station. Rutland House, in the north-east corner of the square, had belonged to Francis Manners, 6th Earl of Rutland, who in 1613 paid William Shakespeare 44 gold shillings for a witty *impresa*.[3] When the earl died in 1632, Davenant

Charterhouse Square viewed from the north (*c.* 1728).

wrote a heartfelt 'Elegie, *On Francis*, Earle of Rutland', which anticipated some of *Gondibert*'s imagery. The earl's widow, Cicely, continued to occupy the mansion in Charterhouse Yard until her death in 1654 but, being a Catholic, her estate was sequestered, the proceeds of her property going to Oliver Cromwell. Davenant leased Rutland House from George Thorn and John Hopkins, who bought the reversion on the death of Lady Manners. Among the neighbours was Lord Willoughby of Parham, who had employed Thomas Cross as his secretary in Barbados when Davenant was in prison.

Davenant set about exploiting his fashionable address. He joined forces with one William Cutler and sought investors for a plan to 'buy a piece of ground near the Charter house and build a Theatre'. By February 1656 the partners had raised £925 and work began on the new venue for 'representations and shows'.

The staging of plays had been banned in September 1642. Since then Shakespeare's theatres, the Globe and the Blackfriars, had been demolished and several others – the Cockpit, Fortune and Salisbury Court – wrecked by soldiers. As recently as September 1655, the Red Bull Theatre had been raided and the actors seized while the spectators fled. The tide, however, was turning.

Sir Balthazar Gerbier, the hysterical courtier who attacked Davenant as one of the 'secret cabale' that opposed him in France, had established an academy at Bethnal Green in 1649, the curriculum including '*Musick, Playing on Instruments, Dancing, Fencing, Riding the Great Horse*' and 'the *Secret Motions of Sceanes*'.

Gerbier placated the Puritans by insisting that his lectures were designed for the benefit of 'godly persons and tender Consciences'. Still, it was a short step from the liberal arts taught at Gerbier's 'select academy' to the 'moral representations' now proposed by Sir William Davenant.

In April 1656, *The Publick Intelligencer* reported that a collection of poems – '*Sportive Wit or The Muses Merriment*' – had been criticised by the Council of State for containing 'much Scandalous, Lascivious, Scurrilous, and profane Matter.' One of the poems was a ballad entitled, 'How Daphne pays his Debts'.

'Daphne' – the Greek word for 'laurel' – was Davenant, the poet laureate. The ballad recounted Sir William's misadventures with his creditors and the failure of *Gondibert* to cover his debts:

> But when this *book* it did come forth
>   As some have given a hinting,
> The gains of his pitifull *Poetry*
>   Scarce paid for paper & printing.

Davenant claimed to have been offered the post of 'master o' th' Revels', which didn't really exist at the time. Accordingly:

> *Already I have hir'd a house,*
>   *Wherein to sing and dance,*
> *And now the Ladies shall have Masques*
>   *Made a la mode* de France.

The ballad suggested that Davenant was surreptitiously mounting productions at Lincoln's Inn Fields and Drury Lane and elsewhere, so that before long he would be ready to settle his accounts. If he had not paid off his creditors 'in two yeares time', the balladeer would 'nere speak for him more'.

The 'structure for representations and shows' he was building near Charterhouse Yard was never finished. Davenant would be charged with fraud by four investors who complained that he had put on performances 'in another place which did not concern them'. That place was a room at the back of Rutland House. An officious Parliamentary snooper wrote up an account of the 'Entertainment by Musick and Declarations after the manner of the Ancients' presented by Davenant at what was then his home:

> Upon Friday the 23 of May 1656 These foresaid Declarations began att the Charterhouse and 5s a head for the entrance. The expectation was of 400 persons, but there appeared not above 150 auditors. The roome was narrow, at the end of which was a stage and on either side two places railed in, Purpled and Guilt [*sic*], The Curtayne also that drew before them was of cloth of gold and Purple

The singers, noted the official, were 'Capt Cooke, Ned Coleman and his wife, a nother wooman and other inconsiderable voyces.' The performance 'lasted an howre and a haulfe and is to continue for 10 dayes by wch time other Declamations wilbee ready.'

After a musical flourish, the curtains had opened for the Prologue. Davenant apologised for the lack of space in '*our Cup-board-Scene*' and invited the audience to:

> *Think this your passage, and the narrow way*
> *To our Elisian Field, the* Opera*:*
> *Tow'rds which some say we have gone far about,*
> *Because it seemes so long since we set out.*

A concert of '*Instrumental Musick*' then heralded the appearance of Diogenes and Aristophanes, both seated on gilded platforms.

Diogenes the cynic argued the Puritan case against public pleasures and railed against 'such as represent the vertuous actions of the *Heroes*' before turning his fire on 'the pleasure of Musick', a 'deceitful Art, whose operations lead to the evil of extreams, making the Melancholy to become mad, and the merry to grow fantastical'. He also attacked stage scenery, 'which is, to be entertain'd with the deception of motion, and transposition of Lights', and poetry, 'the subtle Engine by which the wonderful Body of the *Opera* must move.'

Aristophanes, the comic playwright, countered the quarrelsome Diogenes, who 'in his Age studies revenge … for chastisements receiv'd in his youth':

> This discontented Cynick would turn all time into midnight, and all Learning into melancholy Magick. He is so offended at mirth, as if he would accuse even Nature her self to want gravity, for bringing in the Spring so merrily with the Musick of Birds.

How could a man 'who hath alwayes a Discord within himself' appreciate 'the Ornaments of a publick *Opera*, Musick and Scenes', when 'he can only lift up his feet to a dismal discord, or dance to a consort of groaners and gnashers of Teeth'? Aristophanes concluded that his opponent 'hath much reason to disswade you from Moral Representations, because he is himself the worst representation of Morality; and is justly afraid to be represented in the *Theater*.'

A song was sung by the company:

> *Can Age ere do them harm,*
> *Who chearfully grow old?*
> *Mirth keeps their hearts still warme,*
> *Fooles think themselves safe in sorrow and cold.*

Two more persons then appeared on the rostrums, a Parisian and a Londoner. The Parisian spoke first, criticising the higgledy-piggledy architecture of London and the narrow streets 'where the Garrets ... are so made, that opposite Neighbours may shake hands without stirring from home.' He mocked the low roofs and the houses filled with the 'odor of a certain Weed' (tobacco). The Londoners' diet was unimaginative, their beds were too small, and their servants were trained to be 'rude for the honour *of old England*'. Londoners drank to excess, even in the morning, out of dirty glasses. The Parisian even scorned 'one of your Heroick Games, call'd *Foot-ball*'.

An insight into the psychological roots of extremism was offered in the Parisian's reflections on the English treatment of children, 'to whom you are so terrible, that you seem to make use of Authority whilst they are young, as if you knew it would not continue till their Manhood':

> If you take pains to teach them anything, 'tis only what they should not learn, Bashfulness; which you interpret to be their respect towards you, but it rather shews they are in trouble, and afraid of you; and not only of you, but of all that are elder then themselves; as if youth were a crime, or, as if you had a greater quarrel to Nature then to the Devil; you seem to teach them to be asham'd of their persons, even then when you are willing to excuse their faults.

The Londoner responded. The Louvre, he remarked, 'has a very singular way of being wonderful; the fame of the Palace consisting more in the vast design of what was meant to be, then in the largeness of what it is'. French cuisine was overcomplicated, and whereas Englishmen drank to 'sharpen our Wits when we conclude Bargains', Parisians were more excitable: 'I have a mind to suppose ... that your heads are bottles, and your brains the Cork; for the one, being a little stirr'd, the other fly out, and fill the Room with froth.'

As for their sons, the Parisians dignified them 'betimes with a taste of pleasure and liberty', which made them 'soon turbulent to Supream Authority' (although it was true, of course, that English gentlemen sent their sons to Paris 'to learn the honour and deportment of Manhood'). Crossing the Pont Neuf was just asking to be robbed, while the 'abundant Civility of *Paris*' gave rise to a joke in which two heavily-laden porters spent so long being overly civil to one another that 'they both sunk under their burdens, and so dy'd'.

This Paris-versus-London debate must have occasioned some humorous exchanges between Davenant and his French wife, who was then quite possibly pregnant with their first child. Samuel Pepys certainly enjoyed reading the wry speeches of the Parisian and the Londoner to his French-born wife when she was unwell. The Parliamentarian observer, present that first night, felt that 'the Londoner had the better of itt' – evidently, he failed to notice Davenant's denunciation of killjoy moralists.

The show ended with another song, comparing London's smog of 'Sea-coal Smoak' with the 'clearer Sky' of Paris, and an Epilogue, which claimed that the shillings paid by the audience had been kept 'as simple Tokens of your love.'

What *The First Dayes Entertainment at Rutland-House* lacked in spectacle it more than made up for in audacity. Sir William was fortunate, though, in that Lord Protector Cromwell was fond of 'a good voice and instrumental music'.

Davenant – who had troubled himself to analyse the causes of Puritanism, groping towards the realisation that cruel and abusive parenting created unbalanced, paranoid, obsessive adults – no doubt found Oliver Cromwell intriguing: both men had started out with limited prospects and endured long periods of financial insecurity. One of the defining moments in Cromwell's life came in 1635, when he tried to get his maternal uncle declared a lunatic. This flagrant ploy to seize an inheritance backfired, plunging Cromwell into an emotional crisis from which he emerged, in 1638, convinced that he was one of God's chosen 'elect'.

Like Davenant, Cromwell was not averse to taking risks. His ruthless opportunism, political acumen and military genius had belatedly earned him the wealth and status he hankered for. He now wielded more personal power than any English king before him, and in 1657 Parliament offered him the crown. Cromwell agonised for six weeks before turning the offer down.

Two of Cromwell's daughters were married within eight days of each other in November 1657.[4] The day after Frances Cromwell's marriage to Robert Rich, the wedding feast was held at Whitehall, 'where they had forty-eight violins and fifty trumpets and much mirth with frolics, besides mixt dancing (a thing hitherto counted profane)'. The merriment continued until five in the morning.

Cromwell's Puritanism had served its purpose and – it would seem – could be dispensed with, now that the Lord Protector had all that he ever wanted.

Emboldened by the success of his promotional *First Dayes Entertainment*, Davenant hastened to produce a more theatrical event. This was *The Siege of Rhodes*, which John Dryden would acknowledge as 'the first opera we ever had in England'.

The venue, again, was Rutland House. In a prefatory address 'TO THE READER', dated 17 August 1656, Davenant apologised for the scenery being 'confin'd to eleven foot in height, and about fifteen in depth' and for his cast being limited to seven persons. On 3 September he sent a copy of the text to his friend Bulstrode Whitelocke, the Lord Keeper of the Great Seal, along with a letter:

MY LORD,

    When I consider the nicety of the Times, I fear it may draw a Curtain between your Lordship and our Opera; therefore I have presumed to send your Lordship, hot from the Press, what we mean to represent; making your Lordship my supreme Judge, though I despair to have the Honour of inviting you to be a Spectator

The next day, Whitelocke noted in his journal that '*Sir William Davenant* printed his *Opera*; notwithstanding the nicety of the Times.'

The action was set in 1522, when the Ottoman Turks led by Sultan Suleiman ('Solyman') expelled the multinational Christian forces from the island of Rhodes, although an astute observer might have spotted the parallels with the besieged Royalists at Oxford in 1644. The curtain rose and 'a lightsome Sky appear'd, discov'ring a Maritime Coast, full of craggy Rocks, and high Cliffs … and, a far off, the true Prospect of the City RHODES, when it was in prosperous estate'. The Turkish fleet was also visible, 'making towards a Promontory some few miles distant from the Town.'

Duke Alphonso (played by Captain Henry Cook) and his comrades prepare to defend Rhodes. Meanwhile, the lovely Ianthe (played by Edward Coleman's wife, who thereby became the first woman to act on a public stage in England) resolves to sell all her jewellery and take the money to her embattled husband – just as Queen Henrietta had raised money for King Charles's war effort.

Solyman lands in Rhodes and scorns the behaviour of its Christian defenders:

> Bold in Adult'ries frequent change;
>   And ev'ry loud expensive Vice;
> Ebbing out wealth by ways as strange
>   As it flow'd in by avarice.

Ianthe is brought to him; she has been captured while transporting funds to her husband's army. Struck by her beauty and virtue, Solyman lets her go. He then determines not to attack Rhodes whilst Ianthe is there.

In the town, Ianthe is praised for having sold her jewellery to bring munitions to the beleaguered army when so many kings had failed to contribute:

> *Admiral:*   Look here ye Western Monarchs, look with shame,
>   Who fear not a remote, though common Foe;
>   The Cabinet of one illustrious Dame
>   Does more then your Exchequers joyn'd did do.
> *Alphonso:*   Indeed I think, *Ianthe,* few
>   So young and flourishing as you,
>   Whose Beauties might so well adorn
>   The Jewels which by them are worn,
>   Did ever Musquets for them take,
>   Nor of their Pearls did Bullets make.

Alphonso grows suspicious, though, that Solyman should have treated Ianthe so favourably. Othello-like, his jealousy begins to get the better of him. Solyman, for his part, rages that Ianthe and Alphonso have declined his offer of safe passage from the city, the comparisons with Charles and Henrietta Maria at Oxford continuing:

'Tis such a single pair
     As only equal are
Unto themselves; but many steps above
All others who attempt to make up Love.
Their Lives will noble History afford,
And must adorn my Scepter, not my Sword.

The fifth 'Entry' mirrored the opening of the first, with the Turkish army assailing the town and 'the greatest fury of the Army being discern'd at the English Station' (the scenery, designed by John Webb – who had collaborated with his uncle and father-in-law, Inigo Jones, on Davenant's *Salmacida Spolia* masque in 1640 – was especially innovative in depicting crowds and armies on the painted backcloths, although the attempts by the paltry cast of seven to recreate the final battle in *The Siege of Rhodes* would later be satirised by the Duke of Buckingham in *The Rehearsal*). Ianthe is wounded and Alphonso faces the dilemma of whether to rush to her defence or relieve his commanding officer, the Grand Master Villerius.

The Christian forces prevail. Alphonso is reconciled with Ianthe. A 'Chorus *of Souldiers*' wound up the opera:

You began the Assault
     With a very long Hault;
And, as haulting ye came,
     So ye went off as lame;
And have left our *Alphonso* to scoff ye.
     To himself, as a Daintie,
     He keeps his *Ianthe*;
Whilst we drink good Wine, and you drink but Coffy.

Davenant would revise and enlarge *The Siege of Rhodes* for the opening of the Duke's Playhouse in 1661, adding the part of Roxolana, Solyman's wife, and alternating the first part with a sequel. Somewhat slower than the first part, the second part of *The Siege of Rhodes* took the themes of jealousy and forgiveness about as far as they could go and supplied Samuel Pepys with the words, 'Beauty, retire! Thou dost my pity move!' which the diarist set to his own music.

All in all, Davenant's first 'opera' was an extraordinary achievement. Few productions ever broke more ground or did so in a time of prohibition. Richard Flecknoe

– seldom an uncritical admirer – would remark in his 'Poetical Fiction', *Sir William Davenant's Voyage to the other World*:

> But coming to his Siege of Rhodes,
> It outwent all the rest by odds;
> And somewhat in't that does out-do
> Both th' Antients and the Moderns too.

Thus far, Davenant had mounted his productions at his home. He now sought a licence to reopen the public theatre.

Early in 1657 he wrote to John Thurloe, spymaster and secretary to Cromwell's Council of State, giving his reasons for wishing to resurrect theatrical entertainments. It would, he argued, boost the London economy and prevent the citizens from becoming sad and dejected, 'being otherwise naturally inclin'd to that melancholy that breeds sedition'.[5] Theatre also had a propaganda value:

> If morall representations may be allow'd (being without obscenenesse, profanenesse, and scandal) the first arguments may consist of the Spaniards barbarous conquests in the West Indies and of their severall cruelties there exercis'd upon the subjects of this nation

A trade war with the Dutch had ended in 1654. This freed Lord Protector Cromwell to turn his attention to those traditional enemies of Protestant England – France

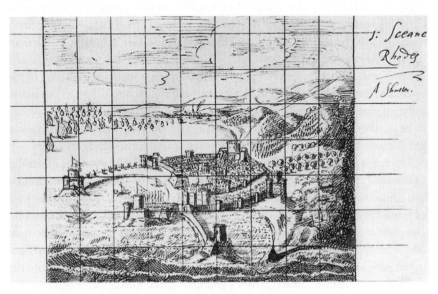

A painted backdrop for *The Siege of Rhodes* designed by John Webb.

and Spain. A massive English force had attempted to take the Spanish-held island of Hispaniola in 1655, the failure of that mission causing Cromwell to fear that God was no longer on his side. Davenant's suggestion that his 'opera' could help to whip up patriotic sentiment was aimed at Oliver Cromwell's ear.

Sir William cultivated influential figures. He wrote an epithalamium, '*The morning after the* Marriage *of the Earl of* Barymore *with Mrs.* Martha Laurence' – Martha being the daughter of Henry Lawrence, President of the Council of State – and a flattering poem '*To Mr.* Edward Laurence', who was Martha's brother. His assiduousness paid off. In the autumn of 1657, Davenant transferred *The Siege of Rhodes* to the Cockpit in Drury Lane, of which he had been appointed manager in 1640, before the outbreak of the Second Bishops' War.

By late July 1658 he had a new 'opera' at the Cockpit, its full title being *The Cruelty of the Spaniards in Peru. Exprest by Instrumentall and Vocall Musick, and by the Art of Perspective in Scenes, &c.* After so many years of colourless Puritanism, London must have been startled by the exotic scenery and fanciful costumes of Davenant's latest extravaganza, which he would later revive as the fourth act of *The Play-House to be Let.*

Over six 'Entries' the 'Priest of the Sun' recounted the history of the people of Peru, the Spanish conquest of the Incas and the arrival of the English 'under whose Ensigns … [the Peruvians] hope to be made Victorious, and to be freed from the Yoke of the *Spaniard*.' Each speech was followed by acrobatic displays and songs. After the sixth speech, a Spaniard loaded with 'Ingots of Gold, and Wedges of Silver' danced himself to sleep; two Apes then appeared, followed by a 'great Baboon', who danced with them before rousing the Spaniard and chasing him into a wood.

Sir Henry Herbert, reinstalled as Master of the Revels, would accuse Davenant of having written and produced 'the First and Second Parts of Peru' – the *Cruelty of the Spaniards* and its follow-up – 'in Olivers tyme, and soly in his favour; wherein hee sett of[f] the justice of Olivers actinges, by comparison with the Spaniards, and endeavoured thereby to make Olivers crueltyes appeare mercyes, in respect of the Spaniards crueltyes'. Herbert was blinded by his habitual opposition to Davenant, but even so this was a superficial assessment. While Davenant might have appeared to be justifying military action in the West Indies, the text could also be read as a searing indictment of the Protestant Reformation and the resulting civil wars.

The Priest of the Sun first described an idyllic society, 'When various sports did Man's lov'd freedom show, / And still the free were willing to obey'. This paradise was ruined by the coming of the 'Bearded People … Idolaters of Gold'. The last king of the Incas had divided the nation by choosing '*for his second Wife the beautiful Daughter of an inferiour Prince … [who] so far prevail'd on his passion, that she made him in his age assign a considerable part of his Dominion to a younger Son*'. Davenant might have been describing Henry VIII's second marriage to Anne Boleyn and the chaos that ensued when King Henry's youngest child, Edward VI, sided with the bearded reformers:

Soft conscience, Nature's whisp'ring Orator,
Did teach us what to love or to abhor;
   And all our punishment was shame.

Civil war had followed, the 'bearded Race' exploiting the divisions in the royal family until they '*did in a short time attain the Dominion over both by Conquest.*' The full horror of life under a repressive regime was shown in the fifth 'Entry', in which two solemnly-dressed Spaniards were seen torturing natives and English mariners. The Priest intoned:

What Race is this, who for our punishment
Pretend that they in haste from Heav'n were sent,
   As just destroyers of Idolatry?

An apt description of the 'godly' fanatics for whom 'The world still waste must lye, / Or else a Prison be to all but them'. Experience of the extremists' predilection for relentless persecution had opened the natives' eyes to the deceitful 'miracles' of these 'dark Divines'. But help was at hand: 'th' *English* Lyon now / Does still victorious grow'. That royal lion was King Charles II, then plotting with Spain to overthrow the republican dictatorship and restore monarchical rule in England.

Davenant's sleight-of-hand – appearing to cheer Cromwell's warmongering while subtly condemning the Protectorate – was brave and timely. The Lord Protector was dying. He succumbed to a urinary infection on 3 September 1658, the anniversary of his victories at Dunbar and Worcester, and was buried in Westminster Abbey in a ceremony modelled on the funeral of King James I.

Oliver Cromwell was succeeded by his son, Richard, who lacked the support of the New Model Army and inherited a colossal state debt. Nicknamed 'Tumbledown Dick', Richard Cromwell would govern as Lord Protector for just nine months.

Davenant continued the expensive task of entertaining the public ('O costly *Opera!*' he wrote of *The Siege of Rhodes*). His next opera, *The History of Sr Francis Drake*, was presented daily at 'Three after noone'. Seats cost a shilling, 'Notwithstanding the great expense necessary to Scenes'. In fact, by shifting the action from Panama to Peru, Davenant was able to recycle the scenery from *The Cruelty of the Spaniards*.

Anticipating the father-reborn-as-the-son motif of his later dramas, he presented 'Drake *Senior*' and 'Drake *Junior*' as two sides of the same character, the prototype Restoration hero. Sir Francis Drake unites the English army and navy to overcome the 'Symerons', 'a Moorish People, brought formerly to *Peru* by the Spaniards, as their Slaves' who 'having lately revolted … did live under the government of a King of their own Election'. The iconic Royal Oak was invoked as 'that Treė which much superiour grows / To all that in this Wood / Have many Ages stood'.

The tree was introduced in the fifth 'Entry'. A 'Beautiful Lady' is discovered tied to it, 'adorn'd with the Ornaments of a Bride, her hair dishevel'd, and complaining with her hands towards Heaven'. She had been taken prisoner by the cruel 'Symerons'. Suddenly, as if by magic, she is freed to return to her joyful Father and Bridegroom. The 'afflicted Bride', we can assume, was England.

He was pushing his luck. On 15 October 1658 a churchman wrote of a citizen's amazement, in the wake of Cromwell's funeral, that 'Sr Wm Davenant (Poet-laureate) hath obtained permission for Stage-plaies'. He hadn't, of course. But his operas were becoming indistinguishable from those forbidden plays. Rachel Newport wrote to her Royalist brother on 14 December: 'It is thought the Opera will speedily go down; the godly party are so much discontented with it.'

Just before Christmas, Richard Cromwell issued an order 'for taking into consideration the Opera shewed at the Cockpit in Drury-lane' and to 'examine by what authority the same is exposed to publick view'. On 5 February 1659, Parliament demanded an inquiry into the staging of plays 'and things of the like nature, called Opera, acted, to the scandal of Religion and Government.'

Davenant held his nerve. John Evelyn recorded his own visit on 5 May 1659 'to see a new opera after the Italian way in recitative musiq and sceanes' – almost certainly The History of Sr Francis Drake. Evelyn chastised himself for going to the theatre: 'my heart smote me for it.'

A month earlier, Parliament had been forced to decide between passing a resolution to banish 3,000 Royalist sympathisers from London and debating 'Sir Wm. Davenant and his opera'. John Thurloe's spy network had warned of a Royalist rebellion scheduled for 5 August. Davenant was one of the suspects rounded up at the start of August, but he was released from prison on 16 August.

Under pressure from the New Model the Rump Parliament had been recalled on 7 May. Richard Cromwell resigned as Lord Protector and faded from view. The public had lost faith in 'godly' government. Pepys would report on 7 February 1660: 'Boys do now cry "Kiss my Parliament" instead of "Kiss my arse," so great and general a contempt is the Rump come to among all the good and bad.'

By then, the recently-appointed commander of Parliament's forces had marched down from Scotland. Davenant excitedly penned 'A Panegyrick to his Excellency, the Lord Generall Monck':

> Auspicious Leader! None shall equall thee,
> Who makst our Nation and our Language free.

The Puritans, he observed, had fettered the people with their intolerance, restraining the English language with 'Scripture-phrase' and misquoting the 'good old Prophets' to make bad laws from 'ill translated Hebrew'.

Monck's army entered London on 3 February. On 16 March the reconstituted Long Parliament dissolved itself, having prepared the legislation for a new, predominantly Royalist parliament to be elected. The next day, Davenant obtained a pass to travel to France. By the end of March he had contracted to lease Lisle's Tennis Court in Lincoln's Inn Fields and turn it into a theatre.

The king was coming home.

Inigo Jones's costume design for Henrietta Maria's role in *Tempe Restored*, 1632.

PART THREE

A Young Man
in London

1622–1638

9

Ffor Avoyding of Inconvenience

Jane Davenant was buried at St Martin's Church, Carfax, on 5 April 1622. She was 53 years old. William, her second son, was 16.

His father was also ailing. John Davenant was halfway through his term as Mayor of Oxford. He drew up his will, which opened with the words 'It hathe pleased god to afflict me these 4 moneths', the nature of the affliction being a 'paine' rather than a sickness. John's last council meeting was held at his bedside on 17 April. He died two days later, two weeks after his wife was buried.

John wished to be buried as close to his wife 'as the place will give leave where she lyeth'. His funeral should be conducted 'in comely manner neither affecting pompe nor too much sparing'. The council decided to attend in their best scarlet apparel, so long as the Vice Chancellor and Doctors of the University did the same. The 'great Mace' of the City of Oxford was 'to be carryed next before the Hearse'. It was with no lack of ceremony that John Davenant was laid to rest in the same grave as his wife on 23 April 1622 – six years to the day after William Shakespeare died.

At least two elegies were written by local admirers. One saw John Davenant's life as exemplary:

What merits hee? Why, a contented life,
A happy yssue of a vertuous wife,
The choyce of friends, a quiet honor'd grave,
All these hee had; what more could Dav'nant have?

Another elegy, 'On Mr. Davenentt, Who Died att Oxford in His Maioralty a Fortnight after His Wife', was more suggestive:

Why should hee dye?
And yett why should he live, his mate being gone,
And turtle[dove]-like sigh out an endlesse moone?
No, no, he loved her better, and would not
So easely lose what hee so hardly gott.

He liv'd to pay the last rites to his bride;
That done, hee pin'd out fourteene dayes and died

There is a hint of possessiveness, even obsession, in the lines – 'No, no, he loved her better, and would not / So easely lose what hee so hardly gott.' The anonymous tribute implied that John had faced such a struggle to win Jane that he could not bear to be parted from her, even in death.

John left £200 to each of his daughters – Jane, Alice and Elizabeth – and £150 to each of his four sons. The family's tavern on Cornmarket would be run by the senior apprentice, Thomas Hallam, under the supervision of a neighbour who had always been 'loving just and kind' to John and Jane Davenant. Their daughters were also to help out in the tavern, and hopefully one of them would marry Thomas Hallam 'if he and shee can fancy one an other'. The eldest daughter, Jane, married Hallam that same year. They proceeded to run the tavern together.

The eldest son was then a 19-year-old scholar at St John's College. His father provided for his university expenses to be paid but insisted that 'my sonne Robert shall not make nor meddle with selling or trusting of wyne nor with any thing in the house but have entertanement as a brother for meals tydes and the like or to take Physicke in sickness'. Robert, who would become rector of several parishes in Pembrokeshire and Wiltshire, would have nothing to do with the family business. The third and fourth sons, John and Nicholas, were students at the Merchant Taylors' School in London. Both would have their school fees paid until they were ready to be 'put to prentice' (Nicholas was indeed apprenticed to a Merchant Taylor, although he then appears to have practised as an attorney: he was involved in the arrangements for leasing the Dorset Garden plot for the Duke's Theatre in 1670).

William was the only son of John and Jane Davenant who was not sent to school in London. He was privately educated in Oxford, 'but I fear he was drawn from school before he was ripe enough', wrote John Aubrey. His father stipulated in his will that 'my sonne William being now arrived to 16 yeares of age shall be put to prentice to some good marchant of London or other tradesman'. He would be given two changes of clothes and £40 in cash and goods to secure an apprenticeship. This should be done, his father resolved, 'within the compasse of 3 moneths after my death ffor avoyding of Inconvenience in my house for mastershippe when I am gone'.

Young William had more than just his father's legacy to trade upon. As the Oxford scholar Antony Wood later recalled, he had inherited his mother's 'very good wit and conversation'. He duly made his way to London within three months of his father's death, but not, as John Davenant had hoped, to become some good merchant or tradesman's apprentice. His first port of call, more or less, was a tailor named John Urswick, from whom William ordered a new outfit. Urswick acquired 'certain stuffe cloth lace and other necessaries', but when the suit was ready, and the tailor presented his bill for £14, young Davenant did not have the money.

An unseemly legal dispute between Davenant and Urswick would run for ten years or more, leading to Davenant being arrested twice, even though he had paid off the original debt by July 1624. The new suit, though, was vital, because young Davenant had found himself a position. As John Aubrey put it, 'he was preferred to the first Duchess of Richmond to wait on her as a page.'

Lady Frances Howard was the granddaughter of Thomas Howard, 3rd Duke of Norfolk and uncle to two of the wives of King Henry VIII. Her first marriage had been to Henry Prannell, the son of a wine merchant and alderman of London. Prannell died in 1599, leaving Frances a very wealthy young widow. She then secretly married Edward Seymour, 1st Earl of Hertford and nephew to Jane Seymour, who had borne Henry VIII's only legitimate son.

Lord Hertford was described as being 'of very small stature, and of timid and feeble character'. He died in his eighties in 1621. Within a couple of months, his widow had married again. Ludovic Stewart, 2nd Duke of Lennox, was a cousin to King James I and the son of James's former favourite, Esmé Stewart. In August 1623, Lennox was created Earl of Newcastle and Duke of Richmond, Lady Frances being known thereafter as the 'Double Duchess'.

John Aubrey did not indicate who had 'preferred' young William to the duchess's service. Davenant's forefathers had been in the same trade as her first husband, and it is notable that Lady Frances consulted the astrologer-physician Simon Forman in 1597 and 1598 about the possibility of her being pregnant (she wasn't). Jane Davenant and her sister-in-law, Ursula Sheppard, had also been consulting Forman at the same time, and about the same matter. It is possible, then, that Lady Frances had known Davenant's mother, and her brothers Thomas and Richard Sheppard, who were employed at Court as the royal perfumer and glove-maker. There is even the chance that young William namedropped his famous godfather, William Shakespeare, who had served the duchess's cousin, Thomas Howard, when he was Lord Chamberlain.

Lady Frances was an elderly snob. There was a theatrical air at Ely House, her mansion in Holborn. A letter from John Chamberlain to Sir Dudley Carleton, dated 8 January 1625, described the 'magnificence' of the duchess 'in going to her chappell at ely house on Sunday last':

> where she had her closet or traverse, her fowre principall officers steward chamberlain Treasurer controller, marching before her in velvet gownes wth their white staves, three gentlemen ushers, two Ladies that bare up her traine, the countesses of Bedford and mungumerie following wth the other Ladies two and two, wth a great deale of other apish imitation

Davenant had landed close to the epicentre of courtly power and influence – the king's cousin, no less! – and, in his fine new apparel, he no doubt drew glances from the likes of that 'universal patroness of poets', Lucy, Countess of Bedford,

The ruins of Ely House and chapel (1828).

and Susan de Vere, whose husband Philip, 1st Earl of Montgomery, was one of the 'Incomparable Paire of Brethren' to whom *Mr. William Shakespeares Comedies, Histories, & Tragedies* were about to be dedicated.

He would later tell John Aubrey that Lady Frances once 'sent him to a famous apothecary for some Unicornes-horne'. Powdered unicorn's horn was understandably expensive. It was believed to cure a range of diseases, as well as being an aphrodisiac and a means of proving a maiden's virginity. Davenant got hold of the substance and revealed his inquisitive nature by making a circle of the powder and placing a spider in the centre. No poisonous insect could cross a barrier of unicorn's horn.

Several times he tried the experiment. The spider repeatedly wandered out of the circle. Presumably, the young page had to report to his mistress that the 'Unicornes-horne' was a dud – but then, maybe the duchess had been in on the joke.

The Duke of Richmond died, aged 49, on 16 February 1624. The 'Double Duchess', after she had cut her hair in mourning, announced that she could not contemplate remarriage to anyone lowlier than a duke. She almost certainly had the king, a widower of five years, in her sights. But King James was in poor health, physically and mentally. Her income reduced, Lady Frances was obliged to curtail her domestic extravagance. She had to let Davenant go.

He was 18 years old and already married. Only his bride's first name is known. John Aubrey noted that she was 'Dr. ... 's daughter, physitian' – and there was the tale of Sir William, arrested for debt in 1654, being rescued by the beggars of the Lombard district who cheered 'the Knight who late did marry / The daughter of our 'pothecary.' One such pharmacist was Gideon Delaune. The son of a French Protestant pastor, Delaune had accompanied his father to London and became apothecary to Anne of Denmark. By 1624 he was apothecary to King James and junior warden of the Society of Apothecaries, making him a candidate for the 'famous apothecary' to whom Davenant was sent for some unicorn's horn. Delaune was appointed an alderman of Dowgate Ward, which bordered Lombard Street, in 1626. He helped to found the Apothecaries' Hall in Blackfriars, where Davenant would rehearse his actors while Lisle's Tennis Court was being converted, and he died in 1659, aged 94.

Davenant told Aubrey that Delaune was 'his great acquaintance'. After returning from exile in France, Davenant visited Delaune, 'being then in his eighties [wrote Aubrey], and very decrepit with the gout':

> and even though he was master of such an estate, Sir William saw him slighted not only by his daughter-in-law, but by the cook-maid, which much affected him – misery of old age.

It could be that Davenant's first wife was the daughter of that 'very wise man', Gideon Delaune, whose estate at his death was valued at £80,000. Perhaps the wily old Duchess of Richmond was privy to the courtship, hence the tomfoolery of the unicorn's horn, which would test whether the girl was a virgin or not.

The marriage appears to have been a shotgun affair.[1] What is known for sure is that on 27 November 1624 the first child of William and Mary Davenant was baptised at St James's Church, Clerkenwell. This was Davenant's 'very beautifull and ingeniose son', William, who would die at the Taverne in Oxford while his father was imprisoned in the Tower of London.

Davenant soon found employment at one of the properties neighbouring Ely House in Holborn. Brooke House was the London residence of the poet, playwright and politician Fulke Greville, who was raised to the peerage in 1621 as the 1st Baron Brooke.

Greville was born on 3 October 1554 at Beauchamp's Court, near Alcester in Warwickshire. His father was recorder of Stratford-upon-Avon until his death in 1606, when his son inherited the post. By then, Greville had been granted Warwick Castle by King James I, and this became his principal home in the Midlands.

The move to Brooke House was an advantageous one for Davenant. Fulke Greville had been a member of the 'Areopagus' circle of poets and spies, which included the courtier-poet Sir Philip Sidney, whose lingering death after the Battle of Zutphen in 1586 affected Greville deeply. He then fell in love with Sidney's sister Mary, who became the mother of William and Philip Herbert, the brothers to whom the First Folio of Shakespeare's plays was dedicated in 1623.

Greville was also a patron to the reigning poet laureate, Ben Jonson, who almost certainly knew of Davenant's existence in London. Jonson had lodged for five years with Esmé Stewart, who became Duke of Lennox on the death of this brother

Ludovic in 1624. When Davenant entered the Duchess of Richmond's household in 1622 it was as a servant to the sister-in-law of Ben Jonson's patron, and this at a time when Jonson, on behalf of another of his patrons – William Herbert, 3rd Earl of Pembroke – was helping to steer Shakespeare's *Comedies, Histories, & Tragedies* through the presses.

One of Davenant's earliest poems was his Ode, 'In remembrance of Master *William Shakespeare*':

(1)

Beware (delighted Poets!) when you sing
To welcome Nature in the early Spring;
 Your num'rous Feet not tread
The Banks of Avon; for each Flowre
(As it nere knew a Sunne or Showre)
 Hangs there, the pensive head.

(2)

Each Tree, whose thick, and spreading growth hath made,
Rather a Night beneath the Boughs, than Shade,
 (Unwilling now to grow)
Lookes like the Plume a Captive weares,
Whose rifled *Falls* are steept i'th teares
 Which from his last rage flow.

(3)

The piteous River wept it selfe away
Long since (Alas!) to such a swift decay;
 That reach the Map; and looke
If you a River there can spie;
And for a River your mock'd Eie,
 Will finde a shallow Brooke.

The River Avon had not really wept itself away at the death of Shakespeare. Davenant was insinuating that, with the Bard of Avon gone, the only poet left in town was the 'shallow Brooke' – Fulke Greville, recorder of Stratford-upon-Avon and recently-created Baron Brooke.

Greville once challenged his servant to write him a poem. The result, 'To the Lord *B.* in performance of a vow, that night to write to him', was published in 1638:

My Lord, it hath beene ask'd, why 'mongst those few
I singled out for Fame, I chose not you
With early speed the first?

'There are degrees, that to the Altar lead;' continued Davenant, 'Where ev'ry rude, dull Sinner must not tread:

> 'Tis not to bring, a swift thankes-giving Tongue,
> Or prayers made as vehement as long,
> Can privilege a zealous Votarie,
> To come, where the High Priest should only be

The impudence of deploying such Catholic images as altars and votaries in a poem to a committed Calvinist like Greville hints at some secret meaning or subtext. The conclusion to the poem returns to the topic on which Greville and Davenant could hardly have seen eye to eye:

> My Vow now kept, I'm loth (my Lord) to doe
> Wrong to your justice, and your mercy too;
> The last, if you vouchsafe; you will excuse
> A strong Religion here, though not a Muse.

The poem says nothing, other than seeking to excuse Davenant's failure to rank Greville among the leading poets on the grounds that he was not yet sufficiently accomplished to applaud his master. It is an oddly noncommittal piece, peppered with subversive 'popish' symbolism, which keeps promising to praise Lord Brooke but consistently avoids doing so. The tone is passive-aggressive throughout.

In February 1623 the Prince of Wales set out on a madcap expedition with his glamorous friend George Villiers, 1st Duke of Buckingham and favourite (some would say lover) of King James, to woo the princess of Spain. Prince Charles declared that 'No one loved a lady more ardently than he did the Infanta', but the Infanta had no intention of marrying a Protestant. Spain demanded an end to the persecution of English Catholics before any marriage contract could be agreed. After six frustrating, fruitless months, Charles and Buckingham returned to England.

En route to Madrid, the pair had visited Paris where, badly disguised, they looked in on the French Court and saw 'nineteen fair dancing ladies' preparing for a masque. Among them was the 13-year-old Henrietta Maria rehearsing the part of Iris, handmaiden to Juno, who was played by Anne of Austria, the wife of Louis XIII and sister to the Spanish Infanta. When negotiations got underway for an Anglo-French alliance, Prince Charles remembered the delicate Henrietta Maria as 'the most admirable sweet creature in this world'. The proposed Spanish match was called off and by May 1624, Henrietta Maria, 'Madame de France', was the openly acknowledged 'mistress' of Charles, Prince of Wales.

Love letters passed to and fro between Charles and Henrietta while their respective courts bickered over the problem of religious toleration. The French wanted 'liberty' for Catholics in England. King James offered only to show them 'favour'.

But James was ill, his thoughts 'a whirl of a thousand fears'. He suffered a stroke and died, during a violent and messy bout of dysentery, on 27 March 1625, his beloved Buckingham at his bedside.

As Davenant settled into his new job at Brooke House, a new age began. Charles Stuart was proclaimed King of England, Scotland and Ireland. He vowed to reform the excesses of his father's Court, promising his subjects 'constancy in religion, sincerity in action' and that he would 'not have recourse to subterfuges in his dealings'.

Charles and Henrietta Maria were married by proxy at Notre-Dame Cathedral on Sunday, 1 May 1625. The king despatched Buckingham 'to hasten and facilitate the journey of my dear wife'. In June a fleet of twenty British ships arrived at Boulogne, firing a 100-gun salute. Henrietta sailed for England. Charles hurried to Dover Castle, where he took the 15-year-old queen in his arms and kissed her 'with all the tenderness which an immaculate and unspotted affection could express'.

This was the couple whom Davenant would serve so faithfully through the difficult years ahead. For now, though, he was a mere servant in an ageing baron's household and about to embark on a new career.

The Cruell Brother. A Tragedy was licensed on 12 January 1627 by Sir Henry Herbert, recently appointed Master of the Revels. Davenant's first play, written when he was not yet 21, was then performed 'at the private House, in the *Blacke-Fryers: By His Majesties Servants*' – that is, by Shakespeare's old company.

The First Folio of Shakespeare's works had been published in December 1623. Davenant, it seems, had read it. There are clear echoes of *Hamlet* and *Othello* in his first theatrical offering, as well as a direct reference to Tarquin's rape of Lucretia, reflecting Shakespeare's long poem, *The Rape of Lucrece*, of 1594.

The scene is '*Italy*'. Count Lucio – a very Shakespearean name – is the favourite of the Duke of Siena, who refers to him lovingly:

My glorious Boy, you are too vigilant:
The Sunne, and you, doe visite me at once.
This courtship is not safe. You must not meete
Your Lover, with a Rivall, glorious
As your selfe.

Count Lucio is secretly in love with Corsa, the sister of his 'Creature' [manservant], Foreste. Humble in origin, Foreste is a man of strict morals. He warns Lucio that 'I would eate your Heart, should it contrive / A way in thought, how to cheate my Sister / Of her pure Chastitie' and refuses to advance a suit presented by a 'Court Satyrist' to establish a money-making monopoly. This '*satyricall* Courtier', Castruchio, is the very image of the playwright Ben Jonson – as Foreste tells him:

You, you must be a Satyrist forsooth,
Calumniate by instinct and inspiration.

As if just Heaven would borrow Gall of you,
Wherewith to write our faults [...]
Why I could never see thee yet but drunke:
Which makes thy Verses reele and stagger so.[2]

Offended, Castruchio challenges Foreste to fight. Foreste wounds him and lets him go – 'Take thy sword. Now get thee home and rayle upon't, / Because t'would fight no better.' To which Castruchio responds:

Yet we may meete i'th' darke. You have a throat,
And there are Knives in *Italy*.

The Duke appoints Foreste his Secretary of State, regardless of his 'birth obscure and base'. Foreste warns his wife, Luinna, that his duties will impact on their married life. Count Lucio then appears, entranced by the singing of his chaste and beloved Corsa. Foreste marries his sister Corsa to his master Lucio, who exclaims 'Excellent wretch!' – the first of two occasions in the play when Davenant steals that line from *Othello*.

Castruchio, meanwhile, declaims that 'The world is altred', reminding the audience of Ben Jonson's first play, *The Case is Altered*. The satirist has written 'a most pestilent Libell' about Foreste, but cannot attack him openly, now that he holds high office. 'Behold society / Amongst the wicked', cries Castruchio, railing against those around him.

Davenant introduces a topical note when Foreste pontificates on the 'forward and affectate violence' of the French: 'T'is a giddy Nation; / And never serious but in trifles.' The Duke corrects him:

    Fruite that is ripe
Is prone to fall, or to corrupt it selfe.
According to the age of Monarchies:
They are now fully ripe: they reach
The height, and top of mortall faculties.
Nature in them doth stand upon the verge
Of her owne youth. The English want
Three hundred yeeres of that perfection.

This comparison of the French with the English – inspired, perhaps, by Davenant's marriage to the daughter of a Frenchman – also reflected the marriage of King Charles to Henrietta Maria, 'Madame de France', and the emotional gulf which had opened up between them, thanks to religious differences and the mutual antipathy of their households. The Duke of Siena seems to stand for the late King James; his 'glorious Boy', Lucio, representing Charles and the virtuous Corsa,

Henrietta. Lucio's 'Creature', therefore, would be the Duke of Buckingham, son of an obscure Leicestershire gentleman and now one of the most powerful individuals in the land.

Lucio confesses to the duke that he has married Foreste's sister. Initially dismayed, the duke is soon charmed by Corsa – 'Excellent wretch! with a / Timerous modesty, she stifleth up / Her utterance. O such a pregnant Eye! / And yet so slow of speech' – and vows, 'Your Mariage we will solemnize with masques / And Revels.'

The duke pays Foreste's wife a secret visit, presenting her with a precious jewel and demanding that she convey an even more costly trinket to Corsa. Troubled by this gift, Corsa is persuaded not to tell her husband about it.

Castruchio seizes on a means of avenging himself on Foreste. He draws up his rival's pedigree 'I'th' shape of a tree (which takes roote in Hell)':

> On that branch appeares a Hangman. Then,
> A Jakes-man [toilet cleaner], then, a Tynker. On's Mothers side
> A Bawde profess'd. then, a Tybb [young prostitute]. then, a Trypewife.
> A Synagogue of Welsh Rabbys; could not
> Expresse more skill in Genealogies,
> Then this includes.

Foreste is outraged that his humble origins have been defamed. Another courtier refers to Davenant's experiment with the spider: 'Know ye not Rogues, that I can muzle up / The testie Unicorne, in a Spinners threed?'

The duke sends Lucio on an unnecessary embassy in order to get Corsa to himself – 'To wrong my boy, unkinde, incestuous heate! / Why is Copulation legal; it gives / Authority to lust'. He enlists the help of Castruchio, bribing him with gold, to which Ben Jonson was ever susceptible. Castruchio exploits his 'interest' in Corsa's maid to secure access to Corsa's chamber, insisting that Corsa 'tooke it willingly!' when the duke, like 'Tarquins Ghost', raped her.

Foreste's jealousy has already been aroused by the duke's gift of a jewel to his wife. He arranges for her to be gang-raped, but when she blurts out 'your Sister's ravish'd by the Duke' he swears a more brutal revenge ('I will be just / Yet cruell too'). He binds his sister to a chair and cuts her wrists:

> Corsa: Oh, oh, oh –
> Fores: A Convulsion in her Arteries!
> Corsa: Mercy Heaven!
> Fores: Hearke!
>   As she ascends, the Spheares doe welcome her,
>   With their owne Musicke. – Her Soule is gone!

So Corsa bleeds to death, to the sound of 'Recorders: Sadly.'

Lucio returns, having been summoned by an urgent letter from Corsa, and finds her 'newly murdered in her Chayre.' Foreste explains: 'The royall Goate (the *Duke*) hath ravish'd her … And finding you betray'd in your owne Fort! / I slit her Wrist-vaynes, and gave perpetuall / Liberty, to her polluted Blood.' Lucio and Foreste vow to kill the duke. They enter his chamber, where Lucio discovers that he cannot murder his 'Royall Master'. Lucio and Foreste make their escape, unaware that the duke has stationed Castruchio and two others outside the chamber. The duke belatedly remembers this and rushes out to warn them, only to be mistakenly slain by the guards – 'O, O, O, I am surpriz'd in my owne snare'. Lucio and Foreste battle with the guards; both are wounded and, forgiving each other, they die. Castruchio and his men are taken prisoner and warned, 'the Law will heere on Earth / Provide such tortures as shall make your deaths / Exemplary to all succeeding times.'

The last words form the moral of the play:

So intricate is Heavens revenge gainst lust,
The righteous suffer here, with the unjust.

Davenant's first venture into playwriting won scant applause, possibly because the duke's behaviour implied that a return to the moral laxity of King James's Court would destroy Henrietta Maria, with her sweet singing voice, the solemn Charles and – the third point of the triangle – the high-climbing Buckingham, who had become a bridge and a wedge between their majesties. Also, by creating a villain so obviously modelled on Ben Jonson, Davenant was distancing himself from the personality cult of the poet laureate. At the time this would have been seen as a provocative and foolhardy way for a newcomer to launch his career.

But Davenant was playing his own game, and if *The Cruel Brother* called into question the probity of the late King James, his next play was dedicated to an infamous victim of the Jacobean Court.

Like *The Cruel Brother*, Davenant's *Albovine, King of the Lombards* was probably written when the plague struck in 1625–26, killing some 40,000 Londoners. Unlike *The Cruel Brother*, it was never performed.

Albovine drew on the ancient history of Lombardy and shared several character names (Paradine, Rhodalinda, Gondibert, Hermegild) with *Gondibert*, written more than twenty years later. A Shakespearean influence is apparent throughout, with strong echoes of *Titus Andronicus* and *Othello*, touches of *Hamlet*, *Macbeth* and *Romeo and Juliet*, and references to *Julius Caesar* and *A Midsummer Night's Dream*.

The warlike Albovine[3] conquers the city of Verona without so much as a fight and announces that he will marry his captive, Rhodalinda. Albovine also has a male favourite, Paradine, who is likewise a prisoner. The king's fondness for his favourite is viewed with disgust by his soldiers: 'the Royall foole greets him with such / Ravenous kisses, that you would thinke, he meant / To eate his lips.' Paradine is in love with Valdaura, and they celebrate their marriage at the same time as Albovine makes Rhodalinda his bride.

At the wedding banquet, Albovine gets roaring drunk and calls for the 'Bowle of Victory'. Paradine protests: 'Sir, you ingag'd your Royall word, never / To present that fatall object.' But Albovine will not be moved – 'I shall delight in fury!'

A skull, made into a drinking bowl, is brought to him:

Welcome, the horrid Trophey of my chief warre!
Rhodalinda, Ile try thy fortitude.
This was thy Fathers Skull: thou shalt pledge a health
Unto his Ghost.

Rhodalinda recoils in horror. She refuses to share a bed with Albovine. And though the king is repentant, his treasurer Hermegild – formerly a counsellor to Rhodalinda's father and now a captive, 'a man / Created in the darke … He dwels in Labyrinths' – seizes his opportunity to set the tragedy in motion.

Hermegild inveigles Paradine into sleeping with the vengeful Rhodalinda, who then blackmails the favourite. She demands that he kill Albovine:

Stay, *Paradine*. If thou dost mocke my hopes
With a slow motion in this just designe,
Expect to finde my anger fatall. Ile to
The King, and make a forfeiture of both
Our lives: but if with hardy sinnewes thou dost march
To 's Throat, and slit the swarthy Pipe, I'le call
Thee then my Souldier.

As Rhodalinda convinces Paradine that his bride, Valdaura, is 'a open whore', the villainous Hermegild lets Valdaura see Rhodalinda whispering in Paradine's ear. Hermegild then instructs Valdaura to give Paradine a slow-acting poison: 'Foure dayes must fully take / Their roome ith'Kalender, ere it effect / Our hopes' – by which time Paradine must be coerced into killing the king.

The onstage death that Davenant had previously contrived for Corsa, tied to a chair and her wrists slashed by her cruel brother, inspired him to go further in *Albovine*. Valdaura, dressed in mourning, tells her husband that she has poisoned him because King Albovine informed her of his – Paradine's – adultery with Queen Rhodalinda. Paradine stabs Valdaura with his poniard and lowers her into a chair. She then admits that she did not poison him after all; neither is she the 'foule loose whore' she claimed to be. Paradine confesses that the 'sinfull Queene' and Hermegild tricked him into committing adultery, and Valdaura, just before she dies, discloses that it was Hermegild who tried to persuade her to poison Paradine.

Paradine steals into Albovine's chamber, only to find (like Lucio in *The Cruel Brother*) that he cannot slay the king. He rouses Albovine and explains: 'Your blacke adulterous Queene betray'd / Me to her lust by wicked Arts.' The king insists on fighting with him and is wounded. Paradine seats the dying Albovine in a chair and discovers the full extent of Hermegild's treachery.

Rhodalinda tells Paradine that '*Hermegild* must die, / He knowes too much.' She pulls Paradine to a chair and kisses him. He chews off her lips and stabs her to death.

Paradine now pretends to be dying of the poison supposedly administered by Valdaura. Hermegild gloats: 'I know th'Ingredients of thy poysnous draught. / 'Twas I that gave it to thy wife.' Paradine snatches Hermegild's sword and reveals Valdaura, Albovine and Rhodalinda, all dead in chairs. Hermegild gasps, 'O triviall Arts, with my / Owne Myne I've blowne my selfe e'en into dust!' Paradine runs him through, and Hermegild dies:

Vaine Arts! Ambition in all sacred Schooles,
Is held the sinne of Heathens, and of Fooles.

The Tragedy of Albovine, King of the Lombards: By Wm. D'avenant was published in 1629 with a dedication to 'The Right Honourable The Earle of Somerset', who had 'read this *Tragedie*, and smil'd upon 't'. The Earl of Somerset no doubt saw something of himself in Paradine, the favourite of the drunken, lascivious king.

Robert Carr was an exceptionally handsome young Scotsman who fell off his horse and broke his leg, winning the heart of King James, in 1607. Carr was willing to tolerate, and even encourage, the king's demonstrative affections. He was swiftly promoted to high office.

Carr fell in love with the youthful beauty of the Court, Frances Howard,[4] who was unhappily married to the Earl of Essex. King James colluded in securing an annulment of the marriage so that Lady Frances could marry his favourite, whom he ennobled as the Earl of Somerset. But Carr's friend, Sir Thomas Overbury, opposed the match. The king arranged for Overbury to be imprisoned in the Tower of London, where he died shortly before Lady Frances was granted her controversial divorce.

By then, King James had fallen for a new favourite – George Villiers, soon-to-be Duke of Buckingham. The Puritans at Court conspired with James's queen, Anne of Denmark, to promote the gorgeous Villiers, simultaneously undermining Somerset and his Howard in-laws. Sir Thomas Overbury's hideous death lent itself to exploitation by Somerset's enemies. Led by Ben Jonson's patron, William Herbert, Earl of Pembroke, the Archbishop of Canterbury, George Abbott, and Fulke Greville, then Chancellor of the Exchequer, an investigation was launched into the alleged murder of Overbury by means of a slow-acting poison. After several minor players had been executed, Robert Carr, Earl of Somerset, and his wife, Lady Frances, were put on trial in May 1616. Both were found guilty of murder.

Neither was executed. The king pardoned Lady Frances on 13 July 1616, although the couple would remain prisoners in the Tower for another six years. Somerset protested his innocence and did not receive his pardon until 7 October 1624. Naturally, the Somersets were ruined. The Puritan faction had won.

Davenant's dedication of *Albovine* to the 'Earle of Somerset' was provocative in the extreme. Though he was employed by the puritanical Fulke Greville he had openly aligned himself with the opposing party. It was a bold move, and one that provoked the acting Master of the Revels, Henry Herbert, who was related to William Herbert, Earl of Pembroke.

Albovine recreated, in the form of a Jacobean tragedy, the downfall of the king's former favourite – a lurid tale of homoerotic fixation, scheming courtiers, lust, adultery, poison and murder. The published text came with several commendatory verses, including one by a 'H. Howard'. But it is the poem by 'Ed. Hyde' that deserves consideration here. Edward Hyde would in time become the 1st Earl of Clarendon and Lord Chancellor of England, before he was rudely dismissed by King Charles II in 1667. He wrote 'To his friend, Mr. Wm. D'avenant':

> *Why should the fond ambition of a friend,*
> *With such industrious accents strive to lend*
> *A Prologue to thy worth? [...]*
> *Thy Wit hath purchas'd such a Patrons name*
> *To deck thy front, as must derive to Fame*
> *These Tragick raptures, and indent with Eyes*
> *To spend hot tears, t'inrich the Sacrifice.*

The dedication of the unacted *Albovine* to the disgraced Earl of Somerset was clearly approved of by Davenant's new friends.

10

The Shade of Gentle Buckingham

Twenty years later, in the Preface to his unfinished *Gondibert*, Davenant told Thomas Hobbes, 'the desire of Fame made me a Writer.' But in dedicating *The Tragedy of Albovine* to the Earl of Somerset, Davenant explained: 'My *Numbers* I [do] not shew unto the publick *Eye*, with an ambition to bee quickly knowne; (for so I covet *noyse*, not *fame*).' The distinction was a subtle one. At the age of 23, Davenant claimed to be less interested in courting adulation than in causing a stir.

One piece of evidence suggests that he was achieving notoriety, if not celebrity. John Taylor – known as the 'Water-Poet' after his seven-year apprenticeship as a waterman ferrying passengers across the River Thames – was a prolific writer with more than 150 publications to his name. In 1628 he produced a joke book entitled, *Wit and Mirth, Chargeably collected out of Tavernes, Ordinaries, Innes, Bowling Greenes, and Allyes, Alehouses, Tobacco shops, Highwaies, and Water-passages*. The 39th quip in the book read thus:

> A Boy, whose mother was noted to bee one not overloden with honesty, went to seeke his Godfather, and enquiring for him, quoth one to him, who is thy Godfather: the boy reply'd his name is goodman Digland the Gardiner: Oh said the man, if he be thy Godfather he is at the next Alehouse: but I feare thou takest Gods name in vaine.

Substitute the verb-noun '*Shakespeare*' for '*Digland* the Gardiner'[1] and you have the tale told of young William Davenant by Thomas Hearne, the sober-minded antiquarian of Oxford, in 1709. The same story was relayed by William Oldys, who heard it from Alexander Pope, who heard it from Thomas Betterton, who knew Davenant well.

The inclusion of the gag in John Taylor's *Wit and Mirth* has been used to downplay the incident, as if it were merely an old chestnut which had somehow been grafted onto Davenant. However, when Taylor published his book Davenant was a young man-about-town who probably frequented the very taverns, bowling-greens and alleyways where the Water-Poet recorded his 'Quirkes'. The joke, as recounted by Taylor in 1628, does not negate the Oxford tradition regarding Davenant's paternity. If anything, it strengthens it. Six years after his arrival in London, Davenant was being talked about, however scandalously. Seeking '*noyse*, not *fame*', that suited him just fine.

An event of 1628 would have added to the gossip surrounding his name. His employer, Fulke Greville, paid a visit to his London home on 1 September. Greville was overheard having a heated discussion with his manservant, Ralph Haywood. The word 'will' was mentioned. This was probably not Greville's will, which Haywood had witnessed.

Greville had been to the lavatory. Haywood was helping to fasten his master's breeches to his doublet (the trousers were attached to the jacket with small hooks). The servant suddenly thrust a dagger into Greville's side, once in the back, between the lower ribs, and again, a little lower down. Haywood then ran from the room, locking the door, and disappeared into his own chamber, where he stabbed himself four times in the chest with the knife he had used against his lordship.

Unaware that his servant had killed himself, Greville 'did desire that if Haywood were escaped out of the house that he should not be prosecuted, desiring not that any man should lose his life for him.' This statement, which was reported the next day in a letter to Greville's friend Sir John Coke, is strangely ambiguous. It could be read as implying that Haywood's grievance was valid, and that Greville recognised it as such. By 'desiring not that any man should lose his life for him', the victim might also have acknowledged that the attack was not the work of a lone servant. Others, perhaps, were implicated, though they had not wielded the dagger.

In the same letter to Sir John Coke, Edward Reed stated: 'My Lord had given Haywood £20 a year for his life now at his [Greville's] coming from Warwick.' The master had been generous to his aged retainer, so why had Ralph Haywood been arguing with Fulke Greville about a 'will' before he stabbed him? John Aubrey, using information supplied to him by William Davenant, would simply indicate that Haywood 'had long waited on [Greville] and his lordship had often told [Haywood] that he would do something for him, but did not, but still put him off with delays.'

It is interesting to note that when *Certaine Learned and Elegant Workes* of Fulke Greville, Lord Brooke, were published five years later the Table of Contents was immediately followed by page 23. Some twenty-odd pages had gone missing, suggesting that someone had removed an introductory epistle at the last minute, presumably because of the matter it contained. Something, it seems, was being hushed up.

Greville's wounds were treated with animal fat. He languished for a month and died on 30 September 1628, three days before his 74th birthday.

Davenant made no comment on his master's murder. As he later told John Aubrey, the death of Lord Brooke 'was scarce taken notice of' because a more high-profile figure had recently been assassinated.

George Villiers, the handsome Duke of Buckingham, remained the loyal favourite of King James after the spectacular downfall of the Earl of Somerset. He also cultivated a relationship with the lonely Prince of Wales, becoming a welcome replacement for Charles's elder brother. They travelled together to Madrid to woo the Spanish Infanta, after which Buckingham was instrumental in hastening the marriage of King Charles to Henrietta Maria, 'Madame de France'.

Buckingham's power far outstripped his abilities. He excelled at making enemies at home and abroad, and his military adventures tended towards disaster. Parliament twice tried to impeach him. In August 1628 he was in Portsmouth, preparing to launch his third assault on La Rochelle. Early on 23 August, Buckingham was fatally stabbed by a disaffected army officer named John Felton.

The nation rejoiced. There was much sympathy for Felton, whose body, mistakenly returned to Portsmouth after his execution, became an object of veneration. Deprived of his feckless friend, King Charles developed a deep attachment to his French queen. The royal marriage, which had begun so well only to grow bitter under Buckingham's influence, rapidly improved.

Davenant – typically – went against the grain. He wrote a poem, '*Elizium*', to Buckingham's widow, imagining a paradise where a '*Vestal's* Shadow' carefully 'attends the *Shade* of gentle *Buckingham*':

> Who there unenvi'd sits, with Chaplets crownd;
> And with wise scorne, smiles on the Peoples wound:
> He call'd it so; for though it touch'd his heart,
> His Nation feeles the rancour, and the smart.

In another poem to the bereaved duchess – whose father, the 6th Earl of Rutland, owned the house where Davenant would one day mount his *First Dayes Entertainment* – he lamented: 'For gone is now the Pilot of the State, / The Courts bright Star, the Clergies Advocate, / The Poets highest Theame, the Lovers flame, / And Souldiers Glory, mighty *Buckingham*.'

It may be that Davenant had been introduced to Buckingham by Fulke Greville. Two letters survive, written by Greville to Buckingham before and during the ill-conceived Spanish jaunt of 1623. In the first, Greville – then aged 63 – referred to Buckingham (aged 30) as his 'grandfather'; in the second, he signed himself the duke's 'loving grandchild and humble servant'. Some reason must be given for Davenant's continued attendance on Greville, a man with whom he had little in common, the most obvious being that William was anxious to exploit Greville's contacts, including the influential Buckingham.

The possibility exists that Davenant volunteered to take part in Buckingham's catastrophic siege of Saint-Martin-de-Ré, near La Rochelle, in 1627 – an operation which saw the deaths of more than 5,000 soldiers out of a total force of 7,000.

This would make sense of Thomas Ellice's remarks in a poem published with Davenant's *Albovine*:

Wise Fame shall sing the prayse of thy deserts,
And voyce thee glorious both in Armes and Arts.
Whilst thou, releast from the Warres sad mishaps,
Rests in soft dalliance on the Muses laps

An introduction to Buckingham in 1627 or thereabouts might also account for the start of Davenant's friendship with Endymion Porter. Raised in Spain, Porter acted as interpreter to Charles and Buckingham during their abortive wooing of the Infanta. He married Buckingham's Catholic niece, Olivia Boteler, who became a lady-in-waiting to Queen Henrietta, and served as Buckingham's Master of the Horse. Porter would support Davenant through thick and thin, and Davenant remained deeply attached to Olivia and her offspring after Endymion's death in 1649.

The assassination of the Duke of Buckingham overshadowed the murder of Fulke Greville, who was stabbed a week later. Greville had no children; his heir was his cousin and adopted son, Robert Greville, who took Parliament's side in the Civil War. Whatever his private feelings about the death of 'Lord B.', the 'shallow Brooke', Davenant found himself, at the age of 22, without employment.

The Anglo-French war sparked by Buckingham's attempts to relieve the Protestants at Saint-Martin-de-Ré in 1627 rumbled on. Eager to be noticed, Davenant put himself forward for a daredevil mission. He sent his proposal to Dudley Carleton, 1st Viscount Dorchester, who became Secretary of State to King Charles in December 1628:

The action I would prefer unto your Lo[rdshi]pp. concernes the Storehowse, or magazin of Dunkerck; and is to be effected, by a secrett illumination of Powder. The meanes to this performance, I arrive at, by the easinesse of a friend; whoe is now Officiall in the Magazin, and his assistance hath given me power to receave imployments there. I have knowledg of a small Engine, that will inforce a usefull fire, at my owne limits, or just when some assualtt upon the Towne shall apoint the distruction of Powder. If ought in this certificate, give hope of advantage to his Ma[jes]tie, I shall performe the service, though with the losse of my life.

Davenant's offer to blow up the magazine at Dunkirk with gunpowder was not taken up. An unsigned and undated copy of his memorandum was endorsed by Dorchester with the words: 'Mr Davenant lodging in ye Middle Temple wth Mr Hide; sonne to my Ld Chief Justice elder brother'. Evidently, Davenant had moved to one of the four Inns of Court where young gentlemen studied law.

Established in 1388, the Middle Temple stood between Fleet Street and the River Thames, close to the Blackfriars and Salisbury Court theatres. Edward Hyde, the nephew of Sir Nicholas Hyde, Lord Chief Justice of England, was then 19 years old. He had entered the Middle Temple in 1625, returning the next year, after an illness, to occupy a pleasant suite on the fourth floor of the Temple's new wing.

Ever grave and serious, Hyde would look back on his Middle Temple years with a certain dismay. 'There never was an Age,' he wrote, 'in which … so many young Gentlemen … were insensibly and suddenly overwhelmed in that Sea of Wine, and Women, and Quarrels, and Gaming'. London was crawling with soldiers back from foreign wars. Hyde wasted much of his time with 'many of those Officers' before he 'had the good Fortune quickly to make a full Retreat from that Company'. Having Davenant as a lodger didn't help, and though their friendship would last for many years the poet invariably reminded the future Lord Chancellor of those riotous times.[2]

The death of Buckingham might have stalled Davenant's advance towards the heart of royal government, but he quickly surrounded himself with bright young men who, as in the case of Edward Hyde, would come to exert great influence over English affairs. Those who provided praise poems for *Albovine* were mostly men of the Inns of Court: Roger Lort was at the Middle Temple, along with Edward Hyde; Richard Clerke (a cousin of the poet Abraham Cowley) was at Lincoln's Inn; Henry Blount and William Habington were at Gray's Inn with Robert and Thomas Ellice, the latter having been admitted on the same day as Davenant's 'great & intimate' friend, Sir John Suckling.

Missing, as usual, from the records is Davenant's wife. They had been married for five years or so, but there is no official mention of Mary Davenant between the baptism of their first child, William, in October 1624 and the burial of their second, Elizabeth, in October 1631. She was most certainly not living with her husband in Edward Hyde's spare bedroom.

While he was sharing Hyde's suite at the Middle Temple, Davenant wrote a new play. Licensed by Henry Herbert on 22 July 1629, *The Colonell* is presumed to have been the play published as *The Siege* in the 1673 collection of Davenant's works. The scene, again, is Italy.

Davenant's close reading of Shakespeare is apparent. The term 'Anthropophagi' (man-eaters), as used in Act One of *Othello*, impressed him so much that he borrowed it in Act Five of *Albovine* – 'Thy flesh is sour, musty … for else / Like th' Anthropophagus, I had devour'd thee up' – and again in Act Four of *The Siege*: 'Shall I mince thee / With thy own Sword; / And like an *Anthropophagus* devour thee, / Thou Rabbet Sucker.' Davenant also invoked the 'walking shadow' from *Macbeth*:

Here I was but a walking shadow, for
My heart was lock'd up there with *Bertolina*,
Foscari's Daughter.

A Florentine army is besieging Pisa, which has rebelled against the Great Duke of Tuscany. Florello, a senior officer in the army of Florence, is in love with Bertolina, the daughter of the Governor of Pisa. He does what he can to prevent the destruction of the city, but the Great Duke demands that the 'Battery' be hastened – '*Pisa is proscrib'd for ruine.*' Florello resolves to 'Commit a sin that will indanger all / Those wreaths my Brow hath merited.' He defects to the enemy. Hailed as 'the greatest Souldier / The World contains', he warns the Pisans that they are about to come under attack.

Bertolina is mortified by Florello's betrayal of his own side for the sake of his love for her: 'Heretofore we lov'd with honor / And ambition; resolv'd to make our issue / Glorious, but now thou hast destroy'd that hope.' She sends him back to his own army, much to the disgust of her father, the governor.

Florello's absence has not gone unnoticed. Questioned on his return by General Castracagnio, he admits that 'Love was the / Witch that drew me from my arms.' The general reinstates his command, even though Florello believes he should be punished for his 'bold enterprise': 'Let me / Beg, not to out-live this infamy … if [Castracagnio] deny / Me one, there is a thousand ways to die –'

So Florello seeks death. He asks Soranzo, whom he appointed captain of his regiment, to kill him, only to learn that Soranzo is also in love with Bertolina. When the battery of Pisa commences, Florello is there in the thick of it, his suicidal frenzy making him immune from injury. He finds Bertolina together with Soranzo and, handing them his pistols – 'Here take you that, assure your / Safety, and destroy me first' – resigns his lover to his captain. But Bertolina protests that she loves Florello:

You were not charitable, to construe
My desires to preserve your fame unstained
(Which made you first precious to me) a
Revolt in my affection; 'twas a jealousie
I could not miss, and love you.

The lovers are reconciled, and though Pisa has fallen, the governor declares:

Now *Pisa* put off thy mourning,
And gather up thy drops of Blood again,
That all may dance to th'Musick of this Peace,
Let Bridal tunes sound high, now the Drums cease.

The Colonell was Davenant's first tragicomedy of love and honour, complete with a storyline in which a captain, promoted from corporal on the basis of his swaggering reputation, proves himself a coward. The comic subplot of the braggart soldier and the impecunious 'Volunteers' owes much to Shakespeare's Falstaff and comes with a tang of personal experience, suggesting that Davenant knew precisely what it meant to be a hungry volunteer, 'come to / The Wars to gain noise' by besieging a fortified town like Saint-Martin-de-Ré.

Licensed on 2 October 1629, Davenant's second tragicomedy, *The Just Italian*, seemed to follow directly on from his first. The scene is Florence. The 'Just Italian' of the title is Altamont, whose brother, Florello, returns penniless from the wars ('Our pay rests in Arrears, and *Pisa's* lost') to find that Altamont has married the noble Alteza. As proud as she is beautiful, Alteza scorns her husband's 'lean and niggard' fate, his inability to shower her with riches, and banishes him from her bed – 'I now divide my house: / This side is mine':

> For here
> My Family and I will rule. That side
> You and your meagre ragged train possess.
> Thou mayst henceforth my Neighbour, but no more
> My Husband be.

Altamont duly introduces the lovely Scoperta to the household to be his concubine and then discovers that his wife has hired Sciolto, a gigolo, for sex. Altamont threatens Sciolto with violence but faints dead away. When he comes round, he is determined on revenge.

Florello disguises himself as Dandolo, 'Count of *Milaine*', and proceeds to woo Alteza's sister, Charintha. The scheme hits a snag, however, when the real Dandolo arrives earlier than expected.

Sciolto, meanwhile, grows impatient with his intended lover, Alteza, 'for she has starv'd me here / With want of natural delight.' He meets Altamont's concubine, Scoperta, and falls in love with her. Scoperta reveals her secret to Sciolto: 'I Sister am / To *Altamont*; not Mistress of his lust.'

Altamont's attempt to provoke his wife's jealousy by getting his sister to pose as his lover appears to have backfired. He plots revenge upon Scoperta, as well as on Sciolto, who has now turned his back on his gigolo career. Sciolto rejects Alteza's advances and insults her. The proud Alteza instantly repents: 'O, I could curse / The giddy judgment of my blood, that thus / Seduc'd me to forsake that Saint [Altamont], and mix / My knowledge with this Devil.' She admits to her husband that 'All springs from the ambition of my guilt' and pleads with Altamont to wreak vengeance on Sciolto.

Altamont confronts Scoperta, showing her his arms covered in blood and claiming to have murdered both Alteza and Sciolto. This is a mere ruse to test his sister's innocence: 'My anger was so just, I would / Not prosecute thy life, until my doubts / Were clear'd.' He then prepares to punish Sciolto in a fair fight. Both are wounded.

Alteza's sister Charintha discovers Florello's real identity: he is being pursued for 'Sums I ow'd when I embark'd for *Pisa*.' She helps him to avoid arrest, and Dandolo is captured when he tries to ambush Florello. Charintha discovers that she loves Florello – 'I ne'er beheld a feature masculine / Till now.' Florello then hears that his brother Altamont is dead.

Word of Altamont's death also reaches Alteza, who is told that, with his last breath, he appointed her judge over Scoperta and Sciolto. The lovers are brought before her, blindfolded and bound. Scoperta and Sciolto profess their true love for each other, and then it is revealed that Sciolto's wealthy uncle died that morning, having made Sciolto his heir. Alteza condemns Sciolto to death for being 'The fatal Instrument that did deprive / My Lord [Altamont] of precious life.' But instead of damning Scoperta, Alteza condemns herself – 'For my stern pride, was the original cause / Of this black Tragedy.'

Altamont, of course, is not dead. His reappearance turns tragedy to tragicomedy. Sciolto, now rich, is given Scoperta. Charintha, swearing that her love is 'sincere, as Holy Hermits vows', is given Florello. Only Dandolo is punished, being forced to ride naked on a mule back to Milan. The play ends with the music of German viols and the Tuscan lute:

> The sacred noise attend, that whilst we hear,
> Our souls may dance into each others ear.

The Just Italian suffers from its uncertain tone, which ranges from the overblown – 'Into my ears thou hast a horrour pour'd / That hath already stiffen'd every hair / On my amazed skull into a reed' – to the unintentionally funny ('Mutes, strangle them!'). The play was not well received when it was performed by Shakespeare's old company, the King's Men, at the Blackfriars. The text was published in 1630 with commendatory verses by 'Will. Hopkins' and Thomas Carew, whose poem 'To my worthy Friend, M. D'AVENANT, upon his excellent Play, THE JUST ITALIAN' confirms that the audience responded negatively:

> *Repine not thou then, since this churlish fate*
> *Rules not the Stage alone; perhaps the State*
> *Hath felt this rancour, where great men and good,*
> *Have by the Rabble been misunderstood.*
> *So was thy Play; whose clear, yet lofty strain,*
> *Wisemen, that govern Fate, shall entertain.*

The point was reiterated by the otherwise unknown Will Hopkins, who noted that the 'giddy fools' of London preferred the noisier entertainments at Paris Garden, or 'the new Motion, the fine Puppet Plays'.

Dedicating his published play 'To the Right Honourable the Earl of *Dorset*', Davenant wrote:

My Lord,

The uncivil ignorance of the People, had depriv'd this humble Work of life; but that your Lordships approbation, stept in to succour it. Those many that came with resolution to dispraise (knowing your Lordships judgment, to be powerful, above their malice), were either corrected to an understanding, or modesty: and this large benefit hath betray'd your Lordship to a Dedication. I am bold to believe, fancies of this composure, have been nobly entertain'd, by the most knowing Princes of the World: The ignorance, that begets the change in this our age, it may become your Lordships example, to correct, me to lament, if so tame a passion can possess a Poet, and one, exalted with a hope to be receiv'd

Your Lordships humble Servant

WILLIAM D'AVENANT.

This smacks of a wounded ego. And yet, there may have been a 'cruel Faction' intent on undermining Davenant's endeavours. A finger could be pointed at Sir Henry Herbert, with whom Davenant was frequently at odds, and, via the Master of the Revels, at Ben Jonson, whose patron, William Herbert, 3rd Earl of Pembroke, died in April 1630.

Jonson's followers – those 'Sons of Ben' who sought to emulate his dramatic achievements and the 'Tribe of Ben' who modelled their poetry on his – were so keen to ingratiate themselves with the poet laureate that they would persecute any pretender who incurred their mentor's displeasure. Ben's jealousy of professional rivals was pathological. His spitefulness was sharpened by the paralytic stroke he suffered in 1628 and the fact that his latest comedy, *The New Inn*, was savagely received when it was presented at the Blackfriars, early in 1629. 'Come leave the lothed stage,' he sulked, after *The New Inn* had bombed, 'And the more lothsome age':

Where pride, and impudence (in faction knit)
    Usurpe the chaire of wit!

He did eventually return to playwriting, but in his embittered Ode '*to himselfe*' Ben Jonson forswore 'The stagers, and the stage-wrights too' and vowed to concentrate solely on praising the king in the elaborate masques he wrote for the Court.

Jonson's first masque had been danced for King James I on Twelfth Night, 5 January 1605. It was a collaboration with the brilliant Inigo Jones, who designed the costumes, scenery and stage machinery. To Jonson, though, it was the words that mattered, not the stunning visuals. Jones would repeatedly feel the lash of the laureate's tongue in verse and on the stage, while in private, Jonson disclosed that 'when he wanted words to express the greatest villain in the world, he would call him an Inigo.'

Chloridia, Ben's last masque for the Court of King Charles I, was performed 'By the Queen's Majesty and her Ladies' at Shrovetide, 22 February 1631. Inigo Jones was outraged that his name had come second, after Jonson's, on the title page of the published text and was omitted altogether when *Chloridia* was reprinted along with another of Ben's masques. Jones's response to this high-handed behaviour provoked a flurry of sarcastic jibes from Ben Jonson, who was warned by a friend that he had 'lighted too foul upon Sir Inigo' and that his 'porcupine quill' was 'dipped in too much gall.' Jonson ignored the warning.

For a quarter of a century, the burly Ben had monopolised the writing of Court masques. His relentless attacks on Inigo Jones meant that his career at Court was now finished. Other poets would finally get the chance to work with the King's Surveyor on the sumptuous courtly entertainments.

The poet who would eventually emerge as Jonson's successor was William Davenant, who was cultivating links with leading courtiers in anticipation of Ben's imminent self-destruction. In 1630, Davenant dedicated *The Cruel Brother* to 'the Right Honourable the Lord Weston, Lord High Treasurer of England' and soon to be created Earl of Portland. A Middle Temple man with Catholic leanings, Richard Weston had succeeded Fulke Greville as Chancellor of the Exchequer in 1621, largely through the Duke of Buckingham's influence, becoming Lord Treasurer in 1628. Ben Jonson considered Weston a personal friend; he regaled the Lord Treasurer with an 'Epistle Mendicant' in 1631, in which he droned on about his poverty. Davenant, by way of contrast, wrote an ecstatic poem 'To the Earle of Portland, Lord Treasurer; on the mariage of his Sonne' in 1633.

By dedicating *Albovine* to the disgraced Earl of Somerset in 1629, Davenant set himself in opposition to Jonson, who had gloated over Somerset's downfall in his 1616 masque, *The Golden Age Restored*. Equally, Davenant's consolatory '*Elizium*' poem to the Duchess of Buckingham was the antithesis of Jonson's delight at the duke's assassination.

With his dedication of *The Just Italian* to the Earl of Dorset, Davenant again trod on the bigger man's toes. Edward Sackville, 4th Earl of Dorset and lord chamberlain to the queen, was a cousin by marriage to the Earl of Somerset and a generous patron to Ben Jonson. Davenant addressed at least two poems to Sackville, including the celebratory 'To EDWARD Earle of *Dorcet*, after his Sicknesse, and happy recovery' and the fawning '*To* EDWARD *Earle of* Dorset', in which he thanked Sackville for having 'adorn'd my Muse and made her known.'

Further evidence that Davenant was winning over Jonson's friends and patrons can be found in the sympathetic poem by Thomas Carew, published with *The Just Italian*. Carew was a paid-up member of the 'Tribe of Ben'. Just as he sought to mollify Davenant for the poor reception of his tragicomedy, so Carew called upon Jonson to curb his 'immodest rage' over the disastrous production of *The New Inn*. But whereas Carew greeted Davenant as the rising star – 'the garlands bloom / From thine own seeds, that crown each glorious page / Of thy triumphant work' – he advised Jonson that his poetic genius had declined from her 'Zenith, & foretells a red / And blushing Evening, when she goes to bed'. Thomas Carew was one of the first to recognise that the old order, in the bulky form of Ben Jonson, was reluctantly yielding place to the new.

Davenant stepped up his campaign to displace Jonson as the Court's favourite poet by composing an Ode, 'To the King on New-yeares day 1630':

> The joyes of eager Youth, of Wine, and Wealth,
> Of Faith untroubled, and unphysick'd Health;
>   Of Lovers, when their Nuptials nie,
>   Of Saints forgiven when they die;
>   Let this yeare bring
>   To *Charles* our King:
> To *Charles*, who is th'example, and the Law,
> By whom the good are taught, not kept in awe.

Three similar stanzas followed, wishing Charles peace and victories 'by Fame obtain'd, / Or pray'r, and not by slaughter gain'd'. Davenant also hoped for a parliamentary 'Session too, of such who can obey … Who not rebell, in hope to git / Some office to reclaime their wit'.

But this was wishful thinking.

Parliament had reassembled in January 1629, no longer able to heap its every grievance on the hated Buckingham. King Charles had allowed himself to be pressured into going to war with Spain and France, not least of all by those 'godly' parliamentarians who welcomed any excuse to massacre Catholics. Those same Puritans refused to vote through sufficient funding for the war effort. They were more anxious to clamp down on the perceived freedoms enjoyed by English Catholics and to resist 'popish' innovations in the Church.

Desperate to raise money for the wars which Parliament had so eagerly promoted, Charles imposed the 'Tunnage and Poundage' levies on imports and exports without Parliament's permission. The MPs reacted with fury. The king had not addressed their trumped-up concerns about 'popery'. Exasperated, Charles dissolved Parliament in March 1629. He would not call another Parliament until 1640.

Davenant's New Year's Ode to King Charles (who, at 29, was just five years older than the poet) was his first serious attempt to catch the king's attention. He had the sense to keep it short and sweet. What it lacked in length, it made up for in political naivety.

More fire was shown in Davenant's uncharacteristically abrasive poem, '*To him who Prophecy'd a Successles end of the Parliament, in the Year* 1630':

> Frantick and foolish too! can any curse,
> Which dying Men still give thee make thee worse?
> Madmen sometimes on suddain flashes hit
> Of Sence, which seem remote, and sound like Wit.
> But thou, most piteously, art Madd and Dull:
> Thy Braines did ly in parcels in thy Skull

The target of Davenant's rage was unidentified, though there are clues:

> He who esteems thy Northern Prophesie,
> Does but encourage Fools to learn to lie […]
> Thou great Informer, canst thou hope I wou'd,
> By dang'rous thee, be plainly understood;
> Whom all, through all thy State disguises know;
> Towards thee, Satyrick numbers must not flow,
> Like Lovers Sonnets, in a soft smooth pace,
> They must be rugged as thy Mistress face.

Ben Jonson, in *The New Inn*, had touched on the disharmony between king and Parliament. The reference to 'thy Northern Prophesie' recalled Jonson's ancestry in the Scottish Borders. Jonson had been accused – by Shakespeare, amongst others – of being an 'Informer'. Ben's infirmity was mentioned ('Swet out thy Blood! in a hot Feaver vext'), as were his perennial appeals for money:

> You have of Monarchs wants a tender sence,
> Meaning to shorten your Lov'd Eloquence;
> And not the fulness of your Loves express,
> By mourning for your Purses emptiness.

Like Jonson, the object of Davenant's wrath was an older man with an interest in the bodily humours: 'Froward with Age, thou seem'st more hum'rous than / A beggar'd Chymist, or rich Curtizan'. Davenant was confident, though, that he had already supplanted the 58-year-old Ben as the foremost poet-seer of the day:

> Why should this Wizard make with Prophecies,
> The People fearful and their Rulers Wise?
> Must all, like Ethnicks to this Divel bow?
> Great Senate know, I am your Prophet now.

It is an extraordinary outburst by Davenant's standards: passionate, angry and assured of his superiority over a celebrated but malignant satirist.

Also in 1630, Davenant began work on his first epic poem, albeit a mock-heroic one.

Jeffrey Hudson was born in 1619, his father a servant to the Duke of Buckingham. He grew to be little more than 18in (46cm) tall, though perfectly proportioned. At a banquet hosted by the Buckinghams in honour of King Charles and Queen Henrietta, the 7-year-old 'rarity of nature' sprang from a large pie, much to the queen's delight. Jeffrey was gifted to Henrietta Maria and became a much-loved addition to her exotic household. He would dance, '*richly apparelled as a prince of hell*', in Ben Jonson's last masque for the Caroline Court.

By the start of 1630, Henrietta Maria was heavily pregnant. Jeffrey, then aged 10, was among the courtiers sent to fetch the royal midwife, Madame de Péronne, from France. On the return journey their ship was captured by Dunkirk pirates. The prisoners were eventually released, however, and on 29 May, Henrietta was delivered of a well-built, dark-skinned son, the future Charles II.

Davenant surely wrote '*Ieffereidos*, Or the Captivitie of *Jeffery*' primarily for the queen's amusement. His dramatic touch was displayed from the outset:

> A Sayle! a sayle! cry'd they, who did consent
> Once more to break the eighth Commandment
> For a few Coles; of which by theft so well
> Th'are stor'd; they have enow to furnish Hell
> With penal heat

The royal ship is boarded. A 'trembling Britaine' – 'tall *Jeff'ry*' – is discovered hiding underneath a candlestick. He is questioned by the pirate chief, who declares: 'This that appears to you, a walking-Thumbe, / May prove, the gen'rall Spie of Christendome'. Jeffrey is taken in chains to Dunkirk, where he refuses to disclose any state secrets, and so he is given a small Icelandic horse on which to make his way to Brussels.

'*Canto* the second' sees Jeffrey thrown from his pony when he 'scarce had driven / Along that Coast, the length of Inches Seven', after which he gets into a fight with a turkey. Luckily, a 'Lady-Midwife now, he there by chance / Espy'd, that came along with him from France'. The embattled dwarf implores her:

> Thou that deliver'd hast so many, be
> So kinde of nature, to deliver me!

Jeffrey is rescued from the savage turkey, and Davenant hinted at further adventures to come:

> Deeds they report, of greater height than these;
> Wonders, and truth; which if the Court-wits please,
> A little helpe from Nature, lesse from Art,
> May happily produce in a Third part.

But there would be no third Canto of this affectionate tribute to the queen's dwarf. Like the more serious *Gondibert*, the saga of *Ieffereidos* was cut short, and for much the same reason.

Davenant was dying.

11

Servant to Her Majestie

'He gott a terrible clap of a Black handsome wench that lay in Axe-yard Westm[inster],' wrote John Aubrey after Davenant's death.
Imprisoned in Cowes Castle on the Isle of Wight, Davenant later recalled the dark-haired siren from whom he had contracted syphilis:

> For a black Beauty did her pride display
>> Through a large Window, and in Jewels shon,
> As if to please the World, weeping for day,
>> Night had put all her Starry Jewels on.

This is the captivating Dalga with the 'dire black Eyes' who appears just before *Gondibert* comes to its premature end – interrupted, as Davenant disclosed, 'by so great an experiment as Dying'. With death on the horizon, and his 'Heroick Poem' never to be completed, Davenant thought back to the attractive wench of Axe Yard, near today's Downing Street, for whose amorous attentions he had so nearly paid with his life, twenty years earlier.

The first recorded outbreak of syphilis in Europe occurred in Italy, late in the fifteenth century, during a French invasion. The French came to think of syphilis as *morbus Neapolitanus*. To the Italians it was *morbus Gallicus*. The English, concurring with the Italians, called it the 'French disease'.

To be 'Frenchified' meant to be infected. Sir John Suckling would later refer to his friend Davenant's 'foolish mischance / That he had got lately travelling in France'. In a similar vein, Davenant's arrest whilst attempting to flee the country after the discovery of the Army Plot in 1641 prompted the balladeer's jest that identifying the fugitive had not been difficult:

> For *Will.* has in his face, the flawes
> Of wounds receiv'd in Countreys Cause.[1]

Davenant had contracted venereal disease 'in Countreys Cause', 'travelling in France'. The first sign was probably a skin lesion. Before long a host of other symptoms would have manifested. The standard treatment at the time was a course of bleeding, purging and bathing, followed by the application of mercury in the form of an ointment, a steam bath or a pill. The mercury was intended to stimulate 'Salivation' which, it was thought, would expel the infection, although the patient ran the risk of gum ulcers, loss of teeth and neurological damage. Davenant would thank the doctor who cured him for 'setting now my condemn'd Body free, / From that no God, but Devill *Mercurie*', listing some of the side-effects which had plagued him: 'revolted Teeth', swollen cheeks, speechlessness, foaming at the mouth and the inability to swallow food.

Reports of his death circulated. He felt obliged, when he was able to hold a quill again, to write a poem 'To the Lady *Bridget Kingsmill*', insisting 'I am no Ghost, nor have beene three weekes dead.' The poem was sent with a gift of melons:

> These Mellons shall approach your pensive Eye,
> Not as a Token but a Legacie.

Lady Bridget was already a widow. She would lose a son to 'a cannon bullet' at the Battle of Edgehill in 1642, where he was fighting for the king.

The combination of the Grand Pox and the 'Devill *Mercurie*' put Davenant out of action. He was soon feeling the effects of poverty on top of his illness. In a poem he wrote 'To *I.C.* Rob'd by his Man Andrew', he complained that his 'sick Joints' would not allow him to join the hunt for the thieving servant, and concluded:

> But hark! who knocks? good troth my Muse is staid,
> By an Apothecaries Bill unpaid;
> Whose length, not strange-nam'd-Drugs, makes her afraid.

But he was not without support. Endymion Porter stayed loyal throughout and was rewarded with a slew of grateful verses. Describing Porter as the 'Lord of my Muse and heart', Davenant recalled the time when he lay 'in darknesse thick':

> More hid than paths of Snakes, to their deep beds,
> Or walkes of Mountaine-Springs from their first Heads

In another poem 'To *Endimion* Porter' he claimed, 'when last I was about to die', to have 'cancell'd my fond Will' and 'Tempted my faith to my Physitians skill' – 'For though our gifts, buy care, nought justly payes / Physitians love, but faith, their art, but prayse':

> If mee (thy Priest) our curled Youth assigne,
> To wash our Fleet-street Altars with new Wine;

I will (since 'tis to thee a Sacrifice)
Take care, that plenty swell not into vice:
Lest, by a fiery surfet I be led,
Once more to grow devout in a strange bed

It was Porter, perhaps, who introduced Davenant to Thomas Cademan, physician in ordinary to Henrietta Maria since December 1626. Cademan, a Catholic, rescued the poet from the devil '*Mercurie*' and set him on the road to recovery, as Davenant acknowledged in his poem 'To Doctor *Cademan*, Physitian to the Queene':

For thy Victorious cares, thy ready heart;
Thy so small tyranny to so much Art;
    For visits made to my disease
    And me, (Alas) not to my Fees

The poet thanked the royal doctor:

May (thou safe Lord of Arts) each Spring
    Ripe plenty of Diseases bring
Unto the Rich; they still t'our Surgeons be
Experiments, Patients alone to thee:
    Health, to the Poore; lest pitty shou'd
    (That gently stirs, and rules thy blood)
Tempt thee from wealth, to such as pay like mee
A Verse; then thinke, they give Eternity.

Davenant could only reimburse Dr Cademan with poetry. The 'Apothecaries Bill' remained unpaid. Years later, on his release from the Tower of London, Davenant would marry Thomas Cademan's widow, Anne.

Other cares upset the recovering poet. His daughter Elizabeth was buried at the Church of St Benet, Paul's Wharf, on 9 October 1631. John Urswick, the tailor, was still pursuing him for debts dating back to his first weeks in London. Davenant was summonsed to attend the Court of the King's Bench in August 1632 but failed to turn up. Urswick protested that the debtor 'did now of Late obscure himselfe and keepe in some private places being hard to bee mete wth all'.

When Davenant did appear in court, that November, Urswick added to the 'principall debts interest and charges of suite' the sum of £9 for 'meate & drinck & apparell makinge for the Compl[ainant's] Wife'. While William was at death's door, it would appear, John Urswick had kindly cared for Mary Davenant.

In his *Albovine* tragedy, Davenant showed that the effects of the pox were well known:

I know
His disease, and whence it came, shortly
You'le see him weare a Curtaine 'fore his Nose;
That's now the newest fashion that came from Paris.

The bridge of his nose collapsed. John Aubrey would remark that 'many wits were too cruelly bold' with this 'unlucky mischance'. Davenant's saddle nose became his defining feature. 'His Art was high, although his Nose was low', wrote George Withers, the presumed author of *The Great Assizes holden in Parnassus*, of Davenant in 1645. Sir John Mennes observed of his own 'journey into France' that he did not go 'like one of those / That doe returne with halfe the nose / They carried from hence.' Among the *Certain Verses Written by Severall of the Authors Friends; to be Re-printed with the Second Edition of Gondibert* (1653) was one that harked back to Davenant's trial for his involvement in the Army Plot:

In answer to which by a speech *Will* showes,
Alas, that his words are drawn through his nose.
Through his nose it was the witnesses cry'd,
But *Will* has none, so again they ly'd.

Another of the *Certain Verses* written by Sir John Denham and others queried '*the Authors writing his name, (as in the Title of his Booke) D'Avenant*' when nobody had heard of any place called Avenant:

Thus *Will* intending *D'Avenant* to grace
Has made a Notch in's name, like that in's face.

The alternative version of his name had first appeared when Davenant signed his dedication of *Albovine* to the Earl of Somerset, 'Your humblest Creature, *D'avenant*'. Such pretentions were not peculiar to Davenant: at Cambridge, in the 1650s, Pepys experimented with styling himself 'Samuel de Pepys'. But to the affectation of slipping an apostrophe into his name, Davenant had added a 'Notch' to his face. He had become a figure of fun to his critics – a saddle-nosed clown.

Davenant returned to the stage, after a four-year absence, with *The Witts. A Comedie*, licensed on 19 January 1634 and presented 'by his Majesties Servants' at the Blackfriars. There was also a performance at Court 'before the Kinge and Queene' on Tuesday, 28 January, which was 'well liked'. When it was published in 1636 the title page described '*The Authour* WILLIAM D'AVENANT' as a '*Servant to Her Majestie*'.

Henry Herbert had been reluctant to license *The Wits*. It took Endymion Porter's intervention, and the personal involvement of King Charles I, to save the play. Herbert's account reads thus:

This morning being the 9th of January, [1634], the King was pleasd to call me unto his withdrawinge chamber to the windowe, wher he went over all that I had croste in Davenants play-booke, and allowing of *faith* and *slight* to bee asseverations only, and no oathes, markt them to stande, and some other few things, but in the greater part allowed of my reformations. This was done upon a complaint of Mr. Endymion Porters in December.

Herbert, who had applied a heavy censorial hand to Davenant's script, had little choice but to obey. He reluctantly 'returned unto Mr. Davenant his play-booke of *The Witts*, corrected by the kinge.' King Charles had refused to accept the script from Endymion Porter, 'but commanded him to bring it unto mee,' wrote Herbert, 'and likewise commanded Davenant to come to me for it, as I believe: otherwise he would not have byn so civill.' Davenant acknowledged Porter's role in defending the play when he dedicated *The Wits* to 'the Chiefly Belov'd of all that are Ingenious, and Noble, ENDYMION PORTER, *of his Majesties Bedchamber*':

SIR,
[…] your goodnesse hath preserv'd life in the Author; then rescu'd his worke from a cruel Faction; which nothing but the forces of your reason, and your reputation could subdue.

The play's original Prologue, '*spoken in Black Fryars*', also referred to this 'Faction':

Blesse mee you kinder Stars! How are wee throng'd?
Alas! whom, hath our long-sick-Poet wrong'd,
That hee should meet together in one day
A Session, and a Faction at his Play?

The first performance occasioned a poem – 'To *Endimion* Porter, When my Comedy (call'd the Wits) was presented at Black-Fryars' – in which Davenant again thanked Porter for standing by him:

I that am told conspiracies are laid,
To have my Muse, her Arts, and life betray'd,
Hope for no easie Judge; though thou wert there,
T'appease, and make their judgements lesse severe.

Whereas his earlier plays had sprung from the grotesque world of Jacobean tragedy, *The Wits* looked forward to the Restoration comedies which flourished in the latter part of the century. The setting was a realistically contemporary London.

The Elder Pallatine, a landed gentleman, has come down from the country with his elderly friend, Sir Morglay Thwack. They plan to live by their wits, finding women to marry for profit, and have agreed that 'The Female Youth o'th towne' are Pallatine's and all 'From forty to fourscore' are Thwack's.

The Younger Pallatine is already in London, living on an allowance from his elder brother. In order to furnish two soldiers recently returned from Holland with handsome clothes, the Younger Pallatine persuades his mistress, Luce, to give him her gold – 'Pendants, Carckanets [pearl necklaces], and Rings' – which he lends to his friends. For this act of charity, Luce is thrown out of her aunt's house. She turns in desperation to Lady Ample, who welcomes Luce but insists that she, too, must learn to live by her wits.

Lady Ample stands to inherit a fortune, for which reason her money-grubbing guardian, Sir Tyrant Thrift, hopes to marry her off to a deformed young gentleman. The Elder Pallatine finds himself attracted to Lady Ample and, especially, her inheritance.

There is a hint of self-projection in Davenant's portrayal of the Younger Pallatine, whose relationship with the Elder Pallatine might have reflected William's attitude towards his brother Robert, the country parson. The Elder Pallatine vows not to pay the Younger Pallatine any more of his allowance and chides his cosmopolitan brother:

> The stock my Father left you, if your care
> Had purpos'd so discreet a course might well
> Have set you up i'th Trade

Much the same might have been said by Robert Davenant to his errant brother, who had chosen not to follow the instructions in their father's will. Rather than become an apprentice to 'some good marchant of London or other tradesman' the younger Davenant had invested in costly apparel, courtesy of the long-suffering tailor John Urswick. The Elder Pallatine, seeing his brother in fancy costume, exclaims: 'What's this, an apparition, a Ghost imbroider'd? / Sure he has got the Devill for his Taylor.'

Later in the play, the Elder Pallatine has cause to admire his brother's resourcefulness:

> This is the wittiest off-spring that our name
> Ere had […]
> My Father was no Poet sure, I wonder
> How hee got him?

Parson Robert's father, the 'very grave and discreet' John Davenant, was certainly no poet. William Davenant, freshly recovered from his life-threatening illness, was apparently happy to let slip that *his* father had been someone altogether more witty.

Lady Ample and the Younger Pallatine join forces to gull the Elder Pallatine and Sir Morglay Thwack, who have quarrelled over which of them has the right to woo Lady Ample. By the end of the play, Lady Ample's puritanical guardian has been apprehended on suspicion of attempting to steal church property; Sir Morglay Thwack has had the satisfaction of seeing his rival locked up in a chest, and the Elder Pallatine is arrested for supposedly stealing the hair of the dead to make wigs. Lady Ample agrees to marry the Elder Pallatine, but obliges him to sign certain bonds – 'hoodwinkt, / And purely ignorant of what they are' – which include the gift of a manor to the Younger Pallatine and £300 to Luce. Sir Morglay makes the Younger Pallatine his heir, and more money is extracted from Sir Tyrant Thrift. The comedy concludes on a note of delirious happiness as the country folk who sought to live 'by our good witts' freely admit that they were outwitted by the city types.

The Wits was revised and enlarged when Davenant opened his Duke's Playhouse in Lincoln's Inn Fields. It was performed on 15 August 1661, with King Charles II, his younger brother James, Duke of York, and the Duchess of York (the daughter of Davenant's old friend Edward Hyde) all present. Samuel Pepys saw it three times during its run of eight consecutive performances and declared it 'a most excellent play', which it is. The Victorian editors of Davenant's *Dramatic Works* described *The Wits* as 'the most perfect comedy as regards plot, character, and language that appeared during the latter portion of the reign of Charles I. or the earlier part of that of his son.'

The contrast between *The Wits* and Davenant's next play is striking. Originally entitled *The Courage of Love*, the author changed this to *Love and Honour* when it was licensed on 20 November 1634. Davenant later asked Henry Herbert to alter the title again – to *The Nonpareilles, or The Matchless Maids* – but it was *Love and Honour* that stuck. It was presented at the Blackfriars Theatre in December 1634 and published, eventually, in 1649.

The playwright had returned to his familiar setting of northern Italy. During an attack on the city of Milan, the young Count Prospero takes two prisoners: Evandra, the beautiful 'heir of *Millaine*', and the wounded Leonel. He sends them both under guard to Turin.

Alvaro, Prince of Savoy, is horrified that his friend Prospero has made a prisoner of 'Faire *Evandra*, the pride of *Italy*':

> Now all the blessings of my faithfull love
> Are lost; she, whom I doated on with my
> Most chast, and early apetite, is sent
> In bonds, t'apease my cruell fathers wrath.

Desperate to make amends, Prospero offers to hide Evandra in a cave.

The Duke of Savoy proclaims that Evandra will 'suffer instant death' as a 'sacrifice for all' – this to fulfil a vow made by the duke 'when those of *Millain* / Took his brother prisoner, and would not be / Appeaz'd without the forfeiture of's head.' The duke's son, Alvaro, meanwhile, meets Evandra at the cave in Prospero's garden and declares his love for her.

Prospero has also fallen for Evandra. But the duke, having failed to discover Evandra's whereabouts, threatens to execute Prospero in her stead. When Alvaro pleads on Prospero's behalf, the duke resolves to sacrifice his own son if Evandra is not found. While the male characters quarrel, Evandra decides to offer herself as a sacrifice to the duke's anger.

A strain of feminism, latent in *The Wits*, now comes to the fore. The 'captive Knight' Leonel, who also loves Evandra, remarks of her intended self-sacrifice:

> this sure is such
> A great example of a female fortitude
> As must undo all men [...]
>   when this is known let women sway
> Counsels, and war, whilst feeble men obey.

Two ambassadors arrive from Milan to sue for the lives of Evandra and Melora, another beauteous prisoner-of-war who is trying to take Evandra's place on the scaffold. The duke admits that he would rather execute 'some man that boasts your masters bloud' than two young women. At which point Leonel reveals himself as son and heir to the Duke of Parma. The ambassadors then remove their false beards to disclose that one of them is the duke's great enemy, Evandra's father, whilst the other is none other than the duke's brother:

> And though ten yeares I have been hidden from
> Your sight, this noble Duke hath us'd me so,
> I cannot call it banishment, but the
> Retir'd and quiet happinesse of life.

And so all is neatly resolved.

Today, the determination of Evandra and Melora, Alvaro, Leonel and Prospero to die in each other's place, for the sake of love and honour, feels forced and tedious. *Love and Honour* was, however, 'more successful than any other of our author's plays', as the nineteenth-century editors of Davenant's *Dramatic Works* observed.

Davenant revised his play for performance at the Duke's Playhouse in October 1661, kitting out the male leads in the coronation suits so recently worn by Charles II and James, Duke of York. Pepys saw it three times in one week – 'and a very good play it is.' *Love and Honour* was revived again at the Duke's Theatre in Dorset Garden, after Davenant's death, and 'often acted with applause'. Andrew Kippis, writing in his *Biographia Britannia* (1778–93), remarked that in 'point of style', *Love and Honour* 'resembled Shakespeare':

> and is more correctly finished than any of Sir William Davenant's former plays,
> which shews that he was not hurt by the applause that he had met with, but

thought himself obliged to labour hard, and take so much the more pains to deserve it.

Produced in the same year – 1634 – *The Wits* and *Love and Honour* displayed Davenant's remarkable dramatic range, from rumbustious city comedy to high-flown tragicomedy. His main aim in writing *Love and Honour* seems to have been to impress Henrietta Maria. It certainly appealed to the queen's romantic sensibility, and when Melora sues for the hand of Prince Alvaro we are reminded of Prince Charles's first glimpse of the teenage Henrietta, rehearsing a masque at the French Court:

> Within my fathers court, when five yeares since
> (Disguis'd you stole to see a triumph there)
> You promis'd if our houses enmity
> Were ever reconcil'd, the church should joyne our hands.

The queen herself revived the play for performance at Hampton Court on New Year's Day 1637, when the public theatres were closed by the plague.

With Ben Jonson no longer writing masques for the Court, after his terminal falling out with Inigo Jones, a vacancy existed. Davenant's friend Thomas Carew had attempted to fill Jonson's shoes – his *Cœlum Britannicum* masque was per-formed at Whitehall on 18 February 1634. But it was Aurelian Townshend's *Tempe Restored*, 'presented by the Queen and fourteen ladies' on Shrove Tuesday 1632, which perhaps offered Davenant his entrée to the world of courtly masques. In *Drama at the Courts of Queen Henrietta Maria*, Karen Britland suggested that the part of Harmony in *Tempe Restored* was sung by Anne Sheppard, a diminutive girl who belonged to the circle of Philip Herbert, one of the two brothers to whom Shakespeare's First Folio was dedicated in 1623. As Britland remarked, 'William Davenant's mother was a Sheppard' and 'Thomas, her elder brother, was a profes-sional colleague of Shakespeare, and … a member of the royal household'. Britland concluded, 'It is likely that Anne Sheppard was a member of this family', meaning that the 12-year-old, who grew no taller than 3ft 10in (1.17m) and would have delighted the queen, was probably related to Davenant.

The need to find a sympathetic poet to provide masques for the Caroline Court intensified after the publication, late in 1632, of *Histrio-Mastix*. Written by the 'godly' lawyer William Prynne, and running to more than 1,000 pages, *The Player's Scourge, or Actor's Tragedy* was a vicious diatribe against the theatre and other popular pleasures, such as Christmas. Prynne's reference to 'Women-Actors' being 'notorious whores' was seen as a criticism of Henrietta Maria, who adored perform-ing in masques (there being no professional actresses then in England). William Prynne was charged with seditious libel and, at his trial in 1634, he was sentenced to be pilloried, imprisoned for life, and fined £5,000.

On Twelfth Night, 5 January 1634, the King's Company under the leadership of Joseph Taylor – from whom Davenant would acquire his portrait of Shakespeare – performed *The Faithful Shepherdess* at Somerset House, the queen's official residence. Davenant wrote a prologue for this revival of John Fletcher's tragicomedy:

> Bless then that Queen whose Eies have brought that light
> Which hither led and stays him [King Charles] here;
> He now doth shine within her Sphear,
> And must obey her Sceptre half this night.

He had prepared the ground, then, when the royal command came, just as *Love and Honour* was going into production at Blackfriars.

Under Charles and Henrietta Maria, Court masques were frequently ordered in pairs – one commissioned by the king, to be presented for the queen's amusement; the other created for Henrietta to perform for King Charles. Davenant's first masque for the Court was '*Presented by the Queens Majestie and her Ladies at Whitehall*' and, uniquely, performed no fewer than four times. It was credited to '*Inigo Jones, Surveyor of his Ma[jes]ties Workes, and William Davenant, her Ma[jes]ties Servant.*'

Inigo Jones was also hard at work on the Queen's Chapel at Somerset House. Henrietta had laid the foundation stone in September 1632; the dedication ceremony would take place in December 1636, when the astonishing chapel attracted crowds to marvel at its interior. To the Puritans, the presence of a Catholic place of worship in London was an abomination. But even the king – no fan of Catholicism – declared that he had never seen anything more beautiful, or more ingeniously conceived, than his wife's chapel.

Though Henrietta's religion had been the cause of ruptures in her marriage to King Charles, in many ways the royal couple walked a very similar moral path. The Royalist antiquary Elias Ashmole wrote that the king 'designed and endeavoured the most complete and absolute reformation of any of his predecessors', in the sense that Charles was committed to imposing conformity on the Church, the Court and the country at large, and leading by his own dignified example. Henrietta, meanwhile, yearned to woo the fractious English heretics back to the Holy Mother Church and to cleanse the Court of immorality.

Improving the morals of the Court, Henrietta-style, required a code of chivalry. The queen's enemies abhorred such civility – a point Davenant would later make in his *First Dayes Entertainment at Rutland-House* – but Henrietta's courtly cult of Platonic love was intended to reintroduce elegance, restraint and good manners. As with her husband's desire to reform the body politic through decorous leadership, the queen's devotion to the principles of chastity and obedience aimed to set the standard for the nation as a whole.

Not all of her courtiers were up to the challenge. In 1633 the queen's favourite, Henry Jermyn, got one of her maids of honour, Eleanor Villiers (a niece of the late Duke of Buckingham), pregnant. Jermyn refused to marry Eleanor. He was imprisoned in the Tower of London and then sent into exile, spending two years in Paris and Jersey. Only the queen's intervention saved him from becoming a pariah.

Such was the background to the first performance of *The Temple of Love* on 10 February 1635. At one end of the banqueting house stood a stage, 6ft high. Surrounded by ornamental decorations symbolising Indian and Asian Monarchy, the words '*TEMPLUM AMORIS*' were inscribed on an Oval set in a 'rich Compartment' of gold.

The curtain flew up to reveal 'a spacious grove of shady trees' representing 'the place where the Soules of the Ancient Poets are feigned to reside.' The figure of '*Divine Poesie*' appeared from 'a great Cloud of a Rosie Colour' and, with a chorus of ancient poets, sang to the king, before the scene changed into 'Mists and Clouds, through which some glimpse of a Temple is here and there scarcely discern'd.' Three magicians emerged from their underground caves, like the witches of *Macbeth*:

> O the Temple of Love, the mists that hid,
> And so reserv'd it from our sinful use,
> (While we seduc'd the more voluptuous race
> Of Men, to give false worship in our own) must be
> Dispell'd! this is the sad ill news; and it
> Is come from Heaven!

Indamora, 'the delight of Destiny', had 'raised strange doctrines, and new sects of Love: / Which must not woo or court the Person, but / The Mind, and practice generation not / Of Bodies but of Souls.' The magicians discussed this 'new sect' of Platonic love, which had been planted in 'a dull Northern Ile, they call Britaine' and, more miraculously, 'in Court'. 'Is there not / One Courtier will resent the cause, and give / Some countenance to the affairs of the body?' demanded one of the magicians, with a sly nod to Henry Jermyn.

The magicians vowed to 'wake our drowsie Art, and try / If we have power to hinder Destiny.' They summoned up their elemental spirits, including those Puritan troublemakers who believed themselves to be among God's 'elect':

> To these I'le add a sect of modern Divels;
> Fine precise Fiends, that hear the devout close
> At ev'ry vertue but their own, that claim
> Chambers and Tenements in heaven, as they
> Had purchas'd there, and all the Angels were
> Their harbingers. With these I'le vex the world.

The social disorder whipped up by the 'godly' extremists was mimed in an '*Antimask of the Spirits*'. Prominent among them was that 'Modern Divel', William Prynne, the author of *Histrio-Mastix* – 'a sworn enemy of Poesie, Musick, and all ingenious Arts, but a great friend to murmuring, libelling, and all seeds of discord, attended by his factious followers'.

The scene changed to a calm sea. Henrietta Maria made her Venus-like entrance as Indamora in a 'Maratime Chariot', the back of which was 'a great Skallop Shell'. Her arrival made visible the 'true temple of Chast Love'. A male figure, representing Sunesis ('Understanding'), and a female representing Thelema ('Free Will'), entered the temple and sang:

> Sunesis: *Come melt thy soul in mine, that when unite,*
> *We may become one vertuous appetite.*
> Thelema: *First breath thine into me, thine is the part*
> *More heavenly, and doth more adorne the heart.*

Amianteros ('Chaste Love') flew down and joined Sunesis, Thelema, Divine Poesie and 'the rest of the Poets' in approaching the king and queen, the 'great *Chorus* following at a distance':

> *To* CHARLES *the Mightiest and the Best,*
> *And to the Darling of his breast,*
>   *(Who rule b' example as by power)*
> *May youthful blessings still increase,*
> *And in their Off-spring never cease,*
>   *Till Time's too old to last an hower.*

The performers retired, and Henrietta and her ladies began 'the Revels with the King and the Lords, which [continued] the most part of the night. Thus ended this Masque,' noted the published text, 'which for the newness of the invention, variety of Scænes, Apparitions, and richness of habits was generally approved to be one of the most magnificent that hath been done in *England*.'

Davenant's fee for *The Temple of Love* was collected for him by Henry Jermyn, who had become a close friend and patron to the poet. But even the £50 he earned for his first Court masque could not make up for his years of indisposition.

In the summer of 1635 he wrote a 'Vacation Play' for performance at the Globe Theatre. *News from Plimouth* was licensed by Sir Henry Herbert on 1 August 1635. A poem of Davenant's – '*The long Vacation in* London, *in Verse-Burlesque, or Mock Verse*' – dates from this time and conjures up the London summer, when the gentry had departed for their country seats and the Inns of Court were emptied:

> Now Man that trusts, with weary Thighs,
> Seeks Garret where small Poet lies:
> He comes to *Lane*, finds Garret shut;

Then not with Knuckle, but with foot
He rudely thrusts, would enter Dores;
Though Poet sleeps not, yet he snores

'From little Lump triangular / Poor Poet sighes, are heard afar', quipped Davenant, no doubt referencing his misshapen nose:

Then forth he steales; to Globe does run;
And smiles, and vowes Four Acts are done:
Finis to bring he does protest,
Tells ev'ry Play'r, his part is best.
And all to get, (as Poets use)
Some Coyne in Pouch to solace Muse.

Times were hard. The 'small Poet', named Will, was forced to hide under the bed when a 'Fierce City *Dunne*' or debt-collector came hammering on the door.

Summer was no time for serious theatre. Davenant acknowledged in his prologue that *News from Plymouth* aimed to '*please those, who not expect too much.*' Three 'Sea-Captaines' – Seawit, Topsaile and Cable – find themselves marooned and penniless in Plymouth, a port where 'they would make us pay / For day-light, if they knew to measure / The Sun-beames by the yard.' The mariners resolve to woo three wealthy women – Widow Carrack, Lady Loveright and Mrs Joynture – without falling into the trap of marriage. So much for the play's '*humble Theame*'.

Among the comic characters is Sir Solemne Trifle, a 'Foolish old Knight' who specialises in manufacturing false news, which he disseminates via his 'Intelligencers' – Scarecrow, Zeale and Prattle:

Trifle: Let me see. Here's something rarer
        But of undoubted truth. The *Spanish* fleet
        That anchor'd at *Gibraltar*, is sunk
        By the *French* Horse […]
            From *France*,
        […] The Cardinal *Richelieu* as he slept in his Tent,
        Had his head cut off with an invisible Sword,
        By the great Constables Ghost.

Trifle's ludicrous 'news' is intended to cause consternation. Arrested, he exclaims 'I am a Traytor / In the highest degree' and confesses that his 'intelligence' came only from playhouses, eateries, almanacs and ballads sung on street corners.

Davenant had put his finger on a growing problem: the spreading of alarmist and seditious tittle-tattle. Trifle's exposure as a sort of tabloid hack, wilfully peddling falsehoods, strikes a discordant note in what is otherwise an undemanding comedy, the tenor of which is summed up in the love song 'O Thou that sleep'st like Pigg in Straw'. The holiday audience might not have appreciated the warning, but Davenant's treatment of Sir Solemne Trifle's cynical rumour-mongering suggests that he could sense the political storm that was soon to break.

He also remained intrigued by the Neo-Platonism that had become so fashionable at Court. The obsession was referred to in a letter written in June 1634 by James Howell to his friend, Philip Warwick, then in Paris: 'This [Platonic] Love sets the Wits of the Town on work; and they say there will be a Mask shortly of it,[2] whereof her Majesty and her Maids of Honour, will be part.' In the prologue to his next play, Davenant admitted that he had no idea what was meant by 'Platonick Love' when he first heard of it.[3] He was worried that the term would not be understood by theatre-goers who read it on the handbills. Nevertheless, The Platonick Lovers was licensed on 16 November 1635 and performed by the King's Men at their indoor venue, the Blackfriars.

Davenant set his latest tragicomedy in Sicily. The young Duke Theander and his neighbouring duke, Phylomont, are in love with each other's sisters. Theander's love for Eurithea is of the Platonic variety:

> the first are Lovers of a pure
> Cœlestiall kind, such as some stile Platonicall:
> (A new Court Epethite scarce understood)
> But all they wooe, Sir is the Spirit, Face,
> And heart

The other couple, Phylomont and Ariola, 'still affect / For naturall ends':

> Why such a way as Libertines call Lust,
> But peacefull Polliticks, and cold Divines
> Name Matrimony

Theander's idealised notion of love causes him to feel outrage at Phylomont's desire to marry and sleep with Ariola – 'Lye with my Sister Phylomont! how vile / And horridly that sounds!' His own courtship of Eurithea is comically strained:

> And thou (my Love) art sweeter far,
> Then Baulmy Incense in the purple smoake,
> Pure and unspotted, as the cleanly Ermine, ere
> The Hunter sullies her with his pursuit,
> Soft as her skin, chaste as th'Arabian bird,
> That wants a sex to woe, or as the dead,
> That are devorc'd from warmth, from objects, and from thought.

There was fun to be had in portraying the effects of a powerful love philtre on a young soldier brought up in ignorance of women – rather like Hippolito, the 'Man who had never seen a Woman', in Davenant and Dryden's later adaptation of *The Tempest*. But there was a serious side to the story, too.

The Platonic Lovers was reprinted, with a dedication to Davenant's friend Henry Jermyn, in 1665 as the second of 'Two Excellent Plays', the first of which was *The Wits*. Excellent or not, *The Platonic Lovers* provides proof of Davenant's moral consistency. The arguments he advanced against the sterility of Platonic love, as it was embraced by the Court in the 1630s, were comparable with his denunciation, in *The Law against Lovers*, of the Puritans' sexual intolerance in the 1650s. Both were irrational attempts to control and alter natural behaviour. Davenant, the happy realist, knew that both fads were unsustainable. For what would become of a country whose people were forbidden, by pretentiousness or prejudice, to procreate?

12

A Mighty Debt

The king's sister, Elizabeth, had married the Elector Palatine, Frederick V, in 1613. In 1619, Frederick was elected king of Bohemia – essentially, the Czech Republic of today.

Bohemia was a sectarian battleground. Protestants threw Catholic councillors out of the windows of the Hradčany castle in Prague, triggering the Thirty Years' War. Frederick's reign lasted a year and four days. He was defeated by the forces of the Holy Roman Emperor at the Battle of the White Mountain, after which Frederick and Elizabeth – now known as the Winter King and Winter Queen – fled to The Hague.

Frederick V died in 1632 and was succeeded by his son, Charles Louis, as Elector of the Palatinate. Charles Louis visited his uncle, Charles I, late in 1635. He was received 'in a private manner but most courteously' by King Charles and Queen Henrietta Maria.

Charles Louis was soon followed to England by his 16-year-old brother, Prince Rupert of the Rhine, an altogether more romantic figure than the stiff and formal Elector. An easy intimacy quickly developed between Rupert and Davenant's friends, Endymion and Olivia Porter, even though Olivia was 'a professed Roman Catholick'.

King Charles had wisely kept Britain out of the Thirty Years' War. With no Parliament to vote through subsidies, Charles instituted financial reforms and avoided heavy expenditure. The result was that Britain was enjoying a period of peace. But the youthful elector and his brother were anxious to secure British support for their bid to regain the devastated Palatinate territories. King Charles knew that a costly involvement in the continental conflict would encourage those Protestant extremists who were ever eager to see Catholics slaughtered and who formed the king's main opposition in the country. The Palatine princes were to be disappointed in their English mission.

One bright moment during the princes' visit came early in 1636. The Inns of Court still celebrated Twelfth Night as a festival of misrule, with a temporary prince presiding over the festivities. At Gray's Inn the Lord of Misrule was known as the 'Prince of Purpoole'; at the Middle Temple, he was the 'Prince d'Amour'. The young lawyer chosen to act as the Prince d'Amour for Christmas 1635 opted to present a grand entertainment in honour of the Palatine princes. It fell to William Davenant to write a masque for the occasion.

Time was short. As Davenant declared in a preface addressed 'To Every Reader' of the printed text:

> The intention of this Entertainement to the Prince ELECTOR, being hastily prepar'd, as from eager hearts that could delay no Ceremony that might render an expression of their Loves: It could not be, but I must share the inconvenience of that hast[e] [...] And this (devis'd and written in three dayes) might happely have found an excuse, if the presentation had beene as suddenly perform'd, as it was prepar'd

Having developed and scripted the masque in just three days, Davenant was frustrated by the delay – caused by the 'sad necessitie' of the queen giving birth to her second daughter on 28 December – and the fact that he was unable to revise his work. This, he felt sure, would come back to haunt him 'when most men strive to raise themselves a reputation of witt, by Cavill and Dislike.' If no account were taken of the speed with which Davenant had been obliged to write the text, his efforts would be criticised by those whose talents extended only so far as resentment and mockery.

The Triumphs of the Prince d'Amour was finally presented at the Middle Temple on Wednesday, 24 February 1636, around the time of Davenant's 30th birthday. The queen entered into the spirit of things by attending in disguise. Henrietta and four of her ladies, dressed as ordinary citizens, were escorted to their seats by Mrs Basse, 'the great Lace Woman of *Cheapside*'. To keep them out of trouble, the ladies were closely followed by four cavaliers: Henry Jermyn, Henry Rich (1st Earl of Holland), Henry Percy (younger son of the Earl of Northumberland) and George Goring, who had previously danced in Davenant's masque of *The Temple of Love*.

The Palatine princes were seated at the upper end of the hall, facing the stage. The curtain rose on a scene of alehouses and tobacco shops. Various characters were seen making ridiculous salutes to one another. After this '*first Anti-Masque*' the scene changed to a 'Campe of Tents', in the middle of which stood 'the Temple of *Mars*'. The Priests of Mars sang, their places then taken by the Knights Templar,[1] whose majestic dance was interrupted by the descent of Cupid. The scene changed again, this time to 'a square Piazza, resembling that of *Venice*', where lovers of several nationalities made fools of themselves. This '*second Anti-Masque*' resolved into a sylvan setting, complete with a 'Temple of *Venus*' from which the Priests of Venus emerged to sing.

The masquers returned, dressed as 'a Troope of noble Lovers'. The 'Temple of *Apollo*' was discovered. Apollo's priests sang of the god's desire to '*unite his wiser Deity*' with Mars and Venus, '*the powers of War and Love*', and called upon the audience to '*Expresse your thankfulnesse in active pleasure*':

Whilst you designe your hearts to Mirth,
   Yours eares to numbers, & your feet to measure.

Baskets of 'precious fruits', covered with blossoms, were carried to the far end of the hall, where they were joined together to form a 'Table richly furnish'd with a Banquet, that look'd as it were hidden in a Grove', and the priests of Mars, Venus and Apollo sang in unison to the Palatine princes. It was simple stuff, but effective nonetheless. Warfare had become romance, allied with wisdom. Such was the triumph of the Prince d'Amour.

The printed text concluded with Davenant's remark: 'Thus, as all Pleasures and Triumphs are full of haste, and aptest to decay, this had an end; yet may live mention'd a while, if the envie of such as were absent do not rebuke the courteous memory of those who vouchsaf'd to enjoy it.' Henrietta Maria certainly enjoyed it. Sir Henry Herbert – whose authority as Master of the Revels was temporarily eclipsed by that of Thomas Maunsell, Master of the Revels to the Prince d'Amour – reported that 'The Masque was very well performed in the dances, scenes, cloathinge, and musique, and the Queene was pleased to tell mee at her going away, that she liked it very well.'

If the Court masque had evolved to reflect the preoccupations and celebrate the policies of the reigning royals, the antimasque represented the disorder which was restored to equilibrium by the intervention of the monarch. Thus, in Davenant's masque of *Salmacida Spolia* (1640) the figure of Discord, '*a malicious Fury*', embodied the forces of division and chaos which were being unleashed by Puritan agitators. That *The Triumphs of the Prince d'Amour*, performed just four years before *Salmacida Spolia*, could find nothing as apocalyptic as a snake-clad 'FURIE' to symbolise social disruption, but only a handful of lowlife camp-followers and some comically affected lovers, is extremely telling.

The 1630s were an exasperating time for the 'godly' extremists who resented the king's insistence on ruling without parliaments. Edward Hyde would refer to the decade as a period of 'the greatest calm and the fullest measure of felicity that any people in any age, for so long time together, have been blessed with, to the wonder and envy of all parts of Christendom'. Only later would 'those men who had the skill and cunning … to compound fears and jealousies' succeed in inflaming those negative emotions 'into the most prodigious and the boldest rebellion that any age or country ever brought forth'. The Civil War was nowhere in sight in 1636, and King Charles was resisting the calls to plunge his country into the religious bloodshed on the Continent. In *The Triumphs of the Prince d'Amour* Davenant had only to strike the right balance between Mars (martial valour), Venus (sexual attraction) and Apollo (perspicacity, intelligence) to configure the perfect scene of natural order and abundance.

The pacific mood of *The Triumphs of the Prince d'Amour* might have dismayed the Palatine princes. Quaint as it was, Davenant's masque gave Charles Louis and

Rupert the message that England had no desire to reclaim their father's Bohemian kingdom if to do so meant going to war.

Eight years later, on 13 June 1644, Davenant found himself writing to Prince Rupert from the hamlet of 'Haleford' in Shropshire, humbly beseeching the prince to forgive his presumption in advising him to continue campaigning against the parliamentary army in the north. Rupert, he observed, was in a position to retake 'the three great mines of England (coal, alum, and lead) immediately in the enemy's possession', an act which would be of greater strategic value than any rush to the king's defence. Had Davenant's previous contact with the hot-headed prince been limited to the anti-war pantomime at the Middle Temple, such unsolicited counsel would have seemed rashly inappropriate. But Rupert had also been treated to Davenant's thoughts in a long poem of 1637.

Frustrated by his uncle's reluctance to commit forces to a European theatre of war, Prince Rupert had dreamt up a different kind of adventure. He had heard of a large island off the coast of Africa. Marco Polo had confused this island with Mogadishu in Somalia and named it 'Madageiscar'.

Rupert took his plans for a Madagascar expedition to King Charles, who commissioned Endymion Porter to look into it. The prince's relations were openly hostile to the scheme, with Rupert's mother Elizabeth, the Winter Queen, writing on 6 April 1637 that her son's dreams of colonising Madagascar sounded 'like one of Don Quixote's conquests, where he promised his trusty squire to make him king of an island.' The plan was 'neither feasible, safe, nor honourable', and by the end of June the prince had given up on the idea and returned to Holland.

Davenant, however, had grasped the potential, if only in his imagination. '*Madagascar*. A Poem written to Prince RUPERT' is a 446-line mini-epic written in early 1637, before Rupert's departure for the Low Countries. The poem opens with a reference to two out-of-body experiences which Davenant had recently undergone:

> My Soule, this Winter, hath beene twice about
> To shift her narrow Mansion, and looke out;
> To aire her yet unpractis'd wings, and trie
> Where Soules are entertain'd when Bodyes die

It was during one of these lucid dreams that Davenant's soul – or so he claimed – travelled to an isle 'Between the Southern *Tropick* and the *Line*; / Which (noble Prince) my prophecie cals thine'. He foresaw, wrongly, the arrival of Prince Rupert at Madagascar, where the natives instantly recognised the prince as a natural leader. A party of 'ambitious Wanderers' also made shore, eager to claim the island, and so it was agreed that to avoid general bloodshed two champions of the privateers should do battle with two seconds chosen by the prince.

Rupert's seconds proved to be Davenant's friends and patrons, '*Endimion*' Porter and '*Arigo*', his new pen-name for Henry Jermyn. Porter and Jermyn defeated their rivals. Prince Rupert's men then saw off an attack by the privateers, making the island theirs – 'And here *Chronologers* pronounce thy stile: / The first true Monarch of the *Golden Isle*'. Gold was extracted from 'virgin Mines'. The sea yielded up her 'Corall Trees' and 'old Oysters' containing 'Pearles whose pond'rous size / Sinks weaker Divors when they strive to rise'. 'Black Suds' of ambergris floated to the shore; precious stones were found among the rocks. The prince appointed '*Endimion*' and '*Arigo*' his deputies on the island, and Davenant dared to hope for some none-too-taxing office of his own, twirling a chain on 'a judiciall Bench' and learning to 'sleep out trials in a gowne of Furre'.

The thought that he was 'destin'd for authoritie, / And early Gowts' startled the dreaming poet:

> my Soule in a strange fright
> From this rich Isle began her hasty flight;
> And to my halfe dead Body did returne,
> Which new inspir'd, rose cheerefull as the Morne.

Davenant's 'Madagascar' poem was about the only thing to come out of Rupert's stillborn scheme to conquer the island. It helped to establish a bond between the poet and the reckless Cavalier, Davenant claiming that he assumed 'when I thy Battailes write / That very flame, which warm'd thee in the fight.' This empathic link would be recalled in the midst of the Civil War, when Sir William Davenant wrote to Prince Rupert of the Rhine, presumptuously offering him military advice.

His out-of-body visionary journeys might have been a sign of recurring ill health, for in the late summer of 1637 Davenant and two friends left London to take the curative waters at Bath. Davenant later told John Aubrey about the trip. Aubrey included it in his brief *Life* of Sir John Suckling.

The third member of the party was Jack Young, a minor poet from Oxfordshire. He made his mark that summer when, walking through Westminster Abbey, he saw a small slab being placed over the grave of Ben Jonson. The poet laureate had died, aged 65, on 6 August and was buried the next day in an upright position in the north aisle of the nave, away from Poets' Corner. Jack Young reputedly paid the masons 18*d* to inscribe the words '*O RARE BEN JOHNSON*' on the gravestone.

Soon afterwards, Jack Young, Will Davenant and Sir John Suckling set out for the West Country. ''Twas as pleasant a journey as ever men had', wrote John Aubrey, 'in the height of a long peace and luxury, and in the venison season.' Suckling travelled 'like a young prince for all manner of equipage and convenience'. Davenant told Aubrey that Sir John 'had a cart-load of books carried down' with them to Bath.

The gallants spent the second night of their journey at Marlborough, where they walked on the Downs before supper and watched the maids laying laundry out to dry on the bushes. Jack Young fell into conversation with a pretty girl and arranged a clandestine meeting with her at midnight. Davenant and Suckling scuppered this assignation by persuading their landlady that Young was prone to dangerous fits and had to be locked in his room and physically restrained.

The party then moved on to Bromham House (later burned to the ground during the Civil War) and thence to the village of West Kington, where Davenant's elder brother was the rector. Robert Davenant, then a 34-year-old bachelor, had the pleasure of their company for a week, 'mirth, wit, and good cheer flowing', before they proceeded to the city of Bath. John Aubrey added that 'Parson Robert Davenant has told me that that tract about Socinianism was written on the table in the parlour of the parsonage at West Kington.'

Sir John Suckling's tract, which he entitled *An Account of Religion by Reason*, was described by an admirer as 'a discourse … which for learning, closeness of reasoning, and elegance of style, may put to shame the writings of men of far greater pretensions on like subjects.' It was a controversial piece, as Suckling admitted in his dedication, dated from Bath on 2 September 1637, to Edward Sackville, Earl of Dorset:

> I send you here, my Lord, that discourse enlarg'd, which frighted the lady into a cold sweat, and which had like to have made me an atheist at court, and your Lordship no very good Christian.

To approach the matter of religion from the direction of reason – 'the best weapon [man's] Creator hath given him for his defence' – was a bold move when the Puritans were promoting their Old Testament brand of blind faith. But this was that Indian Summer, 'the height of a long peace and luxury', and the religious turmoil to come was unimaginable. What Parson Robert would have made of the free-thinkers who came to stay with him in August 1637 is hard to say. His brother's religious views were quite possibly a cause for concern.

A Puritan publication, printed in London in 1644 and entitled *The Cavaliers Bible*, which affected to list the 'Religions, Sects, Societies, and Factions of the Cavaliers now in Armes against the Parliament', placed William Davenant at the head of the 'Valentinians, sometimes called the Gnostici' who 'attribute every thing to the Fates: as if there were so many masculine and feminine gods, as *Davenant* their Commander and the Poets have fained.' Like Suckling's interest in the theories of Fausto Paolo Sozzini (Latin *Socinus*), Davenant's presumed neo-paganism was unorthodox, to say the least.

Matters of life and death were much on his mind that autumn. His friend George Goring was shot in the ankle on 31 August while besieging the Dutch city of Breda. The first reports to reach England indicated that Goring had been killed. This would have been news to *Goring*, who would later conspire with Davenant and Suckling in the Army Plot of 1641. Davenant responded to the initial tidings with a fine tribute, 'Written, When Collonell Goring Was beleev'd to be slaine, at the siege of BREDA', in the form of a quasi-operatic duet sung in a ship at sea by Endymion Porter and Henry 'Arigo' Jermyn:

ENDIMION: Ho! Pilot! change your Course! for know we are
                Not guided by the Sea-mans usuall Starre:
                Storme-frighted Foole! dull, wat'ry Officer!
                Dost thou our Voyage by thy Compasse steere? [...]

ARIGO: If thou wilt Steere our course, thou must rely
                On some majestic, Epick-History;
                (The Poet's Compasse) such as the blind Priest
                In fury writ, when like an Exorcist,
                His Numbers charm'd the Grecian Host; whose Pen,
                The Scepter was, which rul'd the Soules of Men.

'Endimion' and 'Arigo' seek the shore of Elysium, where the shades of 'fierce *Achilles*' and 'bold *Hector*' were to be found alongside the English poet Sir Philip Sidney, whom Davenant had lauded as 'the God-like *Sidney*' in his 'Madagascar' poem. Sidney was shot through the thigh at the Battle of Zutphen in 1586 and died of gangrene twenty-six days later. George Goring was therefore a Doomed Youth in the Sidney mould, or so it appeared at the time.

After singing Goring's praises, 'Endimion' and 'Arigo' wonder whether the ignorant pilot could ever guide them to the Elysian coast. Jermyn commands the pilot to turn back; he has sighted Davenant on the shore, wearing mourning weeds and fearful that his friends may never return to the mortal plane. And so 'Arigo' cries:

Steere back! his Verse may make those Sorrowes last
Which here, wee 'mongst unhallow'd Sea-men waste.

Taken with his '*Elizium*' poem to the bereaved Duchess of Buckingham, it is easy to see why works like his elegy to Lord Goring led his critics to presume that Davenant believed in a pagan afterlife – the Elysian Fields for fallen heroes; astral journeys for departed lovers. There were no heavenly choirs to greet the soul in his vision of the hereafter. This alone would have made Davenant's views suspect to those fundamentalists who were about to turn the world on its head.

Davenant returned from Bath to face his busiest year yet. One of his first tasks was to prepare a collection of his poems for publication.

Madagascar; With Other Poems. By W. Davenant was printed by John Haviland for Thomas Walkley, who had previously published *The Temple of Love*. The volume also bore the 'Imprimatur' of Matthew Clay, dated '*Feb.* 26. 1637'.[2] Davenant's collection was therefore licensed by the stationer roundabout his 32nd birthday.

There was a brief dedication to Porter and Jermyn:

IF
THESE POEMS LIVE,

MAY
THEIR MEMORIES,
BY WHOM
THEY WERE CHERISH'D,
END.PORTER, H.IARMYN,
LIVE WITH THEM.

This was followed by verses by Endymion Porter, Thomas Carew, William Habington and Sir John Suckling, who separately commended both 'Madagascar' and Davenant's other poems.

Carew's poem, 'To Will. Davenant my Friend', compared 'Madagascar' with those ancient epics, the *Iliad* and *Aeneid*, and then quibbled with the issue of paternity:

What though Romances lye
Thus blended with more faithfull Historie?
Wee, of th'adult'rate mixture not complaine,
But thence more Characters of Vertue gaine [...]
So, oft the Bastard nobler fortune meets,
Than the dull Issue of the lawfull sheets.

The cocktail of history and romance produced a kind of poetic truth that neither could achieve on its own. Carew's phrase, 'th'adult'rate mixture', led him to his final couplet, in which he noted that 'the Bastard' often met with 'nobler fortune' than the legitimate – though dull – issue 'of the lawfull sheets.' Couched in terms related to Davenant's merging of the real and the imaginary, these references to adultery and bastards raise questions. Thomas Carew flitted between the rival camps of Ben Jonson and the rising star, Will Davenant. Did he know about William's relationship with Shakespeare?

After the headliner, 'Madagascar', came a miscellany, including the two cantos of '*Ieffereidos*, Or the Captivitie of *Jeffery*'; the odd poem 'To the Lord *B*[rooke]'; the plaintive ode 'In remembrance of Master *William Shakespeare*'; sundry poems addressed to King Charles, Queen Henrietta and the Porters; the operatic elegy for Lord Goring, and poems 'To *Henry Jarmin*' and 'To *Tho: Carew*'. The final poem in the anthology was 'To Doctor *Duppa*, Deane of Christ-Church, and Tutor to the Prince. An acknowledgment for his collection, in Honour of *Ben. Iohnson's* memory', which began:

How shall I sleepe to night, that am to pay
By a bold vow, a mighty Debt ere Day?

Brian Duppa, chaplain to the king and tutor to the princes, Charles and James, was then editing a collection of memorial verses, to be published in 1638 as '*Jonsonus*

Virbius: Or, the Memorie of Ben: Johnson Revived by the Friends of the Muses'. Presumably, Dr Duppa had approached Davenant for a poetic contribution, an error of judgement which can be put down to the clergyman's detachment from worldly affairs, for there is no evidence that Davenant was a friend or admirer of Ben Jonson's.

Above all, Davenant seems to have distrusted Jonson for being a *mis*-informer, a teller of tall tales. He was aware that the vogue for slanderous rumours and hair-raising reports was undermining the stability of the nation. The horrors of the Civil War were the consequence of endless inflammatory stories, wilfully disseminated by seditious rabble-rousers, and Jonson – as far as Davenant was concerned – was the granddaddy of them all.

So Duppa was barking up a very wrong tree if he solicited a praise-poem from Davenant for his *Jonsonus Virbius*. There was no poem from Davenant among the thirty-three lyrics published by Dr Duppa, although Davenant did publish his 'acknowledgement' for Duppa's collection. Jonson's name is not mentioned once. Instead, Davenant harped on about his 'mighty Debt':

> This Debt hereditary is, and more
> Than can be pay'd for such an Ancestor

The 'hereditary' debt was not payable to Ben Jonson, but to Dr Duppa – Davenant wisely choosing to stay on the right side of the royal chaplain, and seeming to hint that, by publishing *Jonsonus Virbius*, Duppa was countering the 'half-Knowers' who had misread Jonson's works:

> Shew them, how full they are of subtle sinne,
> When Faith's great Cable, they would nicely spinne
> To Reason's slender Threads; then (falsely bold)
> When they have weakened it, cry, t'wilt not hold!

Davenant appeared to suggest that Jonson had been overpraised by 'great-faithlesse-Wits' who saw things in his work that were not there. The poem compares with the equally evasive 'To the Lord B.', which spoke of solemn vows and promised to praise Fulke Greville, Lord Brooke, without actually doing so. As Davenant's only known reflection on the death of Ben Jonson, 'To Doctor *Duppa*' lacks any sense of adulation or lament. The contrast with his dramatic elegy for George Goring – who wasn't even dead – could hardly have been much greater.

There had been no masques at Court since *The Temple of Love* in February 1635. Davenant explained the reason for this 'intermission' in the introduction to his next Court masque. The ceiling of the banqueting house at Whitehall was being 'richly adorn'd with pieces of painting of great value, figuring the acts of King James of happy memory, and other enrichments'. The ceiling panels, depicting the birth of

King Charles as the 'Apotheosis of James I', had been painted by Peter Paul Rubens in Antwerp and shipped to London for installation in the Banqueting House, where they can still be seen.

Fearing that the magnificent ceiling 'might suffer from the smoke of many lights', as Davenant put it, the king charged Inigo Jones to create a 'new temporary room of timber' in which masques could be performed. Built of oak, deal and fir, the 'greate new Masking Roome att Whitehall' was 112ft (34m) long, 57ft (17.5m) wide and 59ft (18m) high, with four pairs of stairs 'to goe upp into the same roome' and two tiers of ten windows.

The first masque to be danced in the temporary Masking Room was *Britannia Triumphans*. Conceived by '*Inigo Jones, Surveyor of his Majesties Workes, and William D'Avenant, her Majesties Servant*', it was presented '*by the Kings Majestie and his Lords*' on the Sunday after Twelfth Night, 1638. The Sunday performance outraged the 'godly' fanatics.

The scene opened on a prospect of London and the River Thames. Two characters, signifying Action and Imposture, debated, Imposture threatening that his Puritan affectations were becoming more popular: 'the prosperous, brave / Increasing multitude pursue my steps.' Merlin, the 'prophetic magician', was summoned to conjure up a vision of 'The great seducers of this Isle', and the scene was transformed into a 'horrid hell'.

Scene design by Inigo Jones for *Britannia Triumphans*.

A succession of lowly characters, from 'mock' musicians to such 'rebellious leaders' as Jack Cade, Robert Kett, Jack Straw and others, formed the antimasque. The path from satirical dissent to open rebellion having been mimed, the monster-slaying hero Bellerophon arrived, mounted on Pegasus, and announced that the 'fantastic objects' of the antimasque merely showed 'How dull the imperious were to be so sillily / Misled'. Imposture demanded another vision from Merlin, and the scene changed for a 'MOCK ROMANZA'. In a 'vast forest, in which stood part of an old castle kept by a giant', a dwarf and a squire, a knight and a damsel, contended in burlesque style with the giant.

'How trivial and lost thy visions are!' cried Bellerophon, once the romantic stereotypes had danced themselves off the stage. 'This happy hour is call'd to celebrate / Britanocles, and those that in this Isle / The old with modern virtues reconcile.' A golden palace appeared. The gate of this Palace of Fame opened to reveal Britanocles – King Charles himself – and as the palace sank down beneath the stage the Chorus sang to 'Britanocles, the great and good.'

The scene changed 'to that of Britain' and a new chorus, representing 'our own modern poets raised by Merlin', sang their address to Henrietta Maria, who sat in pride of place at the end of the hall. And then the scene changed again, into a seascape, with the sea-nymph Galatea riding on a dolphin's back and singing of Britanocles's virtues. A fleet of ships appeared while the masquers danced, and the Valediction was sung, wishing 'our royal lover' more 'youthful blessings than he had before' and despatching the assembly 'To bed, to bed!':

Each lawful lover, to advance his youth,
Dream he hath stol'n his vigour, love, and truth;
   Then all will haste to bed but none to rise!

Spectacular as it was, *Britannia Triumphans* seems inchoate and confused, as if Davenant was out of practice. The message – that the king would triumph over his enemies at home and abroad – got lost amid the stage-effects, rather like a modern-day pantomime, in which the plot barely matters.

Henrietta Maria commanded Inigo Jones 'to make a new subject of a Masque for her selfe, that with high and hearty invention, might give occasion for variety of Scenes, strange apparitions, Songs, Musick and dancing of severall kinds'. This was to be the queen's response to the king's masque of *Britannia Triumphans*. Henrietta approved Jones's plan and 'the worke was set in hand, and with all celerity performed in shorter time, than any thing here hath beene done in this kind', as Davenant explained in his introduction. *Luminalia, or The Festivall of Light* was presented 'By the Queenes Majestie, and her Ladies' on the night of Shrove Tuesday, 1638.

The opening scene was 'all of darknesse' – a moonlit wood and river. Night entered in a chariot 'drawne by two great owles' and sang a haunting hymn. Oblivion ('a young man naked') and Silence ('an old man in a skin coat close to his body') then joined Night, and more songs were sung before the 'Attendants of Night' produced their antimasque of night-time activities: thieves and watchmen divided the spoils of a robbery; 'Fayries' danced, with 'Master *Ieffery Hudson*, the Queenes Majesties dwarfe' as their 'principall Captaine'.

From night in the city to the City of Sleep, a dream world of golden mountains and falling towers, which yielded place to the 'beautifull garden of the *Britanides*'. Hesperus and Aurora heralded the dawn, addressing the king, seated opposite the stage, before Queen Henrietta, the 'terrestrial beauty' and the 'earthly star', appeared with her ladies:

> *How dull and uneffectuall is that rage,*
> *   Which swels our Poets when their numbers flow?*
> *Resembling sillily, in ev'ry age,*
> *   Things excellent, to what they least doe know.*
>
> *How poorely have they done, when they compare*
> *   A beauty that can rule severest eyes,*
> *Unto some pretty twinckling senselesse Starre?*
> *   Yet thinke they mend her by such similies.*

The queen took her place beside King Charles. Across the hall, the 'upper part of the heaven opened, and a bright and transparent cloud came forth farre into the Scene'. The cloud carried 'many *Zephyri*' who began a sprightly dance – 'Which Apparition for the newnesse of the Invention, greatnesse of the Machine, and difficulty of Engining, was much admir'd, being a thing not before attempted in the Aire.'

Luminalia is a more satisfying read than *Britannia Triumphans*. It may be that Davenant and Jones found working for the delicate, spirited Henrietta more inspiring than creating a masque for the stiff and sober Charles. Both texts, like Davenant's *Madagascar* anthology, were printed by John Haviland to be sold by Thomas Walkley 'at the flying Horse' on the Strand.

Two masques in as many months made Davenant the *de facto* court poet, a post formerly held by Ben Jonson. The question of who would replace Jonson as poet laureate was still unresolved, although Sir John Suckling had written a humorous poem about it. Suckling's 'A Sessions of the Poets' imagined a gathering of 'the wits of the town' in the presence of Apollo, god of poetry, to determine who should wear the laurel crown. The first to speak was 'good old Ben':

> Prepar'd before with Canary wine,
> And he told them plainly he deserv'd the bays
> For his were call'd works, where others were but plays.

Apollo stopped him, advising Jonson that merit, not presumption, would decide the winner. Jonson turned to leave, angrily, but Apollo called him back.[3]

Thomas Carew was denied the laurels because he had to work too hard on his verses. Next up was 'Will. Davenant: asham'd of a foolish mischance / That he had got lately travelling in France', who:

> Modestly hoped the handsomeness of 's muse
> Might any deformity about him excuse.

However, the company could find no precedent 'in all their records' for a 'laureate without a nose'.

Other poets were considered (Sucking himself wasn't there, being more interested in gambling and dark-eyed women) but none was deemed worthy. The bays were eventually awarded to a wealthy alderman, Apollo declaring that 'the best sign / Of a good store of wit 's to have a good store of coin'. Davenant's reaction to the Alderman's entrance was extraordinary: he began to swear, as if the sight of a local councillor brought out the worst in him.

He was one of the forerunners in the race to become poet laureate. But he still needed to earn a living. His godfather's example would have told him that playwriting alone would not make his fortune. The real money was to be made in theatre management.

Keeping one foot on the public stage, Davenant penned a brace of plays in 1638. The first, *The Unfortunate Lovers: A Tragedie*, was licensed on 16 April and acted 'with great applause' before the queen at the Blackfriars on 23 April. It was performed again at the Cockpit-in-Court in May and at Hampton Court in September.

The Unfortunate Lovers is set in Verona. Altophil, a 'Duke and Generall', is in love with the flawless Arthiopa. But an ambitious courtier named Galeotto wishes to marry his daughter to the duke, and so he bribes two stooges to accuse Arthiopa of 'unchastity'. Galeotto's treachery is discovered and he is arrested. He persuades his guards to let him escape and then betrays Verona to its enemy, Heildebrand, King of the Lombards, whose army is encamped nearby.

With echoes of Shakespeare's *Rape of Lucrece* and *Macbeth*, the plot proceeds to the inevitable muster of corpses and ends with Altophil and Arthiopa sharing a kiss before they both die. *The Unfortunate Lovers* was revived at the Restoration by Thomas Killigrew's company. Samuel Pepys saw it acted by Davenant's company on 7 March 1664, when the house was half-full, and again on 11 September 1667. Pepys also attended the performance of *The Unfortunate Lovers* at the Duke's Playhouse on 8 April 1668, the day after Davenant died. The text was published in 1643, at the height of the Civil War, and reissued in 1649 with a peculiar dedication, signed 'W. H.', to Philip Herbert, Earl of Pembroke and Montgomery.

On 17 November 1638, Davenant's next play was licensed by Sir Henry Herbert. *The Fair Favourite* was performed before the king and queen at the Cockpit-in-Court on 20 November and again on 11 December. The setting, this time, was Naples.

The king does not love his wife; he has always been enamoured of Eumena, the 'Fair Favourite', who was stolen away and pronounced dead so that the king would compact with the neighbouring province of Otranto by marrying the queen. Though the world-weary king still loves Eumena, she remains resolutely chaste. Her brother Oramont, recently taken as a prisoner-of-war, returns to Naples but refuses Eumena's offer to pay his ransom, believing her to be nothing more than the king's whore.

Perhaps the most striking aspect of *The Fair Favourite* is its portrayal of the differences between the sexes. The female leads are virtuous and compassionate. They suffer from the lust and jealousy of the men, who seem inclined to duel over obscure points of honour, and yet, unlike the men, they never lose their moral dignity. This was a surprisingly enlightened attitude. The rise of the 'godly' faction would put women back in their place as the fallible daughters of Eve. By presenting women as moral exemplars, and men as misguided and obsessive, Davenant was way ahead of his time.

Being a tragicomedy, *The Fair Favourite* ends happily, although a darkly prophetic note sounds when Oramont is reprieved from the public executioner:

Lord! How they love to see a proper
Man suffer! And when their wives come home,
Each tells her husband he was like him:
For he behav'd himself with such a
Courtly courage at the block.

Ten years later, these words would gain resonance when Charles I stepped out of the banqueting house in Whitehall to have his head separated from his body.

Finally, two days after Charles and Henrietta saw *The Fair Favourite* for the second time, Davenant was awarded the post of poet laureate. The king issued an order on 13 December to the effect that 'in consideracion of service heretofore done and hereafter to be done unto us by Willm Davenant gentl[eman]' the playwright was to be granted 'one anuitie or yearelie pencion of one hundred poundes of lawfull money of England by the yeare'. This annuity would be paid semi-annually, backdated to the Feast of the Assumption (25 March), and was almost exactly the same as the pension received by Ben Jonson, with the exception of Jonson's additional grant of a 'terse of Canary wine'.[4]

After sixteen years in London, William Davenant had supplanted Ben Jonson as chief writer of masques for the Court and succeeded him as poet laureate. Scorning his father's repressed provincial world he had glided into high-born circles and his godfather's theatrical domain. He had ten full-length plays under his belt and a published volume of poetry. Now all he needed was a theatre to run and a period of relative calm in which to run it.

Such circumstances would not arise for another twenty-two years.

Lincoln College portrait, said to be of William Davenant as a young man.

PART FOUR

A Child in Oxford

1621—1606

13

Shakespears Vncle

*T*he city of Oxford was enclosed by a medieval wall. Four roads pierced this wall and met at Carfax (Latin *Quadrifurcus* – 'four-forked'), where the church of St Martin stood.

There were four smaller gates in the wall. A short distance from the Northgate was a turnstile, recorded in 1590 as 'The hole in the wall called The Turle.' This 'turning gate' gave its name to the alley leading from Broad Street, outside the wall, to Ship Street, which connected Turl Street to Cornmarket, the parallel thoroughfare running from the Northgate to Carfax crossroads.

Number 3 Cornmarket was known as 'Tattleton's House', after John Tattleton, whose tenancy came to an end with his death in 1581. The house was then leased to John Underhill, Doctor of Divinity. The adjacent property – No. 4 – was owned by Pierce Underhill, whose sister married a furrier named William Hough and gifted the garden behind Tattleton's House to her 'naturall and dutifull sonne', Daniel, in 1622. That same year, John Davenant, Mayor of Oxford, died, having expressed the desire in his will that the tavern he had run in Tattleton's House should be managed by his daughters, until one of them married his senior apprentice, and that the rent should be paid to 'Mr Huffe'.

Daniel Hough was a Fellow of Lincoln College, which stood on Turl Street, to the rear of Tattleton's House. He was, to all intents and purposes, the Davenants' landlord. Hough died in 1644, at the height of the Civil War, and left a liberal bequest to Lincoln College for renovations to be carried out 'within two years of a settled peace in this kingdom of England.' His interest in the Davenant family went further than merely collecting the rent. At the time of John Davenant's death, Hough was tutor to his second son, William.

Founded in the 1420s, Lincoln was one of the smaller Oxford colleges. Quite when William entered the college is unclear. The average age for matriculation was between 15 and 18, although Lincoln admitted several students who were 13. It is generally assumed that Davenant's spell at Lincoln began in about 1620, but in *Lincoln College, Oxford*, published in 1908, Stephen A. Warner noted an entry in the college accounts for 1618 – 'For glasse in Slad's, Devonant, and Ford's studdie,

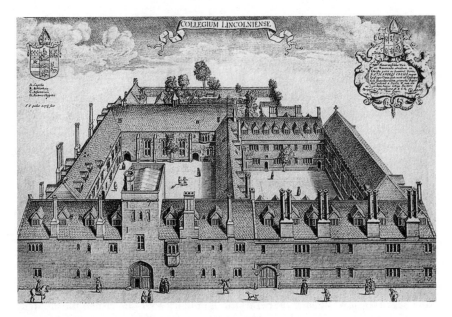

Lincoln College, engraving by David Loggan (1665).

13d.' – which he took to be 'most probably a reference to Sir William Davenant.' This would suggest that William was a student at Lincoln, a stone's throw from his parents' tavern, from the tender age of twelve.

His brothers were sent to London for their schooling, but William was kept closer to home. He was initially educated at Edward Sylvester's private school, near the corner of Turl Street and High Street, but his time there was cut short. William was removed from Sylvester's grammar school and placed in the care of his father's landlord, Daniel Hough, at Lincoln College. The reason for this transfer might have involved a whiff of scandal.

John Davenant was baptised on 6 August 1565 at the church of St Thomas the Apostle, Knightrider Street, in the City of London. His parents had no other children until a daughter, Katherine, was born in 1574, by which time the family had moved to the riverside parish of St James Garlickhythe. On 6 March 1575 John Davenant entered the Merchant Taylors' school on Suffolk Lane – the school to which he later sent three of his four sons.

John Aubrey would describe William's father as 'a very grave and discreet citizen', to which Aubrey's associate Anthony Wood (who drank in the Davenants' Oxford tavern) added that John Davenant was 'yet an admirer and lover of plays and play-makers, especially Shakespeare'. There was a theatrical element in his background. His parents had celebrated their marriage in 1563 with 'a grett dener, and at nyghte a maske', when wedding masques were an expensive rarity. Richard Mulcaster, the master of the Merchant Taylors' school, actively promoted drama as a teaching aid and produced plays and masques for Queen Elizabeth I, in which his students performed.[1]

On 22 June 1590 John Davenant became a freeman of the Worshipful Company of Merchant Taylors, one of the twelve Great Livery Companies of the City of London, his father also being a freeman of the Merchant Taylors' Company. He then followed his father – also called John – into the wine trade. John Davenant senior lived on (Upper) Thames Street, close to where barrels of Bordeaux and Gascony wine were landed at Three Cranes Wharf. He and his son ran a successful business and donated generously to their parish. In late 1592 or early 1593, John Davenant junior married the daughter of the late Robert Sheppard and his widow, Elizabeth. Jane Sheppard was three years younger than her husband. The date and location of the wedding are unknown.

The early years of their marriage were not kind to John and Jane. Their first child was buried in 1593. By Christmas 1597 they had laid a further four children to rest at St James Garlickhythe. Only the fifth child received a christening, on 24 October 1597, and was named after his father, but the bell tolled for him on 11 December. Jane began to show signs of desperation. In January 1598 she visited the amateur physician, Simon Forman, at his Billingsgate lodgings. Forman had an impressive client list, which included persons of influence, and became surprisingly intimate with some of them. Mistress Davenant consulted him about the possibility of her being pregnant again – 'She supposeth herself with child,' wrote Forman, 'but yt is not soe.'

Someone else who appears in Forman's notebooks at this time was Marie Mountjoy. She and her husband Christopher were French Protestants who lived on Silver Street in the Cripplegate district. Within a short while, Shakespeare would be lodging with them. Marie Mountjoy supplied Queen Anne with costly and elaborate headdresses. She was, therefore, in a similar line of work to Jane Davenant's brothers, Thomas and Richard, who were glovers, perfumers and embroiderers to the court of King James. Thomas Sheppard's wife was also consulting Simon Forman about a possible pregnancy. Forman's notes for February 1598 reveal that Ursula Sheppard had not been well: 'She supposeth her self wth child & is very big but I think yt is a false conception.' It is possible that Jane Davenant and her poorly sister-in-law knew Marie Mountjoy, Shakespeare's soon-to-be landlady: all three were visiting Simon Forman over similar issues.

John and Jane Davenant's sixth child was baptised John on 14 January 1599. He cannot have lived long because his parents christened another child John in 1607. On 19 December 1599, Jane's younger sister Phyllis was married at St James Garlickhythe. Soon afterwards, John and Jane left London, transporting their possessions up the River Thames from Three Cranes Wharf to the walled city of Oxford.

During the Civil War, Tattleton's House became known as the Salutation – and, later, the Crown – but during the Davenants' occupancy it was simply the Taverne, identified by the sign of an evergreen bush. It was a four-storey building, registered in 1666 as having twelve hearths and, in 1696, twenty windows. Stretching back some 120ft (36.5m) from Cornmarket, it contained at least twenty rooms, including a kitchen, washhouse and larder at the rear and a couple of parlours fronting the street, with the 'Sheriff's Parlour' behind them. Among the upstairs rooms were John Davenant's 'Study', the 'Elm Chamber', the 'White Chamber', the 'Great Chamber by the Court' and the first floor 'Painted Chamber'. The latter was rediscovered when the seventeenth-century oak panelling was removed in 1927. In addition to images of Canterbury bells, bunches of grapes, arabesques and flowers, the painted murals included two pious inscriptions – a Catholic 'IHS' symbol over the fireplace and a Protestant black-letter text beside it:

> And last of the rest be thou
> gods servant for that hold i best
> In the mornynge earlye
> serve god Devoutlye
> fear god above allthynge.

The wall-paintings date from John Tattleton's tenancy, roughly 1560–81.

It may have been Shakespeare who recommended the property to John and Jane Davenant. The bard broke his journeys between Stratford and London at Oxford and probably knew the Houghs and Underhills who leased the neighbouring tenements on Cornmarket.[2] Joan Underhill – born at the Crosse Inn, No. 5 Cornmarket – ran a celebrated inn called the Angel in Bishopsgate, near where Shakespeare was lodging before he moved in with the Mountjoys. If Shakespeare did suggest Tattleton's House when John and Jane were looking for a fresh start, away from London, it was sound advice. The Davenants prospered in Oxford. All seven of the children they had there survived into adulthood.

The first, born in about 1601, was named Elizabeth, after Jane's mother. Their second daughter was baptised Jane at St Martin's church, Carfax, on 11 February 1602. Robert, their eldest son, named after Jane's father, was christened on 14 April 1603, when he was five weeks old, and five days after Christmas 1604 the Davenants were back at St Martin's for the baptism of their third daughter, Alice. Three more sons followed: William in 1606, John in 1607 and Nicholas in 1611.

Robert resembled his father. He went up to St John's College, Oxford, after his Merchant Taylors' schooling, and then held a succession of incumbencies in the Church of England, marrying Jane Harwich, the daughter of the vicar of Wanborough, Wiltshire, in 1649. His three sisters also appear to have been solidly conformist: Elizabeth married a Fellow of Corpus Christi College, her second husband being Richard Bristow, Rector of Didcot; Alice married Dr William Sherborne of St John's College, who was successively Rector of Talbenny, Rector of Pembridge, Prebendary of Hereford and Chancellor of Llandaff. Jane married the apprentice Thomas Hallam, just as her father had hoped, in 1622, running the Taverne with him until his death, and then by herself; she and Elizabeth lived as widows in Oxford and were both buried at St Martin's Carfax.

The younger Davenant boys were more of a worry. John junior died in a debtors' prison in 1634. Nicholas led a shiftless existence, serving in the First Bishops' War and taking Parliament's side in the Civil War; he lived for a while with his sister Alice and her husband at Pembridge Court, Herefordshire, in the 1650s, and may have been the customs officer named Nicholas Davenant who was in London in 1662.

And then there was William.

John Davenant bought his freedom of the City of Oxford on 4 June 1604. When King James, Queen Anne, Prince Henry and the rest of the Court came to Oxford in August 1605, John would have been one of the dignitaries who, along with representatives of the university, rode out to greet the royal party at Aristotle's Well, north of the city.

In 1615, the churchwardens of St Martin's Carfax listed nearly fifty parishioners who had lent money 'towards the payment of the last yeares surcharge'. The twelfth name on the list was Mr John Davenant. A pencilled note beside this entry reads, 'Jno. Davenant Shakespears Vncle'.

Why 'Shakespeare's Uncle'? Captain Frances Grose's *Classical Dictionary of the Vulgar Tongue*, reproduced in 1811 as *A Dictionary of Buckish Slang, University Wit, and Pickpocket Eloquence*, offers a clue:

> *Uncle*: Mine uncle's; a necessary house. He is gone to visit his uncle; saying of one who leaves his wife soon after marriage. It likewise means a pawn-broker's: goods pawned are frequently said to be at mine uncle's, or laid up in lavender.

The common element appears to be the act of abandonment, of leaving something – a wife, valuables, excrement – behind.

The reference to John Davenant having been 'Shakespeare's Uncle' is a reminder that the relationship between Shakespeare and his godson's family was close and complex. The tales of the young William racing to see his godfather and being admonished not to 'take *God's* name in vain' point to a confusion of roles, with Shakespeare as both godfather and father ('In all probability he got him', wrote Thomas Hearne, the antiquarian of Oxford), while the anonymous elegy 'Upon the Death of Sr WILLIAM DAVENANT' presented the bard and the poet laureate as siblings:

> Then *Shakespear* next a brothers part doth claim,
> Because their quick inventions were the same.

John Davenant was evidently seen as Shakespeare's 'Uncle' – the broker with whom Shakespeare pawned his illegitimate son. Hardly surprising, then, that John should have been 'seldom or never seen to laugh' when such rumours were flying around.

He had set his sights on civic office, purchasing 'a licence of this Cytie to sell Wyne & a Bayliffs place' for £8 in 1604 and, on 2 October 1612, taking a formal oath of allegiance to the university as a burgess with full municipal rights. What cannot be known with any certainty is whether John's ambitions were hampered by the tittle-tattle surrounding his second son, or whether his eagerness to attain the mayoralty was a form of compensation stemming from a desire to be looked up to, rather than sniggered at.

The gossip might have affected his decision to remove William from Edward Sylvester's school at an early age. The Lincoln College accounts suggest that 'Devonant' had a room there in 1618. This was the same year that Robert entered St John's College, just outside the city wall, after three years at school in London. The youngest sons, John and Nicholas, were sent to the Merchant Taylors' school in 1619. With William under the watchful eye of Daniel Hough and his younger brothers despatched to London, John Davenant had purged his household of unruly elements, clearing the way to his becoming mayor of Oxford in 1621.

The evidence points to a troubled relationship between William and his father. Drafting his will in 1622, John Davenant called upon 'my sonne William' to apprentice himself to 'some good marchant of London or other tradesman' and to do so within three months of his father's death 'ffor avoyding of Inconvenience in my house for mastershippe when I am gone'. It is not clear what kind of 'Inconvenience' John anticipated, but the implication is that William's presence was disruptive.

Some years later, in *The Wits*, William amused himself with thoughts of his elder brother's disdain for the use to which he had put his legacy and the firstborn's about-turn when he realises that his cosmopolitan sibling is not without a certain native cunning: 'My Father was no Poet sure, I wonder / How hee got him?'

Anthony Wood, who disclosed that it was Robert Davenant who took after his father, also noted that the sober academic life held little appeal for William – 'but his geny which was always opposite to it, lead him in the pleasant paths of poetry'. A clash of temperaments between the straitlaced father and the wayward son seems to have been inevitable. We recall Sir John Suckling's 'A Sessions of the Poets', in which everything is reasonably orderly until:

> At length who but an Alderman did appear,
> At which Will. Davenant began to swear

Davenant's imagined response to the alderman's entrance was spontaneous and excessive, as if William was known to be hostile to aldermen, maybe because his 'reserved and melancholly' father had been one.

'To swell the records of collegiate fame,' wrote Robert Montgomery, a student at Lincoln College, in his *Oxford* poem of 1831, 'See Lincoln rise, and claim a Davenant's name':

Within her walls the minstrel student wove
Poetic dreams of melody and love.
On him, as yet a verse-enchanted child,
The Soul of nature, Shakespeare's self, had smiled –

Though William left without graduating, Lincoln College still honours him. One of Lincoln's two literary societies is the 'Davenant' and the college boasts a fine portrait which is said to be of him (if so, the artist contrived to depict him before his nose was wrecked by syphilis at the age of 24).[3] As for the 'Poetic dreams' woven by the juvenile Davenant, only 'In remembrance of Master *William Shakespeare*', it has been suggested, survives from his early youth. It seems improbable that the Ode was written at such a tender age as 10 or 12, between Shakespeare's death and Davenant's matriculation, especially if the 'shallow Brooke' of the final line referred to Fulke Greville – Lord Brooke from 1621 – but it is far from impossible that the 'minstrel student' wrote a poem or two in honour of Shakespeare, thereby helping to fuel the rumours.

For the point needs to be made that William Davenant effectively had two fathers. There was John Davenant, vintner and alderman, who seems to have exercised little influence over his second son. And there was Will Shakespeare, the godfather who inspired his entire career, and whose sudden death on 23 April 1616 might explain Davenant's attitudes towards Fulke Greville and Ben Jonson.

The church of St Leonard stands on a hillside above the River Arrow, a few miles north of the Worcestershire town of Redditch. In about 1580, Ralph Sheldon, the lord of the manor of Beoley, built a chapel on the side of the church, complete with a black marble altar which had been blessed by Pope Gregory XIII. The chapel allowed the Sheldon family to fulfil the letter of the law, which required everyone to attend Anglican services, without having to set foot on Church of England premises.

A vault was constructed underneath the Sheldon Chapel.[4] It houses the remains of several Sheldons. Adjoining the vault is an ossuary containing four complete sets of bones, each suggesting a person of large stature. There is also a small skull which appears to be unrelated to the neat piles of bones surrounding it.

The vicar of Beoley in 1884 was the Reverend Charles Jones Langston, a local man born 46 years earlier in the nearby town of Alcester. He had already published a story – *How Shakespeare's Skull was Stolen* – in the October 1879 issue of the *Argosy* magazine. Five years later he completed his strange account, which he released as a privately-printed pamphlet entitled, *How Shakespeare's Skull was Stolen and Found.*

The Reverend Charles Jones Langston claimed to have found 'THE VERITABLE SKULL OF WILLIAM SHAKESPEARE' in the ossuary beside the Sheldon vault beneath Beoley church. It was resting in the funerary urn which had held the viscera of Ralph Sheldon, the man who built the chapel. Ralph Sheldon, a prominent Catholic, died in 1613. He was related to Shakespeare by marriage.

The 'undersized' skull found at Beoley displays some interesting features.[5] There is a depression in the forehead, near the top of the frontal bone. Very similar depressions can be seen on the Shakespeare effigy in the funerary monument at Holy Trinity, Stratford-upon-Avon, and in the 'Unique First Proof' of the Droeshout engraving of Shakespeare, printed in the First Folio of 1623,[6] and on the so-called Davenant Bust of Shakespeare at the Garrick Club. The 'bumpy' texture of the skull above the left eye suggests that the fatty deposits of the eyebrow had slipped (this is also apparent on the Davenant Bust) causing the left eyebrow to droop, as it does in the Shakespeare portraiture; most likely, this brow ptosis was congenital, and it is interesting to note that both the Faithorne engraving and the Lincoln College portrait indicate that Davenant had the same condition – an autosomal dominant inheritance which offers persuasive evidence that Shakespeare was his genetic father.

The lower parts of the skull's eye sockets are broken. Both sides of the upper jaw have been shattered. Jagged burrs of bone protruding from the outer corner of the left eyebrow match the swelling or bulge apparent, in the same position, in the First Folio engraving and the 'Chandos' portrait which belonged to Sir William Davenant. Puncture wounds in the left orbital cavity, near the bridge of the nose, suggest that a sharp-pointed instrument, such as a poniard, was thrust into the eye socket, forcing the eyeball forwards. The scar made by the tip of this weapon can be seen on the death mask of Shakespeare, dated 1616 and housed at Darmstadt Castle, Germany, which also shows that the left eyeball was forced forwards in its socket.

The evidence of the skull, combined with the death mask and portraiture, point to Shakespeare having been the victim of a murderous assault, beginning with the jabbing of a poniard into his eye socket and progressing to a series of ferocious blows to the face.

The recorder of Stratford-upon-Avon at the time of Shakespeare's death was Fulke Greville. The post, which Greville had inherited from his father, combined the roles of registrar and coroner. If there was anything untoward about Shakespeare's demise it would have been Greville's task to investigate. He did no such thing.

An odd connection between Fulke Greville and Shakespeare was made by David Lloyd in *The Statesmen and Favourites of England since the Reformation* (1665):

> One great argument for his [Greville's] worth, was his respect of the worth of others; desiring to be known to posterity under no other notions than of *Shakespear*'s and *Ben Johnson*'s Master, Chancellor *Egerton*'s Patron, Bishop *Overal*'s Lord,[7] and Sir *Philip Sidney*'s friend.

Ben Jonson enjoyed Greville's patronage, but there is no known link between Shakespeare and Greville, apart from the fact that members of the Greville household in Alcester terrorised the Shakespeares in Stratford and caused the death (by a blow to the head) of Shakespeare's friend Richard Quiney, the Stratford mayor whose son married Shakespeare's younger daughter, Judith.

If Greville's desire to be remembered as 'Shakespeare's and Ben Jonson's Master' is puzzling, so is the disappearance of several pages from *Certaine Learned and Elegant Workes of the Right Honorable Fulke Lord Brooke*, published five years after his death. The first page of that volume is numbered 23. Some sort of introductory epistle was apparently withdrawn at the last minute.

William Davenant was working for Fulke Greville when the master was stabbed by his servant, Ralph Haywood. Davenant later told John Aubrey that Greville had often told Haywood 'that he would do something for him, but did not, but still put him off with delays'. Whatever it was that Greville had promised, and neglected, to do for his manservant, they were overheard quarrelling about a 'will' when the fatal wounding took place. Haywood then immediately committed suicide, even though Greville had no intention of prosecuting him.

It was an open secret that William Davenant was Shakespeare's godson and quite possibly his natural son. When Davenant went to work for Fulke Greville, 1st Baron Brooke, might not an aged retainer like Ralph Haywood have felt that the lad deserved an explanation for his godfather's untimely death? As recorder of Stratford-upon-Avon, Greville would have known the facts. Perhaps he agreed to give his servant a full account, but kept avoiding the issue, until Haywood's patience snapped. They argued about Will and Greville was stabbed in the back. Any hints that there might have been in the lengthy preface to Fulke Greville's *Learned and Elegant Workes* were lost when those pages were intercepted at the print-shop and removed.

Greville's murder might have helped to bring on Ben Jonson's apoplectic stroke. On 26 October 1628, Jonson was questioned by the Attorney-General, Sir Robert Heath, in connection with a poem, 'To his confined Friend, Mr. Felton'. John Felton was the discontented soldier who had stabbed the Duke of Buckingham to death that August. The poem, which contains many Jonsonian touches, sought to justify the homicide:

> Enjoy thy Bondage; make thy Prison know
> Thou hast a Libertie thou canst not owe
> To those base Punishments; keep't entire, since
> Nothing but guilt shackles the Conscience.

Jonson denied responsibility for the poem. 'Common fame', he said, attributed it to Zouch Townley, a 'scholar, and a divine by profession, and a preacher' from Christ Church, Oxford. Ben had heard Townley preach at St Margaret's, Westminster, and invited him to supper two nights later, when he presented Townley with 'the dagger with a white haft' which he 'ordinarily wore at his girdle'. Townley avoided punishment for the Felton poem by leaving the country but remained friends with Ben Jonson after his return.

Soon, Jonson was 'strucken with the palsy' which 'made a deep impression upon his body and his mind', in the words of Davenant's friend, Edward Hyde. He had come under suspicion of praising the assassin of the king's favourite and his 'Master', Fulke Greville, had been murdered during an argument over a 'Will'. Either of these recent events could have precipitated his debilitating stroke.

Jonson had been conscious of Davenant's presence in London since at least 1623. Ben's poem 'To the memory of my beloved', published in the First Folio of Shakespeare's plays, includes the lines:

> *Looke how the fathers face*
> *Lives in his issue, even so, the race*
> *Of Shakespeares minde, and manners brightly shines*
> *In his well torned, and true-filed lines:*
> *In each of which, he seemes to shake a Lance,*
> *As brandish't at the eyes of Ignorance.*

Passing over the pun on Shakespeare's name ('shake a Lance') and the mention of a weapon 'brandish't at the eyes', the remark 'Looke how the fathers face / Lives in his issue' can be read in two ways. It could be a mere metaphor, indicating that Shakespeare's personality was reflected in his writing just as a father's features can be replicated in his child. But the imperative '*Looke*' suggests that Jonson was being more specific. Not a metaphorical child, but a genuine chip-off-the-old-block with the same, probably inherited, ptosis of the left eyebrow.

A short while before Ben's poem was published in the 1623 First Folio, Shakespeare's funerary monument was installed in the chancel of Holy Trinity Church, Stratford-upon-Avon. The monument, with its half-length effigy of Shakespeare, bears the inscription:

> STAY PASSENGER, WHY GOEST THOV BY SO FAST,
> READ IF THOV CANST, WHOM ENVIOVS DEATH HATH PLAST
> WITH IN THIS MONVMENT SHAKESPEARE: WITH WHOME,
> QVICK NATVRE DIDE WHOSE NAME, DOTH DECK YS TOMBE,
> FAR MORE, THEN COST: SIEH ALL, YT HE HATH WRITT,
> LEAVES LIVING ART, BVT PAGE, TO SERVE HIS WITT.

The opening lines compare with numerous epitaphs written by Ben Jonson and echo the final quatrain of the anonymous poem, 'To my confined Friend, Mr. Felton':

> If idle Passingers aske, who lies heere,
> Let the Dukes toomb this for Inscription beare.
> Paint Cales and Ree:[8] Make French and Spanish laugh,
> Add Englands shame, And there's his Epitaph.

The final part of the Shakespeare monument inscription – 'Sieh all, that he hath writt, / Leaves living art, but page, to serve his witt' – is ambiguous, to say the least. Had Shakespeare left no more than a page of 'living art' to be remembered by? Or do the lines hint at a living artist, Shakespeare's son, who was then serving as a page to the Duchess of Richmond?

The sole surviving account of Shakespeare's death places Jonson at the scene. Judith Shakespeare, who married Thomas Quiney ten weeks before her father died, was still living in Stratford when Rev. John Ward became vicar of Holy Trinity in 1662. Ward wrote himself a memorandum:

> Shakespear, Drayton and Ben Jhonson, had a merry meeting, and, itt seems, drank too hard, for Shakespear died of a feavour there contracted. – Remember to peruse Shakespears plays and bee versed in them, that I may not be ignorant in that matter.

Ward's notes mention a 'Mrs. Queeny' – presumably Judith Quiney – as well as Shakespeare's nephew, Thomas Hart, who was also in the town. It seems reasonable to infer that Ward's information about the 'merry meeting' came from people who had known Shakespeare and his family.

Michael Drayton, who was at the 'merry meeting', was a Warwickshire poet who spent much of his time at Clifford Chambers, 2 miles from Stratford. He was friends with Shakespeare's 'cousin', Thomas Greene. A minor poet himself, Greene was steward and town clerk of Stratford-upon-Avon from 1603 and lodged with his wife and children at Shakespeare's home, New Place, until Shakespeare's retirement in 1611. A short while after Shakespeare's death, Greene resigned from the Stratford Corporation and moved to Bristol. His replacement as town clerk was one Anthony Langston.

Drayton knew Ben Jonson. Their relationship was a turbulent one. They first fell out in about 1600, when Ben 'stole' Michael's patron, Lucy, Countess of Bedford.[9] The friendship was then patched up until, sometime around 1616, things went wrong again. Drayton would complain that 'Angry OLCON' – his codename for Jonson[10] – had unleashed his 'Roguish swineherds' against him. Jonson, meanwhile, told the Scottish poet William Drummond that 'Drayton feared him'.

Michael Drayton's reference to Jonson's 'Roguish swineherds, that repine / At our flocks like beastly clowns' recalls Davenant's later suffering at the hands of a 'cruel Faction':

> I that am told conspiracies are laid,
> To have my Muse, her Arts, and life betray'd

This 'Faction' almost certainly comprised those 'Tribe of Ben' poets and 'Sons of Ben' playwrights who met regularly with their alcoholic mentor in the Apollo Room of the Devil Tavern in Fleet Street.

According to Rev. John Ward's informants, Shakespeare, Drayton and Jonson had a boozy rendezvous and Shakespeare died 'of a fever there contracted'. Other tales circulated of Shakespeare and Jonson 'being merry at a tavern'. Jonson commenced an epitaph to himself, which Shakespeare completed with a pungent insult. Drayton seemingly confirmed this when describing the 'swineherds' who bullied him:

> Angry OLCON sets them on,
> And against us part doth take,
> Ever since he was out-gone
> Off'ring Rhymes with us to make.

Evidently, something had happened. It affected the Drayton–Jonson friendship, causing Drayton to live in fear of Jonson and his bully boys. Jonson was incapable of keeping the incident entirely to himself – he wrote of shaking a 'Lance' at the 'eyes of Ignorance' and remarked of the First Folio engraving of Shakespeare that 'the Graver had a strife / with Nature, to out-doo the life':

> O, could he but have drawne his wit
>   As well in brasse, as he hath hit
> Hisface ; the Print would then surpasse
>   All, that was ever writ in brasse.

A weapon 'brandished at the eyes'. A 'Graver' who 'hath hit his face'. These were bold hints from a man who had previously slain two rivals – an enemy combatant and an actor. Jonson even tried to justify the murder when he observed, in his posthumously-published *Timber: or, Discoveries Made Upon Men and Matter*, that Shakespeare wrote too candidly, so that 'sometime it was necessary he should be stopped.'

The Burdett-Coutts First Folio in the Folger Shakespeare Library, Washington DC, is the only extant copy which can be traced back to its original owner: William Sheldon, grandson of the Ralph Sheldon in whose funerary urn the Rev. C. J. Langston found the 'veritable skull' of Shakespeare. The First Folio's co-editor was Shakespeare's friend and colleague, Henry Condell. In 1617, Condell purchased land in Worcestershire from relatives of the Sheldons. On 18 August 1619 he conveyed the same property to Edward Sheldon (son of Ralph; father of William). One of the witnesses to that deed was Anthony Langston, recently elected town clerk of Stratford-upon-Avon and almost certainly an ancestor of the Reverend C. J. Langston who 'found' Shakespeare's skull in the Sheldon family vault at Beoley.

According to Langston's 1884 account of *How Shakespeare's Skull was Stolen and Found*, the hunt for Shakespeare's skull was inspired by Horace Walpole, who had probably heard of the skull's whereabouts from his intimate friend and neighbour, Lady Browne (born Frances Sheldon in Beoley).

The 'undersized' skull discovered by Langston betrays the wounds that killed its owner. They include the small holes made in the medial wall of the left eye socket by a poniard or, maybe, the 'dagger with the white haft' which Ben Jonson habitually carried, and which he later gave to the preacher Zouch Townley. This sharp-pointed weapon had been 'brandish't at the eyes' as the assailant 'hit / His face'.

The cause of death, 'a fever there contracted', was probably meningitis.

As he predicted in one of his sonnets, Shakespeare died 'The coward conquest of a wretches knife.' William Davenant was 10 years old. He soon came to doubt that his godfather died of natural causes.

He sought answers from Fulke Greville, the recorder of Stratford-upon-Avon. But Greville was Ben Jonson's patron, and though he promised to give a full account of Shakespeare's death, he kept putting it off. Greville's lingering death at the hands of a servant in a row about a 'Will' no doubt frightened Jonson and helped to bring on his stroke. He lived for another nine years and died impoverished, having seen his rival's 'issue' rise from the lowly status of a page to become writer-in-residence at the court of Charles I.

And so Davenant fulfilled two vows. The first had been to write to 'Lord B.', reminding him, 'There are degrees, that to the Altar lead; / Where every rude, dull Sinner must not tread', for there 'the High Priest should only be'. The 'shallow Brooke', Fulke Greville, had no claim to Shakespeare's greatness, though he wished to be remembered as Shakespeare's 'Master'.

The second 'bold vow' was to repay a 'mighty Debt' – 'This Debt hereditary is, and more / Than can be paid for such an Ancestor'. He honoured this debt when he wrote to Dr Brian Duppa 'An acknowledgment for his collection, in Honour of *Ben. Iohnson*'s memory' which, in revenge for Jonson's disingenuous First Folio poem to Shakespeare's memory, was every bit as equivocal as his earlier poem to Lord Brooke.

Ben might have wielded the dagger – characterising Jonson as the money-grubbing 'Satyrist' Castruchio in *The Cruel Brother* (1627), Davenant had him utter the threat: 'Yet we may meete i'th' darke. You have a throat, / And there are Knives in *Italy*' – but Greville was an accessory. When Fulke Greville succumbed to his infected stab wounds and Ben Jonson's last bedridden years came to an end, Davenant replacing him as Court playwright and poet laureate, the old scores were finally settled.

14

W. H.

*I*f succeeding Ben Jonson as poet laureate was a form of revenge, Davenant surpassed his predecessor when, in September 1643, he was knighted by the king at Gloucester. That same year, *The Unfortunate Lovers* – licensed in April 1638 – was printed in London, to be sold by Francis Coles 'at his Shop in the *Old. Bayley*'. A second edition was published in 1649 by Humphrey Mosely. By then, the king was dead and Sir William was in exile in France.

Both editions were dedicated on Davenant's behalf:

TO THE

RIGHT HONOURABLE

PHILIP

Earle of *Pembroke* and *Montgomery*,&c.

My Noble Lord,

The naturall affection, which by the successive vertue of your Family you have alwayes borne to *Poetry*, ingages me in the absence of the worthy Author, to present your Lordship this piece, that you, the best *Mæcenas* of the age, might Patronize this best of *Playes*. Had Mr *Davenaut* himselfe beene present, hee would have elected no other Patron but your Lordship, and in his absence I beseech you accept this Worke of his; whose excellence, I hope, will excuse his boldnesse, who had no other ambition in the dedication, but that he might by publike profession be knowne to be that which has long time been in his private affection,

The humble honourer of your

Name and Family.

W. H.

There is something mystifying about this dedication to Philip Herbert, 4th Earl of Pembroke and 1st Earl of Montgomery.

He was the son of Henry Herbert and Mary Sidney, the mother of Fulke Greville's friend Sir Philip Sidney, after whom he was named. Philip Herbert was an early favourite of King James I, who persuaded him to marry the Earl of Oxford's daughter, Susan de Vere.[1] His bookish brother, William Herbert, 3rd Earl of Pembroke, was Ben Jonson's patron and served as Lord Chamberlain from 1615.

The First Folio of Shakespeare's plays was dedicated 'To the Most Noble and Incomparable Paire of Brethren. WILLIAM Earle of Pembroke … And PHILIP Earle of Montgomery'. Two years later, in 1625, Philip succeeded William as Lord Chamberlain, with overall control of plays and publications. He inherited the earldom of Pembroke on his brother's death in 1630.

Both brothers were inclined towards Puritanism, and though the royal favours continued under King Charles I, Philip was unable to tolerate Henrietta Maria's Catholicism. He was sympathetic to the Scottish Covenanters during the Bishops' Wars of 1639–40, took Parliament's side in the Civil War, and joined the Council of State after the king's execution in January 1649. Philip fell ill the following May and remained bedridden until he died at Whitehall on 23 January 1650.

To Davenant, Philip Herbert must have seemed little more than a reckless brute, a traitor to his king and country and a 'godly' extremist with blood on his hands. He distanced himself from the dedication of *The Unfortunate Lovers* to the earl: it fell to a proxy to claim, 'Had Mr. *Davenaut* himselfe beene present, hee would have elected no other Patron but your Lordship'. Even so, Davenant, the queen's servant, had seemingly sanctioned the dedication of his play to the queen's sworn enemy.

The Unfortunate Lovers had been performed, in the presence of the queen, by Shakespeare's old company, the King's Men, on 23 April 1638 – the anniversary of Shakespeare's birth and death. When the play was printed in 1643, and reprinted in 1649, it was dedicated to one of the noble brothers to whom Shakespeare's First Folio had been dedicated. The signature – 'W. H.' – spoke of nothing but betrayal.

The most famous 'W. H.' in literary history is the mysterious 'Mr. W.H.' to whom the first edition of *Shake-speares Sonnets* was dedicated in 1609. Much ink has been wasted over the identity of this 'Mr. W.H.', with Philip Herbert's brother William often appearing as the frontrunner.

The dedication, as printed, reads:

TO.THE.ONLIE.BEGETTER.OF
THESE.INSVING.SONNETS.
MR.W.H. ALL.HAPPINESSE.
AND.THAT.ETERNITIE.
PROMISED.
BY.
OVR.EVER-LIVING.POET.
WISHETH.
THE.WELL-WISHING.

ADVENTVRER.IN.
SETTING.
FORTH.

T.T.

A known cipher of the time used full stops to indicate a space between words. Where an actual space occurred, the words on either side were meant to be joined together. Thus, the 'only begetter' of the sonnets was clearly identified as 'Mr. W. Hall'. As Brian Vickers has pointed out, this was just the sort of 'visual pun' that the publisher, Thomas Thorpe, had used elsewhere.

So who was 'Mr. W. Hall'?

Graham Phillips and Martin Keatman argued[2] that William Hall was the codename used by Shakespeare whenever he was engaged in intelligence work. England in the days of Elizabeth and James I was a paranoid state. Rare indeed was the poet who avoided the occasional brush with espionage. Variants of the name 'Will Hall' crop up in the records between 1592 and 1601, and each time Shakespeare was in the vicinity.[3]

The codename was not much of a secret. The satirist Thomas Nashe referred to it in his 'pleasant comedy', *Summer's Last Will and Testament*, produced for the Archbishop of Canterbury in 1592, at a time when 'Will Hall' was working for the archbishop's pursuivant, Anthony Munday, and Shakespeare was collaborating with Munday on *The Book of Sir Thomas More*. Ben Jonson also dropped hints about 'Will Hall'. The inscription on the Shakespeare funerary monument in Stratford abounds with the sort of visual puns so beloved of Jonson's publisher, Thomas Thorpe:

> Stay Passenger, why goest thou by so fast,
> Read if thou canst, whom envious Death hath plast
> With in this monument Shakespeare: *Wl.H* whome,
> Quick nature dide whose name, doth deck this Tombe,
> Far more, then cost: *S.i.e.H all*, that he hath writt,
> Leaves living art, but page, to serve his witt.

Jonson was no stranger to the duplicitous world of spies and informers, and only the latter-day sanitisation of Shakespeare's biography persuades us that Will Shakespeare himself would never have stooped so low. In reality, both Shakespeare and Jonson worked now and then for the state's murdering ministers. As their professional rivalry intensified, Jonson increasingly felt the urge to expose Shakespeare as the double-dealing 'Will Hall'.

In 1609 he was empowered to do just that. The 'onlie begetter' – the father or author – of *Shake-speares Sonnets* was revealed to be 'Mr.W.H. ALL.'

The first reference to Shakespeare's sonnets came in 1598. Francis Meres remarked in *Palladis Tamia. Wits Treasury*:

> As the soule of *Euphorbus* was thought to live in *Pythagoras*: so the sweete wittie soule of *Ovid* lives in mellifluous and hony-tongued *Shakespeare*, witnes his *Venus and Adonis*, his *Lucrece*, his sugred Sonnets among his private friends, &c.

The next year, two of those 'sugared' sonnets were pirated by William Jaggard and released in a volume of twenty poems, ascribed to '*W. Shakespeare*' and published as *The Passionate Pilgrime*. An expanded edition, published in 1612, provoked a response from the playwright Thomas Heywood, who wrote that Shakespeare was 'much offended with M. Jaggard (that altogether unknown to him) presumed to make so bold with his name'.

But by then it was too late. The 1609 edition of *Shake-speares Sonnets*, printed 'By G[eorge]. *Eld* for **T.T.**', contained 154 sonnets, 'Never before Imprinted', and a longer poem, 'A Lovers complaint. *BY* WILLIAM SHAKE-SPEARE'. The order of the sonnets in Thorpe's publication suggested that the sequence fell into two parts – 126 sonnets addressed to a 'Fair Youth' and twenty-eight concerning a 'Dark Lady'. The 'Fair Youth' sequence included nine sonnets dealing with a 'Rival Poet', while the 'Dark Lady' sequence was rounded off with a pair of 'Cupid' sonnets.

Some of the sonnets were circulating amongst Shakespeare's 'private friends' by 1598. Two of them ('When my love sweares that she is made of truth' and 'Two loves I have of comfort and dispaire') were in existence by 1599, when William Jaggard published them in *The Passionate Pilgrime*. Others, though, belong to a later period.

Sonnet 107 refers to events in 1603, when the 'mortall Moone' – Elizabeth I – had endured her 'eclipse' and was succeeded by King James, who liked to think of himself as a peace-maker ('And peace proclaimes Olives of endlesse age').[4] Sonnets 123 and 125 appear to have been prompted by James I's triumphal progress through London on 19 March 1604, when Shakespeare and his colleagues held a rich canopy over the king's head ('Wer't ought to me I bore the canopy …?') and Davenant's uncle, Thomas Sheppard, also walked in the king's train. The procession passed through seven 'great gates' erected for the occasion. These were topped with plaster obelisks or 'pyramids', hence the lines in Sonnet 123:

> Thy pyramyds buylt up with newer might
> To me are nothing novell, nothing strange

The earliest sonnets date from around 1592, when Shakespeare ('Will Hall') was working for the Archbishop of Canterbury's playwright-cum-priest-hunter, Anthony Munday. The first seventeen were almost certainly addressed to Henry Wriothesley, 3rd Earl of Southampton, whose father had died in 1584 whilst under suspicion of having trafficked with the Jesuit Edmund Campion. The young earl came under the purview of Queen Elizabeth's most trusted minister, William Cecil, 1st Baron Burghley, who held the lucrative post of Master of the Court of Wards and Liveries. Burghley was eager to marry the wealthy Southampton to his own granddaughter, Elizabeth de Vere, whose sisters would marry the Herbert brothers, William and Philip. But Southampton resisted the match, and so the 'honey-tongued' Shakespeare was tasked with persuading the orphaned earl to give serious thought to marriage.

Southampton was the only patron acknowledged by Shakespeare, whose long poems – *Venus and Adonis* and *Lucrece* – were dedicated to the earl in 1593 and 1594. The opening lines of the first sonnet[5] in Thorpe's 1609 edition feature a '*Rose*' in what might have been a pun on Southampton's name, Wriothesley (pronounced 'Rose-ly').

The 'Fair Youth' sonnets describe the relationship which developed between Shakespeare – aged 28 in 1592 – and Southampton, who was ten years younger. There was jealousy on Shakespeare's part, both towards the 'Rival Poet' and another lover. The latter figure formed the third corner of a love triangle involving the poet and his glamorous patron.

Shakespeare and Southampton appear to have gone their separate ways in late 1594, when the theatres reopened after two years of closure due to the plague and Southampton began to spend more time at Court. Although sonnets 1 to 126 are usually lumped together as the 'Fair Youth' sequence, at least one can be dated to 1603 and two to 1604, long after the Shakespeare–Southampton relationship had fizzled out. The last sonnet of the sequence stands out from the rest:

O Thou my lovely Boy who in thy power,
Doest hould times fickle glasse, his sickle, hower:
Who hast by wayning growne, and therein shou'st,
Thy lovers withering, as thy sweet selfe grow'st.
If Nature (soveraine misteres over wrack)
As thou goest onwards still will plucke thee backe,
She keepes thee to this purpose, that her skill.
May time disgrace, and wretched mynuit kill.
Yet feare her O thou minnion of her pleasure,
She may detaine, but not still keepe her tresure!
Her *Audite* (though delayed) answer'd must be,
And her *Quietus* is to render thee

Only one other sonnet (145) shares this *aabb* rhyme scheme. All the others follow the standard Shakespeare sonnet pattern of *abab cdcd efef gg*. Furthermore, Sonnet 126 lacks a concluding couplet. A pair of empty brackets at the end of the published version implies that there was once such a couplet, but for some reason it was omitted in Thorpe's 1609 edition.

Sonnet 126 is thought to have ended the 'Fair Youth' sequence, those empty brackets forming a lacuna before the 'Dark Lady' sonnets commence. Coming so soon after two sonnets composed in 1604, however, it would be rash to presume that the 'lovely Boy' of Sonnet 126 was the mature Earl of Southampton. The poem appears to have been written to a very young child whose birth caused his mother's full-moon belly to wane. Some sort of reckoning was expected. But Nature, queen of ruin, had settled the account by creating the little 'minion of her pleasure'. We are left to wonder what the missing lines might have revealed.

Thomas Thorpe's edition of *Shake-speares Sonnets* sold badly. Only thirteen copies survive. Quite possibly, it was suppressed. Thorpe never reissued the sonnets. He died a broken man, in a hospital in Oxfordshire, sometime after December 1635.

A new volume entitled *Poems: Written by Wil. Shake-speare. Gent.*, appeared in 1639. It was printed '*at London* by *Tho. Cotes*' to be sold '*by Iohn Benson*, dwelling in St. *Dunstans* Church-yard' in Fleet Street. Facing the title page was an engraving of Shakespeare by William Marshall, which reversed the Droeshout engraving from the First Folio, beneath which was a mangled version of Ben Jonson's poem, 'To the memory of my beloved':

> *This Shadowe is renowned Shakespear's? Soule of th'age*
> *The applause? delight? the wonder of the Stage* [...]

Jonson was dead by then, his memory honoured by Dr Duppa, who edited the *Jonsonus Virbius* collection of poems in praise of Ben Jonson. John Benson's edition of Shakespeare's *Poems* feels very much like a reaction to *Jonsonus Virbius* and a reminder that a better poet had predeceased the bipolar Ben. Addressing the reader, John Benson stated that Shakespeare's poems '*had not the fortune by reason of their Infancie in his death, to have the due accomodation of proportionable glory, with the rest of his everliving Workes*'. The publisher was hoping to award the same prestige to Shakespeare's poems as that afforded to his plays by the First Folio of 1623 – hence the cut-price parodies of the Droeshout engraving and Jonson's commendation of the same.

There were other links with the First Folio. An Oxfordshire poet named William Basse had written a eulogy, '*On the death* of William Shakespeare', which was omitted from the First Folio, although Ben Jonson referred to it sneeringly in his poem 'To the memory of my beloved'. Basse's tribute was belatedly included in John Benson's 1639 edition of Shakespeare's *Poems*.

Another poet who contributed to the First Folio was Leonard Digges, a gifted translator who had graduated from University College, Oxford, in 1606. Digges's widowed mother married Thomas Russell, whom Shakespeare named as one of the overseers of his will in 1616.[6] Leonard Digges died in 1635, but an extended version of his First Folio poem, 'TO THE MEMORIE Of The Deceased Authour Maister W. SHAKESPEARE', appeared in John Benson's collection of 1639.

Digges's 'Upon Master WILLIAM SHAKESPEARE, the *Deceased Authour, and his* POEMS' contrasted the audiences' delight in '*Brutus* and *Cassius*', 'Honest *Iago*' and other Shakespearean characters with their less enthusiastic responses to Ben Jonson's 'tedious' Catiline and his 'irksome' Sejanus. Even Ben's *Volpone* and *The Alchemist* had barely recovered their production costs. Partisan he may have been, but Digges's testimony indicates that Jonson's work was never as popular as Shakespeare's. The bard outshone the bully every time.

Leonard Digges's posthumously-published paean concluded:

> But why doe I dead *Shakespeares* praise recite,
> Some second *Shakespeare* must of *Shakespeare* write [...]

Was there, then, a 'second Shakespeare' – lacking Shakespeare's brilliance, perhaps, but composed in part of his DNA?

One of the poems in John Benson's edition was left unsigned:

> *An Elegie on the death of that*
> *famous Writer and Actor,*
> M. William Shakspeare.

> I Dare not doe thy Memory that wrong,
> Unto our larger griefes to give a tongue;
> Ile onely sigh in earnest, and let fall
> My solemne teares at thy great Funerall;
> For every eye that raines a showre for thee,
> Laments thy losse in a sad Elegie.
> Nor is it fit each humble Muse should have,
> Thy worth his subject, now th'art laid in grave;
> No its a flight beyond the pitch of those,
> Whose worthles Pamphlets are not sence in Prose.
> Let learned *Iohnson* sing a Dirge for thee,
> And fill our Orbe with mournefull harmony:
> But we neede no Remembrancer, thy Fame
> Shall still accompany thy honoured Name,
> To all posterity; and make us be,
> Sensible of what we lost in losing thee:
> Being the Ages wonder whose smooth Rhimes,
> Did more reforme than lash the looser Times [...]
> How can we then forget thee, when the age
> Her chiefest Tutor, and the widowed Stage
> Her onely favorite in thee hath lost,
> And Natures selfe what she did bragge of most.
> Sleepe then rich soule of numbers, whilst poore we,
> Enjoy the profits of thy Legacie;

And thinke it happinesse enough we have,
So much of thee redeemed from the grave,
As may suffice to enlighten future times,
With the bright lustre of thy matchlesse Rhimes.

Whoever penned this elegy was no fan of Ben Jonson's ('learned *Iohnson*' coming straight after 'those / Whose worthles Pamphlets are not sence in Prose').[7] The 'every eye that raines a showre for thee' line seems to echo Davenant's Ode 'In remembrance of Master *William Shakespeare*':

for each Flowre
(As it nere knew a Sunne or Showre)
Hangs there, the pensive head.

'Sleepe then rich soule of numbers' similarly reminds us that Davenant often referred to poetry as 'Numbers',[8] while the next line ends with 'Legacie', a thought that was much on Davenant's mind in the mid-1630s.

Benson's *Poems: By Wil. Shake-speare* has been roundly condemned on the grounds that Thorpe's 1609 edition of *Shake-speares Sonnets* was the definitive version, arranged as their 'only begetter' had intended. There is no evidence to support that supposition.

Aside from the jibes at Ben Jonson, the Benson volume comprises most of the sonnets, interspersed with poems from *The Passionate Pilgrime*, along with several other verses incorporated, apparently, at random. Eight of the sonnets published in 1609 are missing, including the all-important 'O Thou my lovely Boy', which either concluded the 'Fair Youth' sequence or started the run of 'Dark Lady' sonnets. The versions of sonnets 138 and 144 are those which Jaggard published in *The Passionate Pilgrime*, not the versions published by Thorpe, whose 1609 text appears to have been largely ignored.

Benson's edition presented an alternative arrangement of the sonnets. Some were bundled together in batches of two, three, four or five, and given titles instead of numbers. Thus, Sonnets 8, 9, 10, 11 and 12 were collectively entitled, '*An invitation to Marriage*'; Sonnet 52 was designated '*Familiaritie breeds contempt*'. One of the main complaints about Benson's version is that it altered the gender of the sonnet-recipient, as if trying to obscure the fact that certain poems were written to a man. However, only three titles transferred poems from the 'Fair Youth' sequence to a woman:

Selfe flattery of her beautie = Sonnets 113, 114, 115;
Vpon the receit of a Table Booke [a notebook] *from his Mistris* = Sonnet 122;
An intreatie for her acceptance = Sonnet 125.

These sonnets, in Thorpe's edition, give little or no indication of the sex of their recipients. It is conceivable that they were originally addressed to a woman.

The inclusion of so many extraneous poems – including, bizarrely, Francis Beaumont's '*To Ben. Iohnson*' – argues that Benson's edition was an earnest, if misguided, attempt to produce a complete collection of Shakespearean poetry, as comprehensive, in its way, as the First Folio of Shakespeare's plays. It was a labour of love designed to supplant Thomas Thorpe's earlier edition, with its sly dedication to 'Mr.W.H. ALL.' The question then is: did Benson rearrange Shakespeare's sonnets himself or did someone else edit them for him?

William Davenant was lodging near St Dunstan-in-the-West from about 1629. His *Tragedy of Albovine* was printed that year, to be sold '*in Saint Dunstanes Church-yard*'. He was still in the area in 1632, when he wrote of 'our Fleet-street Altars' after his recovery from illness, and *The Wits*, *The Platonic Lovers* and *The Triumphs of the Prince d'Amour* were all published nearby in 1635–36. In March 1639, Charles I granted Davenant 'full Power Licence and Authority' to build a theatre 'near unto or behind the Three Kings Ordinary in Fleet Street', which would have been in St Dunstan's parish or the adjacent parish of St Bride's. When John Benson opened his bookshop in St Dunstan's churchyard, he moved squarely into Davenant's territory.

Davenant was almost certainly studying Shakespeare's poetry when he wrote *The Platonic Lovers*. In Act Two, Phylomont describes 'False *Tarquines* houre, when he did hide his Torch / From *Lucrece* eies', recalling Shakespeare's *Lucrece* poem of 1594. The sonnets are alluded to in Act Four, when Theander remarks, 'Shee is resolv'd, her better Angell sure / Is ever by her side',[9] and again:

> *Theand:* Thou little, though imperious God of love,
> (Warmely inthron'd within thy mothers lap,)[10]

A little earlier, Eurithea's line:

> whilst neere
> Each Christall brooke the jolly Primrose stands
> Triumphing on his stalke, as he disdain'd
> His hidden roote, ambitious to be worne
> Within a chaste, although a captives breast

mimics the substance of 'The Primrose', one of the additional poems tacked onto the *Poems* of Will Shakespeare. Davenant had surely been reading some of the poems, later published by John Benson, in 1635, when he wrote *The Platonic Lovers* and Leonard Digges, who called upon 'Some second *Shakespeare*' to honour Shakespeare, died. If Davenant composed the anonymous '*Elegie on the death of that famous Writer and Actor*, M. William Shakspeare', he probably wrote it around this time.

Another reason to suspect that Davenant might have been the unacknowl-edged editor of Shakespeare's *Poems* is the inclusion of the songs 'Take, O take those lippes away' from *Measure for Measure*,[11] with an additional verse by John Fletcher, and 'Why should this Desart be' from *As You Like It*. Other poems in the collection read like songs – such as the three 'sonnets' taken from *Love's Labour's Lost* and another, entitled 'Loves labour lost' in the Benson text, which had first been published as a madrigal – while 'The Phoenix and the Turtle' had been set to music by the Catholic composer William Byrd. Davenant's fondness for music was one of his hallmarks. He is likely to have incorporated extracts from Shakespeare's plays in a volume of Shakespeare's poems because he thought of them as lyrics.

John Benson took the credit – and would reap the critical backlash – for the second publication of Shakespeare's sonnets. But it was William Davenant, poet laureate and 'servant to her Majestie', who would perhaps have been most eager to see his godfather's poems issued in a volume designed to supersede Thorpe's unau-thorised original. No one had a better claim than he to be a 'second *Shakespeare*'.

Davenant was three years old when *Shake-speares Sonnets* was published in 1609. If Shakespeare had written Sonnet 126 – 'O Thou my lovely Boy' – to his godson, born in February 1606, this would square with the dating of the preced-ing sonnets (123 and 125) which evoke the king's triumphal progress through London in March 1604.

Several 'Dark Lady' sonnets quibble with the word Will:

135
Who ever hath her wish, thou hast thy *Will*,
And *Will* too boote, and *Will* in over-plus [...]
So thou beeing rich in *Will* adde to thy *Will*,
One will of mine to make thy large *Will* more.
 Let no unkinde, no faire beseechers kill,
 Thinke all but one, and me in that one *Will*.

136
If thy soule check thee that I come so neere,
Sweare to thy blind soule that I was thy *Will* [...]
Will, will fulfill the treasure of thy love,
I fill it full with wils, and my will one [...]
 Make but my name thy love, and love that still,
 And then thou lovest me for my name is *Will*.

The repetition of '*Will*' speaks of sexual obsession ('will' being a slang term for the genitals) and the presence of a 'Will' inside the lover's all-accommodating 'will' or womb.

There soon follows a sonnet which features a housewife and her baby:

143

Loe as a carefull huswife runnes to catch,
One of her fethered creatures broake away,
Sets downe her babe and makes all swift dispatch
In pursuit of the thing she would have stay:
Whilst her neglected child holds her in chace,
Cries to catch her whose busie care is bent,
To follow that which flies before her face:
Not prizing her poore infants discontent;
So runst thou after that which flies from thee,
Whilst I thy babe chace thee a farre behind,
But if thou catch thy hope turne back to me:
And play the mothers part kisse me, be kind.
   So will I pray that thou maist have thy *Will*,
   If thou turne back and my loude crying still.

The poet simultaneously observed this domestic vignette and projected himself into the neglected child. That is, Shakespeare saw *himself* in the infant (named Will?) and felt its crying as his own. The scene might have been the Taverne in Oxford, where Shakespeare was a familiar guest.

Two years after Thorpe published the sonnets, Shakespeare retired from the public stage. *The Tempest*, which Davenant would later rework with John Dryden, was his farewell piece.

The first recorded performance of *The Tempest* was at Whitehall, in the presence of King James I, on 1 November 1611. There had been two vexatious developments that year. A Puritan propagandist, John Speed (patron: Fulke Greville), had linked Shakespeare to Robert Persons, Jesuit rector of the English College in Rome, attacking them in his *Theatre of the Empire of Great Britaine* as 'this Papist and his Poet, of like conscience for lies, the one ever faining, and the other ever falsifying the truth'.[12] Like his 'Will Hall' pseudonym, Shakespeare's Catholic sympathies were hardly a secret.

Worse, in many ways, was the first performance of Ben Jonson's *Catiline* by Shakespeare's theatre company. The production was not a success, as Jonson revealed in his dedication of the play to his patron, William Herbert. Leonard Digges would justly describe *Catiline* as 'tedious (though well laboured)' in comparison with *Julius Caesar*, although Jonson was actually responding to another of Shakespeare's Roman tragedies – *Coriolanus*.

'Rome' was a loaded concept in Shakespeare's day. Adherents of the old religion might refer to it, metaphorically, as 'love' (Latin *amor*, the mirror-image of *Roma*). A subsidiary image was that of 'more', which was both an anagram of 'Rome' and a tribute to the martyr, Sir Thomas More. From the Greek *moros* came the notions of impending doom and foolishness; those who remained true to the Catholic faith were 'more fools' – 'God's lunatics', as the Puritans called them. When Shakespeare wrote of 'love' in his sonnets he was coyly referring – some of the time – to his proscribed religion.

Coriolanus was the last of his Roman tragedies. The opening scene was inspired by the Midlands Rising against rapacious landlords, which erupted on the eve of May Day 1607, and James I's 'Proclamation for the preventing and remedying of the dearth of Grain, and other Victuals', issued on 2 June 1608. The rest of the play drew on events surrounding the Gunpowder Plot of 1605.

The ringleader of the 'powder' plot was Robert Catesby, whose ancestral home of Bushwood Hall was part of the manor of Stratford-upon-Avon. Like Catesby, Shakespeare's Coriolanus is a brilliant swordsman, arrogant and disdainful. He takes part in a battle against Rome's enemies and is wounded in the arm at the gateway to the city of Corioles, just as Catesby was wounded at the entrance to the City of London during the failed Essex Rebellion of 1601.

Coriolanus then stands for election to the senate. His Puritan enemies turn the people against him. So he goes over to the enemy and conspires with Tullus Aufidius to destroy Rome with fire.

Aufidius gives Coriolanus all the help he needs, from making him 'joynt-servant with me' to letting him 'choose / Out of my Files, his projects, to accomplish / My best and freshest men'. Meanwhile, the friends of Coriolanus plead with him not to betray Rome. Menenius, a caring and jovial patrician, attempts to mollify him, but it is only the intervention of the women of his family that produces results. Coriolanus abandons his plan to burn the city. Tullus Aufidius then arranges for him to be treacherously slain, so that 'His Tale pronounc'd, shall bury / His Reasons, with his Body.'

As a veiled account of the Gunpowder Treason, *Coriolanus* is wildly at odds with the official story of Catholic militants plotting to blow the king and Parliament to smithereens. So fiendish was the alleged conspiracy that it turned young men like John Pym and John Milton into rabid anti-Catholics and paved the way for the English Revolution. However, Shakespeare's account is closer to the truth than the popular myth. Evidence exists to suggest that Catesby ('Coriolanus') was working for Robert Cecil ('Aufidius'), Secretary of State and son of the scheming Lord Burghley. Cecil gave orders that Catesby and his fellow *agent provocateur*, Thomas Percy, were to be killed, rather than taken prisoner, when the fugitive plotters were cornered.

Shakespeare knew more about the plot than most of his contemporaries. It was hatched in his Warwickshire back yard by men of his acquaintance. And he was 'Will Hall', the Catholic insider and informer.

There is no evidence that *Coriolanus* was performed during Shakespeare's lifetime. The mere fact that he had written it, though, was a threat to Robert Cecil and the government fiction of the 'powder treason'. The success of Cecil's scheme to discredit the Jesuit mission in England depended on an unquestioning belief that the plot was genuine. Shakespeare implied that Catesby was Cecil's 'joint-servant' with access to his secret files. He had challenged the myth of the Gunpowder Plot.

Cecil counterattacked. He commissioned an answer to *Coriolanus* from his pet poet and occasional spy – Ben Jonson. The riposte was delayed, partly because Jonson was appointed chaperone to Sir Walter Raleigh's son on a dissipated European tour. When it finally appeared, *Catiline His Conspiracy* retold the story from the government's point of view.

The audience proved hostile. Jonson's attempt to translate Robert Cecil from Shakespeare's Aufidius, sworn enemy of Rome, into the great orator and statesman, Cicero, evinced a slavish obsequiousness which outraged the spectators at the Globe. A suggestive subplot, meanwhile, offered an insight into the inner workings of the 'powder treason'.

Curius Quintus is intimate with the conspirators. He takes their sacred oath and appears committed to Catiline's plot to destroy the state by means of fire and a 'violent blow'. But Curius has a mistress: a vain, proud, married woman who has grown tired of his attentions. Her name is Fulvia.

When Curius drops hints about Catiline's conspiracy, she changes her tune. Fulvia leads Curius on, trading sexual favours for information, which she forwards to Cicero. The Cecil-character thanks her profusely and courteously invites her lover to become his inside man. Together, Curius and Fulvia betray Catiline and his fellow plotters. Cicero concedes that the couple 'must receive reward, though 't be not knowne'.

In *The Tragedy of Coriolanus*, Shakespeare disclosed some of the secrets of the Gunpowder Plot – that it was an operation cooked up by Secretary of State Cecil and his agent, Robert Catesby. Jonson's *Catiline His Conspiracy* implied that the details of the plot were divulged to Cecil by a pair of adulterous lovers.

But *Catiline* was not ready for production until at least two years after Shakespeare wrote *Coriolanus*. A more immediate response was called for. It came in the form of *Shake-speares Sonnets*, issued by Ben Jonson's publisher.

Shakespeare's intimate thoughts were exposed to the public gaze: his relationship with Southampton, his affair with the 'Dark Lady' and the birth of his 'lovely Boy' – along with his private musings on Catholic 'love'. Thorpe's edition came with a mischievous dedication to the 'onlie begetter' of the sonnets, Mr W. Hall. Shakespeare's cover was blown.

Davenant must have been aware of some, if not all, of this history when he brought Will Hall back from the grave. His play, *The Unfortunate Lovers*, already had Shakespearean associations. It was performed by Shakespeare's old company on the anniversary of his birth and death.

When religious extremism and anti-Catholic hysteria plunged the country into civil war, Davenant took the play's links with his godfather further. He arranged for

The Unfortunate Lovers to be printed – in his absence – in London, with a dedication to the 'godly' rebel Philip Herbert, the brother of Ben Jonson's patron and joint-dedicatee of *Mr. William Shakespeares Comedies, Histories, & Tragedies* (First Folio). As if to remind Herbert of past treasons and betrayals, and the horrors unleashed by Puritan delusions, Davenant allowed Shakespeare's ghost to sign the dedication:

> The humble honourer of your
> Name and Family.
> *W. H.*

15

Babes and Beggers

St Martin's Church, Carfax, was half a minute's walk from the Taverne on Cornmarket. An entry in the church register recorded the baptism on 3 March 1606 of 'William Devenet, the sonne of John Devenet vintener.'

The family name could be spelt in a variety of ways: 'Devnet', 'Dabenett', 'Dennant', 'Davenaunte'. But it was William's decision to insert an apostrophe – 'D'Avenant' – that would cause his critics so much mirth. The French *avenant* could signify 'comely', the contraction *av'nant* (from the Old French *avenant*) meaning 'affable', a fitting epithet for William Davenant. 'D'Avenant', though, implied that Davenant's family came from somewhere called Avenant.

St Martin's Church, Carfax, before 1820.

Among the *Certain Verses Written by Severall of the Authors Friends; to be Re-printed with the Second Edition of Gondibert* (1653) was a skit on Davenant's name:

> As severall Cities made their claim
> Of *Homers* birth to have the fame;
> So after ages will not want
> Towns claiming to be *Avenant* [...]
> Some say by *Avenant* no place is meant,
> And that this *Lombard* is without descent;
> And as by *bilke* men mean ther's nothing there,
> So come from *Avenant*, means from *No-where*.

An anonymous 'Elegy on Sir William D'avenant', published after his death, returned to the theme:

> Though hee is dead th'imortall name
> Of William, who from Avenant came,
> Who mixt with English Lombard Flame,
> Shall live in ye records of Fame.

The elusive Avenant had somehow come to be associated with the Italian region of Lombardy, although some had their doubts:

> Your Wits have further, than you rode,
>   You needed not to have gone abroad.
> *D'avenant* from *Avon*, comes.
>   Rivers are still the Muses Rooms.

This verse, from *The Incomparable Poem Gondibert, Vindicated from the Wit-Combats of Four Esquires* (1655), was joined by another:

> Wash thee in Avon, if thou flie,
> My wary *Davenant* so high.

So there was some dispute in the matter. 'D'Avenant' might have referred to Lombardy, or perhaps it indicated that William came from the Avon – the river which, in his ode 'In remembrance of Master *William Shakespeare*', Davenant suggested, had 'wept it selfe away'.

Davenant seems to have been the source of the rumour that 'D'Avenant' linked him with Lombardy. Of the eleven plays he wrote before the outbreak of the Civil War, eight were set in Italy – six of them[1] in those parts of Italy which had been conquered by the

Germanic 'Langobards' in the sixth century AD. *Albovine, King of the Lombards* and *The Unfortunate Lovers* shared their setting in Verona, to which Davenant returned with his 'Heroick Poem', *Gondibert. The Unfortunate Lovers* features 'Heildebrand, King of the Lombards'; in *Gondibert* it is Aribert who rules the Langobards.

The inspiration might have come from Shakespeare. *The Two Gentlemen of Verona* was probably Shakespeare's very first play, and *Romeo and Juliet* was also set in Verona, the city captured by Alboin ('Albovine') in AD 569. Moreover, *The Two Gentlemen of Verona* involves two young friends setting out for – but never quite reaching – Milan. *The Tempest*, Shakespeare's last play for the public stage, concerns an old duke (and his heiress) who wants to get back to Milan. Davenant took the hints, incorporating a 'Count of Milan' in *The Just Italian* and a 'Duke of Millain' (and his heiress) in *Love and Honour.*

When Prospero[2] stood poised to 'retire me to my *Millaine*' at the end of *The Tempest*, Shakespeare's theatrical career had come full circle, returning – as it were – to the beginning of *The Two Gentlemen of Verona*, when Valentine has 'parted hence to embarque for *Millain*.' Milan is the capital of Lombardy. It was also the epicentre of the Counter-Reformation; when Shakespeare was 16 his father signed a 'Testament of the Last Will of the Soul' which had been composed by Cardinal Carlo Borromeo, Archbishop of Milan.

Davenant appears to have been drawn to northern Italy, just as his godfather was. If not more so, since Davenant seemingly encouraged the notion that his roots lay in Lombardy. The place Shakespeare circled in his imagination, setting out for and returning to at the beginning and the end of his career, became the imaginary origin of his godson.

'*D'avenant* from *Avon*, comes' quipped one of the wits who took advantage of Davenant's incarceration in the Tower of London to publish their scabrous verses about him. His father's family came from the Sible Hedingham and Halstead area of Essex, where there is no Avon to be found. His 'other' father, Shakespeare, was dubbed '*Sweet Swan of* Avon!' by Ben Jonson in his poem for the First Folio. Anthony Wood subsequently hailed Davenant as the 'sweet Swan of Isis' (Isis being the name of the River Thames as it winds through Oxford).

Another Avon rises in the west of England, and it is there that we must seek Davenant's maternal roots.

A genealogy, drawn up by the College of Arms for William Davenant's grandson, was entered 'by Order of Chapter dated 20th April 1727' and signed:

> I Henry Molins Davenant Esqr. late his Majesty's Envoy Extraordinary to the Italian Princes, do certifie this Pedigree to be true to the best of my knowledge, and therefore desire that the said Pedigree may be Registred in the Colledge of Arms London, Witness my Hand the 3d. of April 1727.
> Hen. Davenant.

The pedigree begins, thirteen centuries before William, with 'Johannes Davenant', a soldier in the time of Henry III and Edward I, and states that William's father died on 23 April 1622.[3] His mother is identified simply as *Jana filia … Shepherd de Durham* ('Jane daughter of … Shepherd of Durham'). Jane's father was in fact Robert Sheppard, who died when Jane was 5 years old and was buried at Westminster on 19 August 1574. Jane Sheppard was baptised at St Margaret's, Westminster, on 1 November 1568. The will of her uncle, William Sheppard, reveals that she was familiarly known as 'Jennet'.

'*Shepherd de Durham*' is one of those references which send researchers off in the wrong direction. The seventeenth-century Dyrham Park mansion in south Gloucestershire was built by the Denys family on a site previously occupied by the manor house of Dyrham. The village is associated with the Battle of Deorham, fought between the West Saxons and the Britons in AD 577. Eighteenth-century maps referred to the village as *Durham*.[4] It is a mere 4 miles from West Kington, where Davenant visited his clergyman brother Robert in 1637.

Several springs rise in Dyrham Park to feed the River Boyd, of which John Dennys wrote in his *Secrets of Angling*:

> And thou, sweet Boyd, that with thy watry sway,
> Dost wash the cliffs of Deignton and of Weeke;
> And through their Rockes with crooked winding way,
> Thy mother Avon runneth soft to seeke.

The Boyd joins the River Avon at Bitton, between Bristol and Bath.

The Reverend Henry Nicholson Ellacombe, Vicar of Bitton and author of *Shakespeare as an Angler* (1883), argued that Shakespeare possibly knew John Dennys, the angler-poet, who died in 1609. Dennys married a Warwickshire woman and lived at Pucklechurch, the neighbouring parish to Dyrham. Also in the area were individuals bearing 'Shepherd' surnames: an Ambrose Sheperd died at Pucklechurch in 1571; a Robert Smith, alias Sheperde, at Dodington in 1582; and a John Sheperde at Bitton in 1588.

On 26 May 946, King Edmund I was celebrating the St Augustine's Day mass at Pucklechurch when he was stabbed to death by an exiled thief. Edmund was eventually succeeded by his son, Edgar the Peaceful.

In all of the known works of Shakespeare the word 'godson' appears only once – in *King Lear*, when Regan says, 'What, did my Fathers Godsonne seeke your life? / He whom my Father nam'd, your *Edgar*?'

Shakespeare drew his inspiration from a *True Chronicle History of King Leir*, published in 1605, to which he added 'the unfortunate life of Edgar, son and heir to the Earl of Gloucester'. His *True Chronicle History of the Life and death of King Lear and his three daughters* was performed 'at Whitehall before his Majesty', James I, on 26 December 1606 and the text published in 1608. A revised version, *The Tragedie of King Lear*, was included in the First Folio of 1623. Davenant later produced '*The Tragedy of King* Lear', '*Acted* exactly as *Mr. Shakespear* Wrote it', at his theatre in Lincoln's Inn Fields.

King Lear has three daughters – the troublesome Goneril and Regan and the 'silent' Cordelia. He compares, then, with Shakespeare, whose first biographer, Nicholas Rowe, remarked in 1709 that Shakespeare 'had three Daughters, of which two liv'd to be marry'd'.[5] As well as being the father of three daughters, Lear is godfather to Edgar, the legitimate heir of the Earl of Gloucester. The earl also has an illegitimate son:

> though this Knave came somthing sawcily to the world before he was sent for: yet was his Mother fayre, there was good sport at his making, and the [w]horson must be acknowledged.

The boy is called Edmund ('*Bastard*', in the First Folio text). He rails against his illegitimacy: 'Now Gods, stand up for Bastards!' Like William Davenant, he is a second son. He is the rival brother to Edgar. At the end of *King Lear*, when Edmund dies by an unknown hand, it is Edgar who becomes joint King of England with the Earl of Kent – much as the historical Edgar ruled jointly with Eadwig, King of Wessex and Kent, after his father Edmund was murdered at Pucklechurch, near Dyrham.[6]

As Lear descends into madness, betrayed by his two elder daughters, a parallel theme to Edmund's illegitimacy arises. Lear becomes obsessed with female sexuality and adultery:

> I pardon that mans life. What was thy cause?
> Adultery? thou shalt not dye: dye for Adultery?
> No, the Wren goes too't, and the small gilded Fly
> Does lecher in my sight. Let Copulation thrive:
> For Glousters bastard Son was kinder to his Father,
> Then my Daughters got 'tween the lawfull sheets.
> [...]
> Downe from the waist they are Centaurs, though Women all above: but to the Girdle do the Gods inherit, beneath is all the Fiends. There's hell, there's darkenes, there is the sulphurous pit; burning, scalding, stench, consumption: Fye, fie, fie; pah, pah

Lear's outburst calls to mind Shakespeare's 129th sonnet, entitled '*Immoderate Lust*', in John Benson's edition of the *Poems*:

> Th'expence of Spirit in a waste of shame
> Is lust in action, and till action, lust

Is perjurd, murdrous, blouddy full of blame,
Savage, extreame, rude, cruell, not to trust,
Injoyd no sooner but dispised straight,
Past reason hunted, and no sooner had
Past reason hated as a swollowed bayt,
On purpose layd to make the taker mad [...]
   All this the world well knowes yet none knowes well,
   To shun the heaven that leads men to this hell.

This is only the third of the 'Dark Lady' sonnets, coming soon after 'O Thou my lovely Boy'. It is not too much to suggest that Shakespeare was writing about an actual incident – the release of 'Spirit' (semen) in a shameful waste, and the self-loathing that followed the deed. The image of the 'swallowed bait' implies that Rev. Henry Nicholson Ellacombe was right: Shakespeare was an angler, like John Dennys of Pucklechurch. The angling imagery recurs in *King Lear*, when Lear encounters Edgar disguised as 'poore mad Tom', a beggar: '*Fraterretto* cals me, and tells me *Nero* is an Angler in the Lake of Darknesse.'

Shakespeare's *History of King Lear*, which dates from around the time of Davenant's birth, not only included his sole use of the word 'Godsonne' but also dwelt obsessively on illicit sex and bastards.

Davenant's mother was, by all accounts, strikingly attractive. John Aubrey described her as 'a very beautiful woman, and of very good wit, and of conversation extremely agreeable', to which Anthony Wood[7] (who first met Aubrey at the Taverne in Oxford) added that Jane was imitated in her beauty and wit 'by none of her children but by this William.' Her second son was probably her favourite, the child who least resembled her stolid husband. It may be that William inherited those dark eyes which gaze at us from the Lincoln College portrait from his mother, as well as his abiding love of music.[8]

John Aubrey recalled that William was born 'about the end of February' 1606. For the country at large this was a nervous time. Shortly after midnight on 5 November a 35-year-old Yorkshireman had been arrested in the undercroft beneath the House of Lords. He gave his name as John Johnson. His real name was Guy Fawkes. He was executed, along with seven others, at the end of January 1606. By then, the government was referring to the Gunpowder Plot as the 'Jesuits' Conspiracy'.

Robert Cecil's chief target was Father Henry Garnet, superior of the Jesuit mission in England, whom Shakespeare would characterise as the kindly Menenius in *Coriolanus*. Garnet was captured at Hindlip Hall, north of Worcester, on 27 January. Four days earlier his servant Nicholas Owen had given himself up in the vain hope that the hunt for Father Garnet would be called off. Known in Catholic circles as 'Little John', Owen was born in Castle Street, Oxford, and apprenticed in February 1577 to a joiner named William Conway. His speciality was constructing priest-holes – ingenious hiding places in wealthy Catholic houses.

Nicholas Owen was brutally tortured by Cecil's goons. He died of a ruptured abdomen in the Tower of London, early in the morning of 2 March 1606. Just hours later, William Davenant was baptised at St Martin's Church in Oxford. The public execution of Father Garnet on 3 May 1606 provoked a bitter response from Shakespeare. This was his *Tragedie of Macbeth*, which conflated Garnet's execution with the murder of the saintly Duncan by Macbeth and his 'Fiend-like' wife.

Samuel Pepys saw Davenant's 'alter'd' version of *Macbeth* on Saturday 5 November 1664 – the fifty-ninth anniversary of the Gunpowder Plot. He thought it 'a pretty good play'. Naturally, Davenant has since come under fire for mangling Shakespeare's original. But the times had changed.

Shakespeare's *Tragedie of Macbeth* was written in the wake of an alleged attempt to kill King James I, although Shakespeare knew that the plot had been manipulated and – to some extent – manufactured by Cecil, so he presented Robert Catesby and his fellow conspirators as 'Artificiall Sprights' straight out of Reginald Scot's *The Discoverie of Witchcraft* (1584), conjured up by government ministers to beguile the twitchy king. Davenant's *Macbeth: A Tragædy* was written after the actual beheading of King Charles I and the dictatorship of Oliver Cromwell. Behind Shakespeare's *Macbeth* there were only rumours; behind Davenant's, there was regicide. History had altered the nature of the tragedy.

Both versions open with '*Thunder and Lightning*'. Three witches agree to meet with Macbeth. In Davenant's version they exeunt '*flying*'.

Shakespeare's witches were inspired by events at Oxford. On Tuesday, 27 August 1605, King James and his Court rode into Oxford, accompanied by dignitaries of the university and the town, for a three-day visit. Approaching the Northgate, the procession halted at the gate to St John's College. Three youths appeared in a bower, dressed as if they had emerged from a forest 'in habit and attire like nymphs or sibyls'. They addressed the king in Latin, 'putting him in mind of that ancient prophecy' made to his supposed ancestor, Banquo:

> Word is that prophetic sisters once sang of a never-ending reign for your race, renowned king […] We three likewise sing to you of destiny, as, a worthy sight for your subjects, you approach from forest to city. And we give you greetings, you whom Scotland obeys.
>> Hail, you whom England obeys.
>> Hail, you whom Ireland obeys […]
> You whom previously-divided Britain worships, hail.

This was six months before William Davenant was born. His father, John Davenant, followed the royals as they rode along Cornmarket, past the Taverne. Shakespeare, we can assume, was also there on that warm late August day in 1605.

Shakespeare's witches conclude their short opening scene with 'faire is foule, and foule is faire, / Hover through the fogge and filthie ayre.'[9] Their words are echoed by Macbeth on his first appearance: 'So foule and faire a day I have not seene.' At about the same time, presumably, Shakespeare was juggling *fair* and *foul* in his 'Dark Lady' sonnets – 'To put faire truth upon so foule a face' (137); 'For I have sworne thee faire: more perjurde eye; / To swere against the truth so foule a lie' (152); and the pertinent Sonnet 127:

> In the ould age blacke was not counted faire,
> Or if it weare it bore not beauties name:
> But now is blacke beauties successive heire,
> And Beautie slanderd with a bastard shame,
> For since each hand hath put on Natures power,
> Fairing the foule with Arts faulse borrow'd face,
> Sweet beauty hath no name no holy boure,
> But is prophan'd, if not lives in disgrace.

Several sonnets share *Macbeth*'s imagery of falsehood disguised by a mask of innocence. Macbeth's couplet – 'Away, and mock the time with fairest show, / False Face must hide what the false Heart doth know' – finds its counterpart in Sonnet 93, in which the poet, 'Like a deceived husband', struggles to gauge his lover's true feelings, for while in many 'the falce hearts history / Is writ in moods and frounes and wrinckles strange', his lover excels at dissembling:

> But heaven in thy creation did decree,
> That in thy face sweet love should ever dwell,
> What ere thy thoughts, or thy hearts workings be,
> Thy lookes should nothing thence, but sweetnesse tell.

The woman's deceptive beauty is compared with Eve's apple, hiding its latent chaos, much as Lady Macbeth advises her husband to 'looke like th'innocent flower, / But be the Serpent under't.'

Shakespeare's *Macbeth* also abounds in images of generation – of seeds planted and growing – and, especially, children. The witches tell Banquo that his children shall be kings. Later, Macbeth attempts to murder Banquo's son and slaughters Macduff's offspring ('He ha's no Children', groans Macduff when the news is brought to him). Lady Macbeth has 'given Sucke'. She knows 'How tender 'tis to love the Babe that milkes me'. And yet she would 'while it was smyling in my Face, / Have pluckt my Nipple from his Bonelesse Gummes / And dasht the Braines out', rather than deviate from her resolution. Macbeth finds her ruthless determination irresistible:

> Bring forth Men-Children onely:
> For thy undaunted Mettle should compose
> Nothing but Males.

Still, he wrestles with his conscience. Weighing up the consequences of killing King Duncan, Macbeth realises that the evil deed will rebound on him:

> But in these Cases,
> We still have judgement heere, that we but teach
> Bloody Instructions, which being taught, returne
> To plague th'Inventor. This even-handed Justice
> Commends th'Ingredience of our poyson'd Challice
> To our owne lips.

The same ideas are expressed in Sonnet 114:

> Or whether doth my minde being crown'd with you
> Drinke up the monarks plague this flattery?
> Or whether shall I say mine eie saith true,
> And that your love taught it this *Alcumie?*
> To make of monsters, and things indigest,
> Such cherubines as your sweet selfe resemble,
> Creating every bad a perfect best
> As fast as objects to his beames assemble:
> Oh tis the first, tis flatry in my seeing,
> And my great minde most kingly drinkes it up,
> Mine eie well knowes what with his gust is greeing,
> And to his pallat doth prepare the cup.
>   If it be poison'd, tis the lesser sinne,
>   That mine eye loves it and doth first beginne.

The poisoned cup or chalice, and the '*Alcumie*' that can turn monsters into cherubs, are present simultaneously in Macbeth's soliloquy and Shakespeare's sonnet. The king, whom Macbeth must murder if he is to fulfil the witches' prophecy, is no ordinary mortal:

> Besides, this *Duncane*
> Hath borne his Faculties so meeke; hath bin
> So cleere in his great Office, that his Vertues
> Will pleade like Angels, Trumpet-tongu'd against
> The deepe damnation of his taking off:
> And Pitty, like a naked New-borne-Babe,
> Striding the blast, or Heavens Cherubin, hors'd
> Upon the sightlesse Curriors of the Ayre,
> Shall blow the horrid deed in every eye,
> That teares shall drowne the winde.

The fearsome storm which breaks on the night of Duncan's murder resembles the 'Great Storm' which blasted England after Father Garnet was condemned to death at the end of March 1606. And when Shakespeare needed an image of pity there was one ready to hand in the shape of his godson, baptised at Oxford at the start of that month.

Davenant omitted the references to the poisoned chalice and the new-born babe in his version of *Macbeth*, streamlining the passage:

> Besides, this *Duncan*
> Has born his faculties so meek, and been
> So clear in his great Office; that his Vertues,
> Like Angels, plead against so black a deed

One wonders whether it ever occurred to him that he was the 'naked New-borne-Babe' whose cherubic pity blew the 'horrid deed' of Father Garnet's execution 'in every eye', causing tears to drown the 'Great Winds' of March 1606.

Spurred on by the unnatural mother who would rather suckle 'murthering Ministers' than her own baby, Macbeth approaches Duncan's chamber 'With *Tarquins* ravishing s[tr]ides', evoking *The Rape of Lucrece*.

Ben Jonson also invoked *Lucrece* in his *Catiline* (1611), when he sought to sign-post the adulterous couple who betrayed the Gunpowder Plot to the authorities. Quintus Curius threatens to rape his married lover – 'How now? / Will *Lais* turne a *Lucrece*?' Fulvia replies, 'Ile not be put to kill my selfe, as shee did / For you, sweet *Tarquine*.' Jonson hinted at the identities of the proud woman who had tired of her persistent lover, and the reluctant informer who tells her to pluck off her tragic mask, by citing both of Shakespeare's long narrative poems, *Lucrece* and *Venus and Adonis*:

> Come, Ladie *Cypris*,
> Know your owne vertues, quickly. Ile not be
> Put to the woing of you thus, afresh,
> At every turne, for all the *Venus* in you.

Most of Davenant's alterations can be explained by his need to make *Macbeth* acceptable to Restoration theatregoers. Shakespeare's language was updated and, where necessary, prudently pruned – 'their Daggers / Unmannerly breech'd with gore' became 'their Daggers / Being yet unwip'd'; 'The multitudinous Seas incarnadine' was rendered as 'add a tincture to / The Sea'. The low comedy of the drunken porter (one of the clearer links between *Macbeth* and the Gunpowder Plot) was dropped and the play's gory violence restrained.

Lennox and Macbeth are both killed onstage, Macbeth repeatedly stabbed by Macduff:

This for my Royal Master *Duncan*,
This for my dearest Friend my Wife,
This for those Pledges of our Loves, my Children.

But whereas Shakespeare had Macbeth's head brought back onstage by Macduff, Davenant had Macduff return with only Macbeth's sword.

Davenant also established a delicate balance of the Macbeths and the Macduffs. Whilst Macbeth and Macduff are putting down a rebellion against King Duncan at the start of the play, Lady Macduff is staying with Lady Macbeth and fearing for her husband's safety. Thereafter, Macbeth's discussions with his lady about the steps they must take to secure the crown are counterpointed by Macduff's dialogues with his lady concerning the double-edged nature of 'Ambition'.

This symmetry is taken further. Davenant's Macduffs have their own encounter with the witches after the murder of King Duncan. Just as the witches foretold Macbeth's future, now they prophesy to Macduff:

1 *Witch:*   Saving thy bloud will cause it to be shed;
2 *Witch:*   He'll bleed by thee, by whom thou first hast bled.
3 *Witch:*   Thy wife shall shunning danger, dangers find,
        And fatal be, to whom she is most kind.

The Macbeths' dance of death is nicely counterpoised by the Macduffs. Both men abandon their wives – Macbeth reluctantly ('The Spur of my Ambition prompts me to go / And make my Kingdom safe, but Love which softens me / To pity here in her distress, curbs my Resolves') and Macduff because he misjudges Macbeth ('He will not injure you, he cannot be / Possest with such unmanly cruelty; / You will your safety to your weakness owe / As Grass escapes the Syth by being low'). The counterbalancing of the couples adds to, rather than detracts from, Shakespeare's original.

Most criticism has been heaped on Davenant for the additional songs and dances, including an aerial ballet, which he introduced for the witches. But there is no reason to presume that Davenant took his witches less than seriously; he cast Samuel Sandford, a 'Round-shoulder'd, Meagre-fac'd, Spindle-shank'd, Splay-footed' actor whom King Charles II admired as 'the best *Villain* in the World', in the role of '*Heccate*', Queen of Witches. Pepys spotted no defect in Davenant's production, considering it 'most excellently acted, and a most excellent play for variety' when he saw it on 28 December 1666.

He saw it again, a few days later, confiding that it 'yet appears a most excellent play in all respects, but especially in divertisement, though it be a deep tragedy; which is a strange perfection in a tragedy, it being most proper here, and suitable.' After his fourth viewing in April 1667, Pepys declared Davenant's *Macbeth* 'one of the best plays for a stage, and variety of dancing and musique, that ever I saw.' Evidently, Davenant had caught the right mood, making the most of the stage technology available to him, along with the musical talents of Matthew Locke and the choreography of Luke Channell and Joseph Priest. His version, it should be remembered, was a success. Shakespeare's had received little acclaim.

Shakespeare's witches presented Macbeth with the vision of a crowned child, who 'weares upon his Baby-brow, the round / And top of Soveraignty', and misled him by stating that 'none of woman borne / Shall harme *Macbeth*.' This preoccupation with childbirth and children continued right up till the moment when, in Davenant's version, Macbeth and Macduff confront each other:

> *Macb:* I have a Prophecy secures my Life.
> *Macd:* I have another which tells me I shall have his Blood,
> Who first shed mine.
> *Macb:* None of Woman born can spill my Blood.
> *Macd:* Then let the Devils tell thee, *Macduff*
> Was from his Mothers Womb untimely Ript.

It is churlish to claim, as many have done, that Davenant ruined his godfather's masterpiece. Given that Shakespeare wrote his dark and troubled tragedy, with its recurring imagery of sons and motherhood, so soon after his naked new-born godson came into the world, it might be admitted that Davenant had a special relationship with *Macbeth*. He updated it with flair and sensitivity.

The year 1606 was exceptionally productive for Shakespeare. *Macbeth* was first performed that summer, and *King Lear* at Christmas, both before King James I at Whitehall.

A third tragedy was written in 1606. Shakespeare seems to have felt a certain empathy for Mark Antony, the unconventional, pleasure-loving hero of his *Julius Caesar*. He gave Antony a passing mention in *Macbeth* (which Davenant left out of his version) and returned to the subject later that year for his sprawling epic of love and power, *The Tragedie of Anthonie, and Cleopatra*.

The play opens in 40 BC, when Mark Antony was 42 years old – as was Shakespeare in 1606.[10] Anthony, the 'triple Pillar of the world', has become 'a Strumpets Foole.' He is infatuated with Cleopatra: his 'goodly eyes … now bend, now turne / The Office and Devotion of their view / Upon a Tawny Front'. Cleopatra, it was assumed, was tanned – 'with Phœbus amorous pinches blacke' – and so, like the 'Dark Lady' of the sonnets, she is unfashionably tawny, 'a woman collour'd il'.

At the start of the play the never 'Lust-wearied' Antony is married to the 'shrill-tongu'd *Fulvia*'. He has abandoned her to dally in Alexandria, where he 'fishes, drinkes, and wastes / The Lampes of night in revell' with his beloved queen of the Nile. Cleopatra wonders 'Why did he marry *Fulvia*, and not love her?' and – in an echo of Sonnet 152 ('In loving thee thou know'st I am forsworne, / But thou art twice forsworne to me love swearing') – chastises Antony:

Why should I thinke you can be mine, & true [...]
Who have beene false to *Fulvia*?
Riotous madnesse,
To be entangled with those mouth-made vowes
Which breake themselves in swearing.

Fulvia is also the name of the vain, capricious woman with whom the would-be conspirator Quintus Curius is besotted in Ben Jonson's *Catiline*. Her character in Jonson's play mirrors Cleopatra's headstrong wilfulness, a quality which appeals to her 'idolator', Curius – 'I would have my Love / Angry, sometimes, to sweeten off the rest / Of her behaviour'. As well as evoking Shakespeare's long poems, then, Ben Jonson glanced at *Antony and Cleopatra* when composing his propagandist counterblast to Shakespeare's *Coriolanus*.

The hints could not have been heavier: Jonson was highlighting a discordant relationship between a Mark Antony-figure and his imperious lover, an affair which had run its course but was reignited at the time of the Gunpowder Plot, when William Davenant was conceived.

Cleopatra shares Mark Antony's love of fishing:

And when good will is shewed,
Though't come to short
The Actor may pleade pardon. [...]
Give me mine Angle, weele to'th'River there
My Musicke playing farre off. I will betray
Tawny fine fishes, my bended hooke shall pierce
Their slimy jaws: and as I draw them up,
Ile thinke them every one an *Anthony*,
And say, ah ha; y'are caught.

The imagery recalls that of Sonnet 129 ('Past reason hated as a swollowed bayt, / On purpose layd to make the taker mad') and Sonnet 137 – 'Why of eyes falsehood hast thou forged hookes, / Whereto the judgement of my heart is tide?' Shakespeare apparently knew what it was to be hooked and played by that 'false Soule of Egypt', the dazzling, infuriating Cleopatra.

The historical Cleopatra proclaimed herself the 'New Isis'. In Shakespeare's play, the Nile-goddess is invoked as 'sweet *Isis*', 'good *Isis*', 'deere *Isis*'. The River Thames, as it flows through Oxford, is known as the Isis.

Cleopatra, the queen 'Worth many Babes and Beggers', died of a self-administered snakebite, aged 38. In November 1606, when Shakespeare was putting the finishing touches to his *Antony and Cleopatra*, Jane Davenant, mistress of the Taverne and mother of William, turned 38 years old.

Davenant left *King Lear* much as it was and substantially 'alter'd' *Macbeth*. His approach to *Antony and Cleopatra* was very different: he sent it up in the fifth act of *The Play-House to be Let*, which he produced in 1663.

It was most likely a last-minute addition, but Davenant's comic treatment of 'trusty *Tony*' and his Cleopatra set a remarkable precedent. His parody introduced burlesque to the Restoration stage.[11] Davenant expunged every last drop of tragedy from the tale. As Cæsar, Cleopatra and Mark-Anthony enter, a character quips:

> There *Tony* is, our *Cleopatra* leading;
> Her eyes look blew; pray Heav'n she be not breeding?

Anthony calls Cleopatra 'Chuck', as Mark Antony does in Shakespeare's telling, and Cæsar says, 'What have I heard? shall it be said in Hist'ries, / That *Marcus Tony* squabl'd with his Mistress.' Anthony is reproached by Pompey's widow:

> Man, Woman, and Child, you chief should be killing,
> But 'stead of bombasting you are a billing [kissing]
> With Queen who should be her Parishes pattern,
> Good Housewife in House not sauntring young slattern.

(Compare Cleopatra's line from Shakespeare: 'No, let me speake, and let me rayle so hye, / That the false Huswife Fortune, breake her Wheele, / Provok'd by my offence'). Davenant's Cleopatra responds with a Shakespearean allusion:

> Bodikins! pray why a gog Mistress *Pompey*?
> As high as you are; a *Joan* may out-jump ye,
> Be an example before y'are a Tutress!
> You want a *Tarquin* to make you a *Lucress*.

But Cleopatra's airs and graces cannot hide the fact that she is really a dark-skinned creature from a tavern: 'For all your new Gown, y'are but a black *Gipsey*, / Sure *Tony* and you have drunk till y'are tipsy.'

That Davenant created a pantomime burlesque of the Antony and Cleopatra story hints at a reluctance to confront the gravity of his godfather's play. For, if he saw himself in *King Lear*, with its unique-for-Shakespeare mention of a 'Godsonne', and in *Macbeth*, of which he could claim to be the 'naked New-borne-Babe' and the man-child brought forth by Macbeth's '*dearest Partner of Greatnesse*', the *Tragedy of Antony and Cleopatra* was exclusively Will Shakespeare's and Jane Davenant's. Their love story was played out onstage – in the treachery of the Macbeths and the mutual betrayal of Mark Antony and Cleopatra – and, more privately, in the sonnets, where Shakespeare wondered 'why should others false adulterat eyes / Give salutation to my sportive blood?' in tones reminiscent of his Antony.

Even in his 50s, Davenant dared not revisit the electromagnetic attraction-repulsion of his mother's relationship with Shakespeare without earthing the energy in mock-heroic couplets. Making fun of it all was a way of insulating himself from the hair-trigger emotions and the exquisite pathos of his own conception.

16

1605: A Lover's Complaint

'And sir William Davenant of oxford's mother
with her cup of canary for any cockcanary.'
James Joyce, *Ulysses*

The plague struck with abnormal severity in 1636. By mid-May, the theatres were closed. The Court left London on its summer progress, arriving at Oxford on 29 August.

The entrance, via the Northgate, of King Charles and Henrietta Maria was not unlike the arrival of King James and Queen Anne in the city on 27 August 1605. As with that earlier visit, the royals were treated to a hit-and-miss selection of entertainments. The first evening they sat through *The Floating Island* by William Strode, Doctor of Divinity and Orator of Oxford University. Though the play attacked Puritan agitators like William Prynne, Charles and Henrietta found it 'grave' and hard to understand. Other plays were performed – *Love's Hospital* and *The Royal Slave* – but none by professional playwrights. The royals left Oxford on 31 August.

Davenant had no desire to return to a plague-ridden London and the long-running dispute with his tailor. Oxford, too, held little appeal (his brother-in-law, Thomas Hallam, had died, leaving Davenant's sister in charge of the Taverne). Davenant opted to set out for the Cotswolds with a few friends. He wrote a breezy account of the trip in his poem, 'A Journey into *Worcestershire*'.

The party – Davenant, Endymion Porter, a 'Captaine' and 'my Lord' – took horse, leaving behind them 'ill Playes, sowre Wine, / Fierce Serjeants and the plague'. The weather broke. The riders were lashed with rain until 'no man gave breath to thought; / But like to silent Traytors in a Vault, / Digg'd on our way'. At last, they 'reach'd Wickham, with the early Night'. They had followed the old Roman road which descended Broadway Hill and passed through the village of Childs Wickham, near the Worcestershire border.

The manor of Childs Wickham was then in the hands of the Sheldon family.[1] The steward of the adjoining manor of Wickhamford was Robert Dover, who had taken over that role from Anthony Langston.

Robert Dover inaugurated the Cotswold Olympicks. This annual jamboree of country sports was held in Whitsun week on Kingcombe Plain – now Dover's Hill

– above the town of Chipping Campden, and was conceived as an antidote to the creeping Puritanism which forbade amusements. Because Dover also acted as legal agent to Endymion Porter, whose estate at Ashton-sub-Edge was nearby, Porter had used his influence to secure King James's blessing for the games.

Prince Rupert attended the games in 1636. Also that year, a collection of verses was published under the title *Annalia Dubrensia* ('Doverian Annals'). The poems in praise of Dover and his Olympicks had been penned by such luminaries as Thomas Heywood, Michael Drayton and Ben Jonson. Davenant's offering, 'In celebration of the yearely Preserver of the Games at COTSWALD', was published later that year. 'Heare me you Men of strife!' he began, targeting the Puritans 'that toyle for pow'r to doe Men wrong ...

> *Dover* (the Gentry's Darling) know this flame,
> Is but a willing tribute to thy Fame,
> Sung by a Poet, that conceals his name.

Davenant had missed out on the first edition of *Annalia Dubrensia*. He no doubt intended to meet Robert Dover at 'Wickham' and insinuate his own poem into a later edition. His 'Journey into *Worcestershire*' described the first day's jaunt and heaped praise on 'brave *Endimion*', whose wit kept them amused that first night. But it broke off before the friends had even entered Worcestershire:

> Our other Sallies, and th'adventures wee
> Achiev'd, deserve new braine, new Historie.

What were those 'other Sallies' and 'th'adventures' they achieved?

Sir John Suckling and Endymion Porter contributed prefatory verses to the *Madagascar* collection of 1638, which included 'A Journey into *Worcestershire*' and Davenant's poem to Robert Dover. Other commendatory verses were provided by Thomas Carew and William Habington. The latter lived at Hindlip Hall, north of Worcester.

Davenant hinted that Hindlip was the intended destination of the Worcestershire excursion when he compared the rain-swept travellers with 'silent Traytors in a Vault'. William Habington was born at Hindlip on 4 November 1605, a few hours before Guy Fawkes was discovered lurking in the vault beneath the House of Lords. Habington was a mere swaddled babe when Hindlip was surrounded by armed men, and when Nicholas Owen gave himself up, and when – on 27 January 1606 – Father Henry Garnet emerged from his cramped hiding place to be whisked away for interrogation, trial and execution.

It is likely that Davenant would have wanted to visit the Worcestershire home of his friend, William Habington, and see the space where Father Garnet had hidden for eight painful days in early 1606.[2] The Jesuit superior loomed large in his background.

John Davies of Hereford: the frontispiece to *The Writing Schoolemaster* (1636).

John Benson's 1639 edition of Shakespeare's *Poems* included a long poem entitled 'A Lovers Complaint'. The same poem, 'A Lovers complaint, *BY* WILLIAM SHAKE-SPEARE', concluded Thomas Thorpe's 1609 edition of *Shake-speares Sonnets*.

For many years Shakespeare's authorship of 'A Lover's Complaint' was doubted. It was not until the 1980s that the poem was again published with the 154 sonnets of William Shakespeare. Then, in 2007, Brian Vickers produced a convincing argument that 'A Lover's Complaint' was not by Shakespeare at all. It was written by John Davies of Hereford.

The issue of who wrote 'A Lover's Complaint', and why it was published in Thorpe's Quarto of 1609, is crucial to an understanding of the sonnets. The timing of Thorpe's publication, along with the dedication to 'Mr.W.H. ALL.', suggests that the release of *Shake-speares Sonnets* was calculated to discredit Shakespeare, whose *Coriolanus* of the previous year had challenged the official account of the 1605 Gunpowder Plot. Ben Jonson's more considered riposte, *Catiline His Conspiracy*, would not appear until 1611. The publication of the sonnets was an interim measure: a shot across Shakespeare's bows.

Ben Jonson would remark of Shakespeare, 'sometime it was necessary he should be stopped.' Jonson underlined the point, noting that the Emperor Augustus (Octavius Caesar, Mark Antony's enemy) had said of the eloquent speaker Quintus Haterius, '*Sufflaminandus erat*' – 'The brake had to be applied'.

The publication of 'A Lover's Complaint' in 1609 was part of a concerted bid to stop Shakespeare's mouth. It offered a key to the mysteries of the sonnets.

A woman sits on a riverbank, 'Tearing of papers breaking rings a twaine, / Storming her world with sorrowes, wind and raine.' Neither young nor old, she retains some of her youthful beauty. A 'reverend man' happens to be grazing his cattle nearby. He approaches the 'fickle maid', demanding to know 'the grounds and motives of her wo.' She addresses him as 'Father' and begins to tell her tale.

Years before, she was wooed by a brown-haired, honey-tongued womaniser – 'one by natures outwards so commended, / That maidens eyes stucke over all his face'. The young man was prone to sudden outbursts: 'His rudenesse so with his authoriz'd youth, / Did livery falsenesse in a pride of truth.' He was also an accomplished horseman. With his 'subduing tongue' and 'craft of will' the young man had seduced many a woman, including a 'Nun, / Or Sister sanctified of holiest note'. But the maid, he insisted, was his 'origin and ender'. He begged her to have 'some feeling pitty' for his 'suffering youth' and to 'be not of my holy vowes afraid' – he was already married – since 'Thats to ye sworne to none was ever said'.[3]

The 'fickle maid' was eventually won over by the 'witch-craft' of his tears: 'Aye me I fell, and yet do question make, / What I should do againe for such a sake':

> O that infected moysture of his eye,
> O that false fire which in his cheeke so glowd:
> O that forc'd thunder from his heart did flye,
> O that sad breath his spungie lungs bestowed;
> O all that borrowed motion seeming owed,
> Would yet againe betray the fore-betrayed,
> And new pervert a reconciled Maide.

The implication at the end of the poem is that the maid has allowed herself to be seduced again, more recently. And so she is sobbing on the riverbank and tossing love tokens into the water.

The seven-line stanzas and *ababbcc* rhyme scheme of 'A Lover's Complaint' matched Shakespeare's *Lucrece* poem of 1594 and Samuel Daniel's 'Complaint of Rosamond' (1592), which Daniel reissued in 1594 with his *Tragedy of Cleopatra*. By echoing those two examples – *The Rape of Lucrece* and 'The Complaint of Rosamond' – the author of 'A Lover's Complaint' was seemingly harking back to 1594, although the poem itself was written later.

The opening lines established the location of the riverbank:

> From off a hill whose concave wombe reworded,
> A plaintfull story from a sistring vale
> My spirrits t'attend this doble voyce accorded,
> And downe I laid to list the sad tun'd tale

The poet alluded to two local legends – that of King Lludd, who dug a pit on Carfax Hill to snare two warring dragons, and that of Fair Rosamund (otherwise known as Jane Clifford), the mistress of King Henry II, who was buried at Godstow, near Oxford. Like Lludd's dragons, carried away from Oxford in a satin sheet, Rosamund's remains were removed for reburial in a 'silken scented bag'.[4] The legend of Carfax therefore 'reworded' the sad tale of Fair Rosamund from the 'sistring vale'.

The poem's narrator had walked from Carfax to Christ Church Meadow, a triangular expanse of ground, bounded by the Isis and Cherwell rivers, where local farmers grazed their cattle. He had laid down to hear the 'doble voyce' of Great Tom, the Christ Church bell, which had been known as 'Mary' when it belonged to Oseney Abbey. And it was there that he espied the 'fickle maid' sitting beside the River Isis.

It was a scene that John Davies of Hereford knew well. He was based at Magdalen, Samuel Daniel's old college, a little further up the Cherwell. Davies, the probable author of 'A Lover's Complaint', almost certainly tutored Prince Henry, who visited Oxford with his parents in August 1605 and was enrolled at Magdalen that same year.

John Davies also knew Shakespeare. That is, he knew his work.[5] In a poem he published in 1603, Davies addressed the matter of the stage:

> Players, I love thee, and your Qualitie,
> As ye are Men, that pass-time not abus'd:
> And some I love for painting, poesie,
> And say fell Fortune cannot be excus'd,
> That hath for better uses you refus'd

He added a margin note – 'W. S. R. B.' – to indicate that those he loved for 'painting, poesie' were Richard Burbage and William Shakespeare.

In *The Scourge of Folly* (1611) Davies addressed an epigram to Shakespeare:

> SOME say good Will (which I, in sport, do sing)
> Had'st thou not plaid some Kingly parts in sport,
> Thou hadst bin a companion for a King;
> And, beene a King among the meaner sort.

This followed epigrams to 'my worthily disposed friend' Samuel Daniel and 'my well-accomplish'd friend' Ben Jonson, and came immediately before a snippy epigram *'To his most constant, though most unknown friend; No-body'*:

> You shall be serv'd; but not with numbers now;
> You shall be servd with nought; that's good for you.

The pronoun '*his*' implies that this '*No-body*' was Shakespeare's '*most constant, though most unknown friend*', since the preceding epigram was '*To our English Terence Mr. Will: Shake-speare*'. John Davies, it seems, knew more than he was letting on.

First and foremost, John Davies was a master of writing. Davenant's cousin, Thomas Fuller, would describe him as 'the greatest master of the pen that England in her age beheld' for 'Fast-writing', 'Fair-writing' and 'Close-writing' ('a mystery indeed, and too dark for my dim eyes to discover'). His remarkable speed as a copyist has led to the suggestion that Davies was responsible for certain 'stolen reports' – playscripts transcribed during live performances and published without the playwright's consent. Two Shakespeare plays, *King Lear* and *Pericles*, appeared in relatively good editions in 1608 and 1609, around the time that Shakespeare's sonnets were published by Thomas Thorpe, and the author of 'A Lover's Complaint' appears to have been acquainted with those plays, as well as *Antony and Cleopatra* (1606). Indeed, that Shakespearean tragedy probably bore Davies in mind of Samuel Daniel's *Tragedy of Cleopatra* (1594) and 'The Complaint of Rosamond', from which he directly drew inspiration for 'A Lover's Complaint'.

The year 1594 also saw the first publication of *Willobie His Avisa or The true Picture of a modest Maid, and of a chast and constant wife*. It is one of the great curiosities of English literature. Its author went to inordinate lengths to disguise when, why and by whom it was written, and whether or not the 'modest Maid' was a real person. 'Avisa', he admitted, was a 'fained name', although he 'would not have *Avisa* to be thought a politicke fiction, nor a truthlesse invention, for it may be, that I have at least heard of one in the west of England, in whome the substance of all this hath bene specified':

> *Againe, if we marke the exact descriptions of her birth, her countrie, the place of her abode; and such other circumstances [...] me thinkes it a matter almost impossible that any man could invent all this without some ground or foundation to build on.*

A prefatory poem, '*In praise of* Willobie *his* Avisa', cited Shakespeare's *Lucrece*, first published that year:

> Yet Tarquyne *pluckt his glistering grape,*
> And Shake-speare, *paints poore* Lucreece *rape.*

Just as John Davies would later take pains to specify the setting of 'A Lover's Complaint' on the riverbank in Oxford, so the author of *Willobie His Avisa* began by locating the scene:

At wester side of Albions Ile,
Where Austine pitcht his Monkish tent,
Where Sheapheards sing, where Muses smile,
The graces met with one consent

St Augustine ('Austin') met with native British bishops in about AD 603, somewhere near the mouth of the River Severn. The poet was possibly thinking of Aust, some 10 miles north of Bristol, or the monastery of St Augustine, which is now Bristol Cathedral.

About a mile east of the cathedral stood Bristol Castle, near the junction of the River Frome with the River Avon. Parts of Shakespeare's *Richard II* (c. 1594) were set in the precincts of Bristol Castle, which in Shakespeare's day was practically derelict (the castle was destroyed on Cromwell's orders in 1656).

From the castle, the River Avon flowed across the plain towards the Severn. Erosion had exposed the old red sandstone deposits which gave names to the suburbs of Redland and Redcliffe. William Camden wrote in 1584 that the earth here is 'of a red colour'. The author of *Willobie His Avisa* noted this reddishness, remarking that not far from the spot where St Augustine pitched his monkish tent there lies a 'rosie vale in pleasant plaine'.

Just as the river turns northwards, past Brandon Hill and the steep-sided valley of the Sandbrook, to carve its way through the Avon Gorge, a hot spring bubbled up through the riverbank at the foot of St Vincent's Rock. The existence of this spring was recorded in 1480 by William Worcestre, who observed that a 'hermitage and chapel' dedicated to St Vincent of Saragossa, patron saint of vintners, stood halfway up the cliff above the hot spring.

The Hot Well was accessible only at low tide and was said to start flowing in March to April. The effervescent, mineral-rich water gushed out of the ground at the rate of 60gal (270l) per minute and at a temperature of 76° Fahrenheit (24° Centigrade). It was believed to cure a range of ailments, from diabetes to 'obstinate Venereal Complaints'. The seventeenth-century traveller Celia Fiennes considered the Bristol water 'As warm as new milk and [with] much of that sweetness'.

Willobie His Avisa drew the reader's attention to Bristol Castle and the Hot Well:

At East of this, a Castle stands,
By auncient sheepheards built of olde […]
    At west side springs a Christall well;
    There doth this chast *Avisa* dwell.

More specifically, 'Avisa' dwelt on the downs above the 'rosie vale' of the River Avon:

Along this plaine there lyes a downe,
Where sheepheards feed their frisking flocke;

Her Sire the Maior of the towne,
A lovely shout of auncient stocke,
    Full twentie yeares she lived a maide,
    And never was by man betrayde.

The maid's 'Sire' (poetically, a male ancestor) had been the 'Mayor of the town'. The wealthy merchant John Shipwarde or Shippward[6] had been Mayor of Bristol in 1455, 1463, 1469 and 1470; he paid for the construction of the tower of St Stephen's, the parish church of Bristol, and died in 1471. Amongst other things, he owned an inn – the 'Guillows' – in Bristol High Street. But the family's fortunes had suffered. When courted by a nobleman, 'Avisa' declares 'I am too base to be your wife'. Subsequent editions of *Willobie His Avisa* revealed that the maid was linked 'both by Syre and spouse … to men of meanest trade'. She was the 'Child of an innkeeper, wife of the same'.

Shake-speares Sonnets, as published in 1609, end with a visit to a hot spring:

153
Cupid laid by his brand and fell a sleepe,
A maide of *Dyans* this advantage found,
And his love-kindling fire did quickly steepe
In a could vallie-fountaine of that ground:
Which borrowed from this holie fire of love,
A datelesse lively heat still to indure,
And grew a seething bath which yet men prove,
Against strang malladies a soveraigne cure

Sonnet 154 tells the same story. The 'fayrest votary' of the local nymphs found the 'little Love-God' lying asleep and quenched his 'heart inflaming brand' in 'a coole Well by':

Which from loves fire took heat perpetuall,
Growing a bath and healthfull remedy,
For men diseasd

The poet found no respite in the warm water: 'but I my Mistress thrall, / Came there for cure and this by that I prove, / Loves fire heates water, water cooles not love.' Sonnet 153 concludes likewise:

I sick withall the helpe of bath desired,
And thether hied a sad distemperd guest.
    But found no cure, the bath for my helpe lies,
    Where *Cupid* got new fire; my mistres eye.

The language compares with that of *Willobie His Avisa*, in which 'Nimphes' frequent the 'rosie vale', '*Venus*' framed the modest maid's 'sweete aspect' and Cupid's mother 'bent her wil, / In this to shew her utmost skill', while '*Diana*' presented the maid with a 'Golden shaft, / To conquer Cupids creeping craft' and gave her the name '*Avisa*'.[7] It is as if the author of *Willobie* had read Shakespeare's 'Cupid' sonnets and borrowed their imagery.

Regardless of their ordering in Thorpe's 1609 edition, there is no reason to presume that sonnets 153 and 154 were the last ones Shakespeare wrote. They were placed at the end of the 'Dark Lady' sequence in anticipation of the supplementary poem, 'A Lover's Complaint', because they pointed to the Hot Well on the outskirts of Bristol and hinted at the identity of Shakespeare's lover. She was one and the same as the Bristol-based 'A.D.' of the *Avisa* poem of 1594.

The Sheppard family, headed by Robert Sheppard of '*Durham*' or Dyrham, 10 miles east of Bristol, had moved to London in search of better fortune. The fact that three of Jane Sheppard's brothers were employed at Court suggests that they had been able to namedrop an influential figure.

The composer John Sheppard had been *Informator Choristarum* of Magdalen College, Oxford, and, from 1552, a Gentleman of the Chapel Royal. His first wife, 'Jane Shepperde', was buried at St Margaret's, Westminster, on 9 April 1555. 'John Scheperde' himself was interred at St Margaret's on 21 December 1558 (he was denied burial in Westminster Abbey, probably because he was Catholic).[8] Ten years later, Jane Sheppard, daughter of Robert, was baptised at St Margaret's on 1 November 1568. A 'John Shepard, son of Robert', born at Westminster on 1 November 1571, was possibly the 'Shepperd' who became a Gentleman of the Chapel Royal on 1 December 1606.

When the plague broke out in 1592 Jane would have been sent away for safety to the 'countrie hills' near Bristol. At the same time, William Shakespeare found sanctuary with his patron, Henry Wriothesley, at the earl's Titchfield estate near Southampton. There he wrote some of his 'Fair Youth' sonnets and his *Venus and Adonis*, which he published in 1593 with a dedication to the 19-year-old earl. *Venus and Adonis* contains a hint that Shakespeare, the expert horseman, had already been intimate with a 'breeding Jennet, lustie, young, and proud'. Jane Sheppard was familiarly known as Jennet.[9]

Around April 1593, Shakespeare and Southampton set out for Bristol,[10] hoping perhaps to catch up with some theatrical colleagues who were touring the country.[11] Being in such close proximity to his 'breeding Jennet', Shakespeare found that the Hot Well could not cure his malady. Henry Wriothesley was similarly struck by Jane's tawny beauty:

> Such fainty qualmes I never found,
> Till first I saw this westerne ground.

Published the following year, *Willobie His Avisa* divulged that 'H. W.' was 'sodenly affected' at his first sight of the maid. He betrayed 'the secresy of his disease unto his familiar frend W. S. who not long before had tried the curtesy of the like passion, and was now newly recovered of the like infection'. W. S. persuaded his 'frend Harry' that the woman might yield – 'She is no Saynt, She is no Nonne, / I thinke in tyme she may be wonne':

> Thus this miserable comforter comforting his frend with an impossibilitie, eyther for that he now would secretly laugh at his frends folly, that had given occasion not long before unto others to laugh at his owne, or because he would see whether an other could play his part better then himselfe, & in viewing a far off the course of this loving Comedy, he determined to see whether it would sort to a happier end for this new actor, then it did for the old player.

Willobie His Avisa then relayed the increasingly fraught exchanges between 'H. W.' and the spirited maid, which took place at the inn 'where hanges the badge / Of Englands saint', where she worked. This was possibly the Green Dragon on St Michael's Hill, which had Davenant connections.[12] The poet claimed that 'H. W.' enjoyed no more success in assailing the maid's chastity than any of the other '*Ruffians, Roysters, young* Gentlemen, and lustie Captaines' who tried her.

Shakespeare's sonnets, however, reveal a different story:

> That thou hast her it is not all my griefe,
> And yet it may be said I lov'd her deerely,
> That she hath thee is of my wayling cheefe,
> A losse in love that touches me more neerely.

'Thou doost love her, because thou knowst I love her,' protested Shakespeare. 'Take all my loves, my love, yea take them all'. Southampton, he argued, had broken a 'two-fold truth':

> Hers by thy beauty tempting her to thee,
> Thine by thy beautie beeing false to me.

Sonnet 35 even points to the place of the betrayal:

> No more bee greev'd at that which thou hast done,
> Roses have thornes, and silver fountaines mud

Henry 'Rose-ly', the 'Rose-cheekt Adonis', had slept with Shakespeare's mistress near the warm spring which bubbled up through the mud of the Avon. The Green Dragon stood just a mile from the Hot Well, in the suburb of Kingsdown.

St Michael's Hill, Bristol, early nineteenth century.

At the very least, *Willobie His Avisa* publicised Henry Wriothesley's juvenile obsession with the wife of an innkeeper[13] – for by then, Jane had married John Davenant.
The order to smear the young earl must have come from Lord Burghley, Queen
Elizabeth's most trusted minister, who held the post of Lord High Steward of Bristol.
Burghley was Southampton's legal guardian. He wanted the earl to marry his granddaughter, Elizabeth de Vere, and with Southampton's 21st birthday in October 1594
approaching, Burghley decided to up the pressure on his wilful ward.

Southampton's family network was Catholic. The persecution of Catholics reached
new heights in the early 1590s. Catholic homes around London were violently raided
in March 1594, and in April a supposed conspiracy came to light. Ralph Sheldon of
Beoley was reputedly preparing to fund a rebellion in Wales. Southampton was a
potential figurehead for any such Catholic uprising. The unscrupulous Burghley had
plenty of motive in 1594 to commission a muck-raking poem on the subject of 'H. W.'s
infatuation with the married maid of the Green Dragon.

'*D'avenant* from *Avon*, comes'. Not the mythical town of Avenant in Lombardy,
but the downs above the Bristol Avon, where his mother had dwelt 'in publique
eye, / Shut up from none that list to see'.

Twelve years had passed since Shakespeare's visit to the Hot Well and
Southampton's crush on 'A.D.' Jane Davenant was now the mistress of the Taverne
in Oxford, where Shakespeare was a frequent guest. He was probably in Oxford
on 27 August 1605 – the prophecy uttered to King James that afternoon by three
students dressed like 'nymphs or sibyls' would soon be evoked in *Macbeth*. Three

days later, the Court left Oxford. That same day a party of pilgrims set out from Essex. Among them were several Jesuit priests and their servants, including Nicholas Owen, the Oxford-born priest-hole constructor.

Father Garnet had announced his intention to go on a pilgrimage two days earlier, on 28 August. The Jesuit superior was 50 years old, portly and short-sighted. He answers the description of the 'reverend man' who sat down beside the 'fickle maid' on the Oxford riverbank in 'A Lover's Complaint':

Sometime a blusterer that the ruffle knew
Of Court of Cittie, and had let go by
The swiftest houres observed as they flew[14]

The maid addressed him as 'Father' and proceeded with her confession. She had been seduced, all those years before. Now she had fallen again. The items she had thrown into the Isis – 'folded schedulls', 'letters sadly pend in blood' – and her pathetic cry, 'O false blood thou register of lies, / What unapproved witnes doost thou beare!' explain the cause of her distress. She was pregnant.

She was wearing a sunhat – a 'plattid hive of straw, / Which fortified her visage from the Sunne'. It had been warm and sunny when King James and his courtiers arrived in Oxford on 27 August 1605. Jane Davenant was pregnant at the time. She would give birth to her second son, Shakespeare's 'Godsonne' William, six months later.

Father Garnet used the alias 'Mr Farmer'. The image of the 'reverend man' grazing his cattle on Christ Church Meadow would have brought to mind, when the poem was published in 1609, the Jesuit who set out on the pilgrimage to North Wales on 30 August 1605. From Oxford, the pilgrims travelled to Stratford-upon-Avon and then across the Midlands to the shrine of St Winefride at Holywell in Flintshire.

James, Duke of York, the patron of Davenant's theatre company, became King James II in 1685. On 29 August 1686, James and his Catholic queen visited St Winefride's Well to pray for a son and heir. More than a century earlier Shakespeare's father named 'saint Winefrid' as his special patron in a Jesuit 'Testament of the Last Will of the Soul', which was later found hidden among the rafters of the Shakespeare Birthplace in Stratford. John Shakespeare's first two children had died in infancy. If he visited St Winefride's Well – illegally – to pray for a healthy son, his prayers were answered when William Shakespeare was born.

There is another meaning of the French avenant. It can be an amendment to a contract, or something that makes 'amends'.

By 27 August 1605, Shakespeare must have known that his 'Dark Lady', Jane Davenant, was pregnant with his child. He would have prayed for a son, his only legitimate male heir, Hamnet, having died in 1596.

But an act of penance was required. Shakespeare summoned Father Garnet to hear Jane's confession and no doubt accompanied the pilgrims on at least part of

The White Bear, formerly the Green Dragon.

their journey to Holywell. Garnet was glad to be on the move. Robert Catesby had spent much of that summer trying to coax him into condoning an atrocity against the state.

What the Jesuit didn't know was that the net was closing. Once Catesby had recruited Sir Everard Digby (who went on the Holywell pilgrimage) into his 'Gunpowder' treason, the Secretary of State, Sir Robert Cecil, would have all that he needed to annihilate the Jesuit mission in England.

Cecil had learnt much from his father, Lord Burghley. The best weapon in his war against Catholicism was compromised Catholics.[15] Shakespeare knew Robert Catesby, to whom he was distantly related, and other plotters, like John Grant and Robert Wintour, whose homes the pilgrims visited. He was ideally placed to monitor their movements.

When Shakespeare exposed the truth about the Gunpowder Plot in *Coriolanus*, revealing that Catesby had been used and betrayed by Cecil, other Catholics were set to work blackening Shakespeare's name. Thomas Thorpe, a Catholic publisher, was provided with Shakespeare's private sonnets. John Davies of Hereford, a Catholic poetaster, was commissioned to write 'A Lover's Complaint'. The methodology was the same as that of *Willobie His Avisa*, published in 1594 and reissued in 1609 to coincide with the release of *Shake-speares Sonnets*. The final pair of sonnets linked up with *Willobie*, signposting where Shakespeare's 'Dark Lady' was living in 1593, and 'A Lover's Complaint' proclaimed that the affair had been rekindled. Jane had become pregnant with Shakespeare's son. Father Garnet heard her confession. Thorpe's volume was pointedly dedicated to the 'only begetter' and 'well-wishing adventurer', 'Mr. W. Hall'.

That 'well-wishing' adventure was the Holywell pilgrimage – part of Shakespeare's penance for his adultery. William Davenant was, therefore, *avenant*, since his father sought to make 'amends' for having impregnated his married lover. The sonnets and 'A Lover's Complaint' gave notice that Shakespeare had consorted with the Jesuits and the supposed perpetrators of the Gunpowder Plot.

Worse was to come. In 1611, two years after the sonnets were published, John Speed – a Puritan – denounced Shakespeare as a Jesuit mouthpiece and Ben Jonson produced his response to *Coriolanus*. Jonson's *Catiline His Conspiracy* stuck to his master's line by portraying Sir Robert Cecil as the gifted statesman who foiled the plot and indicating that an associate of the gunpowder plotters had blabbed to his married mistress, who then passed on the information to Cecil. The fact that Shakespeare's adultery was now common knowledge, as were the roles he and his lover had played as Cecil's informants, led to his prompt retirement from the public stage.

This explains why Sir Kenelm Digby was so keen to fight a duel with Davenant in France in 1648. Kenelm was the son of Sir Everard Digby, the first of the gunpowder plotters to be executed on 30 January 1606. He was also a friend and literary executor of the late Ben Jonson, who effectively told the world that Will Shakespeare and Jane Davenant were rewarded for betraying the plotters to Sir Robert Cecil. Sir Kenelm Digby was desperate to punish Sir William Davenant for the sins of his parents.

Davenant's 'A Journey into *Worcestershire*' makes sense if we assume that he and his Catholic friends were making their way to Hindlip Hall, the home of William Habington, where Father Garnet and his servant, Nicholas Owen, were captured in January 1606.

Garnet had heard his mother's confession. Perhaps it was the Jesuit who recommended that Shakespeare should take some responsibility for Davenant's upbringing by becoming his godfather. But Jane also helped to ensure the grisly execution of the 'reverend man' – like Lady Macbeth, who would have murdered the saintly Duncan herself, 'Had he not resembled / My Father as he slept'. If, as seems likely, Davenant was editing Shakespeare's poems for John Benson's edition of 1639, he might have wanted to make his own amends in an act of contrition and remembrance.

His parents' love affair inspired great works of literature and brought a holy man to the scaffold. It also produced a poet laureate and one of the most influential impresarios the English stage has ever known.

Selected Bibliography

Acheson, A. (1913), *Mistress Davenant, The Dark Lady of Shakespeare's Sonnets*. London: B. Quaritch.

Adolph, A. (2012), *The King's Henchman: Henry Jermyn, Stuart Spymaster and Architect of the British Empire*. London: Gibson Square Books.

Anon. (1888), *The Life and Times of that Excellent and Renowned Actor Thomas Betterton*. London: Reader.

Barber, R. (ed.) (1982), *John Aubrey: Brief Lives*. Woodbridge: The Boydell Press.

— (1987), *Fuller's Worthies: Selected from The Worthies of England by Thomas Fuller*. London: The Folio Society.

Barnard, E. A. B. (1930), *New Links With Shakespeare*. Cambridge: Cambridge University Press.

— (1936), *The Sheldons: Being Some Account of the Sheldon Family of Worcestershire and Warwickshire*. Cambridge: Cambridge University Press.

Bevis, R. W. (1898), *English Drama: Restoration and Eighteenth Century, 1660–1789*. London: Longman.

Britland, K. (2006), *Drama at the Courts of Queen Henrietta Maria*. Cambridge: Cambridge University Press.

Butler, M. (1984), *Theatre and Crisis 1632–1642*. Cambridge: Cambridge University Press.

Cambers, A. (2013), *Godly Reading: Print, Manuscript and Puritanism in England, 1580–1720*. Cambridge: Cambridge University Press.

Collins, H. S. (1967), *The Comedy of Sir William Davenant*. The Hague: Mouton & Co.

Davenant, W. (1629), *The Tragedy of Albovine, King of the Lombards*. London: R.M.

— (1630), *The Cruell Brother*. London: John Waterson.

— (1635), *The Triumphs of the Prince D'Amour*. London: Richard Meighen.

— (1636), *The Platonick Lovers: A Tragœcomedy*. London: Richard Meighen.

— (1636), *The Witts*. London: Richard Meighen.

— (1637), *Luminalia, or The Festivall of Light*. London: Thomas Walkley.

— (1638), *Madagascar; With Other Poems*. London: Thomas Walkley.

— (1639), *Salmacida Spolia*. London: Thomas Walkley.

— (1643), *The Unfortunate Lovers: A Tragedie*. London: Francis Coles.

— (1649), *Love and Honour*. London: Humphrey Robinson/Humphrey Moseley.

— (1651), *Gondibert: An Heroick Poem*. London: John Holden.

— (1656), *The Siege of Rhodes*. London: Henry Herringman.

— (1659), *The History of Sr Francis Drake*. London: Henry Herringman.

— (1668), *The Rivals*. London: William Cademan.

— (ed.) (1669), *The New Academy of Complements [etc.]*. London: Samuel Speed.

— (1670), *The Tempest, or The Enchanted Island*. London: Henry Herringman.

— (1673), *The Works of Sr William D'avenant Kt Consisting of Those which were formerly Printed, And Those which he design'd for the Press*. London: Henry Herringman.

— (1674), *Macbeth, A Tragœdy*. London: P. Chetwin.

D'avenant, W. (1678), *Notitia Historicorum Selectorum [etc.]*. Oxford: Richard Davis.

De Chambrun, C. L. (1938), *Shakespeare Rediscovered*. New York: Charles Scribner's Sons.

Defoe, D. (1966), *A Journal of the Plague Year*. Harmondsworth: Penguin.

Donaldson, I. (2011), *Ben Jonson: A Life*. Oxford: Oxford University Press.

Downes, J. & Summers, M. (eds) (1886), *Roscius Anglicanus*. London: The Fortune Press.

Edmond, M. (1987), *Rare Sir William Davenant*. Manchester: Manchester University Press.

Ellacombe, H. N. (1883), *Shakespeare as an Angler*. London: Elliot Stock.

Elton, C. I. (1904), *William Shakespeare: His Family and Friends*. London: John Murray.

Evans, J. (1824), *Chronological Outline of the History of Bristol*. Bristol: John Evans.

Fraser, A. (1979), *King Charles II*. London: Book Club Associates.

— (1989), *The Weaker Vessel: Woman's Lot in Seventeenth-Century England*. London: Mandarin.

Green, M. A. E. (ed.) (1857), *Letters of Queen Henrietta Maria, including Her Private Correspondence with Charles I*. London: Richard Bentley.

Greville, F. (1633), *Certaine Learned and Elegant Workes of the Right Honorable Fulke Lord Brooke, [etc.]*. London: Henry Seyle.

Grosart, A. B. (ed.) (1880), *Willobie's Avisa, 1594*. Blackburn: Printed for the Subscribers.

Grose, F. (1971/1811), *Dictionary of the Vulgar Tongue: A Dictionary of Buckish Slang, University Wit, and Pickpocket Eloquence*. Chicago: Follett Publishing Company.

Gurr, A. (1992), *The Shakespearean Stage 1574–1642* (3rd Edition). Cambridge: Cambridge University Press.

Hamilton, E. (1976), *Henrietta Maria*. New York: Coward, McCann & Geoghegan, Inc.

Hammerschmidt-Hummel, H. (2006), *The True Face of William Shakespeare*. London: Chaucer Press.

Hammond, B. (ed.) (2010), *Double Falsehood or The Distressed Lovers (The Arden Shakespeare)*. London: Methuen Drama.

Hammond, P. (ed.) (2002), *Restoration Literature: An Anthology*. Oxford: Oxford University Press.

Harbage, A. (1935), *Sir William Davenant: Poet Venturer 1606–1668*. Philadelphia: University of Pennsylvania Press.

Harley, J. (2010), *The World of William Byrd: Musicians, Merchants and Magnates*. Farnham: Ashgate.

Heylin, C. (2009), *So Long as Men Can Breathe: The Untold Story of Shakespeare's Sonnets*. Philadelphia: Da Capo Press.

Hibbert, C. (1993), *Cavaliers and Roundheads: The English at War 1642–1649*. London: HarperCollins.

Hill, C. (1991), *The World Turned Upside Down: Radical Ideas During the English Revolution*. London: Penguin.

Hotson, L. (1928), *The Commonwealth and Restoration Stage*. Cambridge: Harvard University Press.

Howarth, R. G. (ed.) (1959), *Minor Poets of the Seventeenth Century*. London: J. M. Dent & Sons.

Howe, E. (1992), *The First English Actresses: Women and Drama 1660–1700*. Cambridge: Cambridge University Press.

Hugo, V. (1905), *William Shakespeare*. London: George Routledge and Sons.

Jacob, J. R. & Raylor, T. (1991), *Opera and Obedience: Thomas Hobbes and A Proposition for*

Advancement of Moralitie by Sir William Davenant. The Seventeenth Century: Volume VI, No. 2.

Jonson, B. (1611), *Catiline his Conspiracy*. London: Walter Burre.

Jordan, D. & Walsh, M. (2013), *The King's Revenge: Charles II and the Greatest Manhunt in British History*. London: Abacus.

Kenyon, J. P. (1987), *The Stuarts*. London: Fontana.

Kroll, R. (2007), *Restoration Drama and 'The Circle of Commerce': Tragicomedy, Politics, and Trade in the Seventeenth Century*. Cambridge: Cambridge University Press.

Leacroft, R. & H. (1985), *Theatre and Playhouse*. London: Methuen.

Leech, J. (1884), *Brief Romances from Bristol History, with a Few Other Papers from the Same Pen*. Bristol: William George and Son.

Leech, R. H. (2000), *The St Michael's Hill Precinct of the University of Bristol: Medieval and Early Modern Topography*. Bristol: Bristol Record Society.

Lewcock, D. (2008), *Sir William Davenant, the Court Masque, and the English Seventeenth-Century Scenic Stage, c.1605–c.1700*. Amherst: Cambria Press.

Lindley, D. (1995), *Court Masques: Jacobean and Caroline Entertainments 1605–1640*. Oxford: Oxford University Press.

Little, P. (ed.) (2009), *Oliver Cromwell*. Houndsmill: Palgrave Macmillan.

Lowe, R. W. (1891), *Thomas Betterton*. London: Kegan Paul, Trench, Trübner & Co.

Loxley, J. (1997), *Royalism and Poetry in the English Civil Wars: The Drawn Sword*. Houndsmill: Macmillan.

Maidment, J. & Logan, W. H. (eds.) (1872–74), *The Dramatic Works of Sir William D'avenant with Prefatory Memoir and Notes* (5 volumes). Edinburgh: William Paterson.

Maguire, N. K. (1992), *Regicide and Restoration: English Tragicomedy, 1660–1671*. Cambridge: Cambridge University Press.

Major, P. (ed.) (2013), *Thomas Killigrew and the Seventeenth-Century English Stage*. Farnham: Ashgate Publishing Limited.

Marchant, E. C. (1936), *Sir William Davenant*. Oxford: Oxford University Press.

Milhous, J. (1979), *Thomas Betterton and the Management of Lincoln's Inn Fields 1695–1708*. Carbondale and Edwardsville: Southern Illinois University Press.

Milton, J. (1997), *Complete English Poems, Of Education, Areopagitica*. London: J.M. Dent.

Morrill, J. (ed.) (1990), *Oliver Cromwell and the English Revolution*. London: Longman.

Neale, F. (2000), *William Worcestre: The Topography of Medieval Bristol*. Bristol: Bristol Record Society.

Nethercot, A. H. (1967), *Sir William D'avenant: Poet Laureate and Playwright-Manager*. New York: Russell & Russell.

Nicholl, C. (2007), *The Lodger: Shakespeare on Silver Street*. London: Allen Lane.

Ollard, R. (1988), *Clarendon and His Friends*. Oxford: Oxford University Press.

Phillips, G. & Keatman, M. (1994), *The Shakespeare Conspiracy*. London: Century.

Picard, L. (2003), *Restoration London*. London: Phoenix.

Pilkinton, M. C. (ed.) (1997), *Records of Early English Drama: Bristol*. Toronto: University of Toronto Press.

Potter, L. (1989), *Secret Rites and Secret Writing: Royalist Literature, 1641–1660*. Cambridge: Cambridge University Press.

Purkiss, D. (2007), *The English Civil War: A People's History*. London: Harper Perennial.

Raddadi, M. (1979), *Davenant's Adaptations of Shakespeare*. Uppsala: Uppsala University.

Raymond, J. (2005), *The Invention of the Newspaper: English Newsbooks 1641–1649*. Oxford: Oxford University Press.

Rees, J. (1971), *Fulke Greville, Lord Brooke, 1554–1628: A Critical Biography*. London: Routledge & Kegan Paul.

Salter, H. E. (1921), *The Historic Names of the Streets & Lanes of Oxford Intra Muros*. Oxford: The Clarendon Press.

Schoenbaum, S. (2006), *Shakespeare's Lives*. New York: Barnes & Noble.

Scott, W. (1826), *Woodstock, or The Cavalier*. Kindle edition.

Seymour-Smith, M. (ed.) (1963), *Shakespeare's Sonnets*. London: Heinemann.

Shakespeare, W. (1609), *Shake-speares Sonnets*. London: Thomas Thorpe.

— (1640), *Poems: Written by Wil. Shake-speare. Gent*. London: John Benson.

— (1996), *The First Folio of Shakespeare* (2nd Edition). New York: W.W. Norton & Company.

Somerset, A. (1998), *Unnatural Murder: Poison at the Court of James I*. London: Phoenix.

Spencer, T. J. B. & Wells, S. W. (eds.) (1980), *A Book of Masques*. Cambridge: Cambridge University Press.

Stokes, F. A. (ed.) (1886), *The Poems of Sir John Suckling*. New York: White, Stokes, & Allen.

Stone, L. (1985), *The Family, Sex and Marriage in England 1500–1800*. London: Peregrine Books.

Stubbs, J. (2011), *Reprobates: The Cavaliers of the English Civil War*. London: Viking.

Summers, M. (1935), *The Playhouse of Pepys*. London: Kegan Paul, Trench, Trubner & Co.

Taylor, J. (1628), *Wit and Mirth, Chargeably collected out of Tavernes, [etc.]*. London: Henry Gosson.

Tennant, G. B. (ed.) (1908), *The New Inn or The Light Heart by Ben Jonson*. New York: Henry Holt and Company.

Tomalin, C. (2003), *Samuel Pepys: The Unequalled Self*. London: Penguin.

Tomlinson, H. (ed.) (1983), *Before the English Civil War: Essays on Early Stuart Politics and Government*. Houndmills: Macmillan.

Trease, G. (1973), *Samuel Pepys and his World*. London: Book Club Associates.

Trussler, S. (ed.) (1969), *Burlesque Plays of the Eighteenth Century*. Oxford: Oxford University Press.

Underdown, D. (1987), *Revel, Riot, and Rebellion: Popular Politics and Culture in England 1603–1660*. Oxford: Oxford University Press.

Vickers, B. (2007), *Shakespeare, A Lover's Complaint, and John Davies of Hereford*. Cambridge: Cambridge University Press.

Walters, R. (2011), *Naughty Boys: Ten Rogues of Oxford* (eBook).

Walton, I. (1982), *The Compleat Angler*. Oxford: Oxford University Press.

Warburton, E. (1846), *Memoirs of Prince Rupert, and the Cavaliers* (Vol. II). London: Richard Bentley.

Warner, S. A. (1908), *Lincoln College Oxford*. London: Sidgwick & Jackson.

Wedgwood, C. V. (1970), *The Trial of Charles I*. London: Fontana.

Whitaker, K. (2010), *A Royal Passion: The Turbulent Marriage of Charles I and Henrietta Maria*. London: Phoenix.

Wilcher, R. (2001), *The Writing of Royalism 1628–1660*. Cambridge: Cambridge University Press.

Williams, J. D. E. (1905), *Sir William Davenant's Relation to Shakespeare*. Strassburg: Kaiser-Wilhelm-Universität.

Wilson, D. (2004), *All the King's Women: Love, Sex and Politics in the Life of Charles II*. London: Pimlico.

Wilson, I. (1994), *Shakespeare: The Evidence*. London: Headline.

Winn, J. A. (1987), *John Dryden and His World*. New Haven: Yale University Press.

Worden, B. (2009), *The English Civil Wars 1640–1660*. London: Phoenix.

Wulstan, D. (1994), 'New Light on John Sheppard: Where There's a Will'. *The Musical Times*, Vol. 135, No. 1811.

Notes

Chapter 1. Orare Sir Will. Davenant

1. Davenant died intestate, leaving no will or inventory of his belongings, and so his wealth is an unknown quantity.
2. The quotation is from William Hayley's *Essay on Epic Poetry* (1782).
3. Samuel Butler (1613-80) published *Hudibras*, his satirical poem on religious sectarianism, in three parts between 1662 and 1678. His birthplace was Strensham in Worcestershire, where the lord of the manor was Sir William Russell (see Chapter 2).
4. Scott helpfully provided a footnote, explaining that 'D'Avenant actually wanted the nose, the foundation of many a jest of the day.'

Chapter 2. His Sacred Majestie's Most Happy Return

1. This arrangement soon broke down, mainly because Davenant and Killigrew were intent on crushing the competition, and so Herbert took Michael Mohun and his company to court.
2. Herbert remained Master of the Revels throughout the Interregnum, even though the office was effectively dormant.
3. Samuel Pepys saw them on 23 March 1661 at the Red Bull in Clerkenwell.

Chapter 3. A Teeming Muse

1. See Chapter 8.
2. 'The truth of Resurrection is by *You* / Confirm'd to all,' wrote Davenant of King Charles II, 'and made apparent too'.
3. i.e. Puritans.

Chapter 4. His Exit

1. The Oxford scholar Anthony Wood was frequently to be found at 'Morrell's' in the 1660s. He met John Aubrey there on 2 January 1668. Both men would later write about Davenant.

2. Old Style – 16 June in the modern calendar.
3. In 1669, the year after Davenant's death, a book was published, entitled *The New Academy of Complements, Erected For Ladies, Gentlewomen, Courtiers, Gentlemen, Scholars, Souldiers, Citizens, Country-men, and all persons, of what degree soever, of both Sexes*. Sir William Davenant was named as one of the compilers of this curious volume which, in addition to a host of useful expressions and sample letters, included 'An Exact Collection Of the Newest and Choicest *Songs à la Mode*' composed '*by the most Refined Wits of this Age.*' Whether or not it was Davenant's decision to juxtapose his own poems with those of William Shakespeare, it seems unlikely that he would have chosen to insert this ditty into the collection:

> Take a pound of Butter made in *May*,
> Clap it to her Arse in a Summers day,
> And ever as it melts, then lick it clean away;
> 'Tis a Med'cine for the Tooth-ach, old wives say.

4. William's translation was published as *Notitia Historicorum Selectorum, or Animadversions upon the Antient and Famous Greek and Latin Historians* (Oxford, 1678).
5. Shakespeare's first biographer, Nicholas Rowe, wrote scathingly in the Epilogue to his first play, *The Ambitious Stepmother* – performed at Lincoln's Inn Fields in 1700 – of the theatregoers who had flocked '*to the other House*' to see foreign dancers: '*Must* Shakespear, Fletcher, *and laborious* Ben / *Be left for* Scaramouch *and* Harlequin?' The implication is that Shakespeare, John Fletcher and Ben Jonson were among the presiding geniuses of Davenant's old playhouse, represented (perhaps) by their terracotta 'Heads'.

Chapter 5. Davenant the Poet

1. The royal office of Poet Laureate was first conferred on John Dryden by letters patent issued two years after Davenant's death in 1668. Ben Jonson's royal pension of £100 was transferred to William Davenant in 1638, making him the recognised, quasi-official laureate.
2. The occasion, perhaps, of Suckling's poem 'To Mr. D'Avenant for Absence', which included the lines:

> Where there is a traitor eye,
> That lets in from th' enemy
> All that may supplant an heart,
> 'Tis time the chief should use some art:
> Who parts the object from the sense,
> Wisely cuts off intelligence.

3. For comparison, Davenant's service in the Second Bishops' War of 1640 earned him £40.
4. They were tipped off by an insider – most likely the queen's confidante Lucy, Countess of Carlisle, once the Earl of Strafford's lover and now infatuated with John Pym.

Chapter 6. Davenet the Poet (Now Knighted)

1. Published, in 1673, as *The Distresses*.
2. The Parliamentarian officer who killed him, Thomas 'Butcher' Harrison, gave a fundamentalist rationale for the execution: 'Cursed is he that does the work of the Lord negligently!'

3. 'Mistress Sayers' was Mary, the wife of John Sayer, a loyal servant who became chief cook to King Charles II; Pepys would refer to him as 'Mr. Sayres, the Master Cook'.

Chapter 7. Gondibert

1. The term 'Whig' derives from a radical faction of the Scottish Covenanters.
2. According to John Aubrey, Davenant also recruited thirty-six weavers from the prisons of Paris to work in the American plantations.
3. Aripertus in the eighth-century *Historia Langobardorum*.

Chapter 8. How Daphne Pays His Debts

1. See Chapter 9.
2. Named after one of the MPs, Praise-God Barebone.
3. An emblem and motto to adorn a ceremonial shield.
4. Davenant was later accused by Sir Henry Herbert of having written an epithalamium or wedding poem for one of these occasions.
5. The argument was much the same as that advanced by Davenant in *A Proposition for Advancement of Moralitie*, published anonymously in 1653, in which he had insisted that theatrical entertainments could divert the people 'from Vices and Mischiefe'.

Chapter 9. Ffor Avoyding of Inconvenience

1. There was a brisk trade in cheap, no-questions-asked marriages, especially in the Fleet Street area. Young men could make money by marrying a gentlewoman who was already pregnant.
2. Ben Jonson was a heavy drinker, especially of the sweet wine known as Canary.
3. Based on Alboin, a Germanic warlord who invaded northern Italy in the sixth century AD.
4. A distant cousin of Davenant's first employer, the Duchess of Richmond.

Chapter 10. The Shade of Gentle Buckingham

1. Shakespeare's horticultural interests were explored by Janick, Paris and Daunay in their 2012 paper, 'The Cucurbits and Nightshades of Renaissance England: John Gerard and William Shakespeare' (*Horticultural Reviews*, Vol. 40), and Shakespeare has recently been identified as one of the four individuals featured on the cover of Gerard's *The Herball, or Generall Historie of Plantes* (1597). One also wonders whether John Taylor the Water-Poet knew that Shakespeare's father-in-law, Richard Hathaway, was alternatively known as Gardner.
2. In the prologue to a performance at the Inner Temple, in the presence of Lord Chancellor Hyde, on 2 February 1663, Davenant addressed his former roommate:

> My Lord, you in your early youth did sit,
> As Patron and as Censor too of Wit …
> As you were then our Judge, so now we come,
> In yearly trial to receive our doom.

Chapter 11. Servant to Her Majestie

1. The sense here is the same as that in Hamlet's ribald exchange with Ophelia:

   Ham: Ladie, shall I lye in your Lap?
   Oph: No my Lord.
   Ham: I meane, my Head upon your Lap?
   Oph: I my Lord.
   Ham: Do you thinke I meant Country matters?

2. The 'Mask' was Davenant's *The Temple of Love*.
3. Possibly in Ben Jonson's *The New Inn* (1629).

Chapter 12. A Mighty Debt

1. The Middle Temple had once been Templar property.
2. 1638 in the modern calendar.
3. Jonson's presence at the 'Sessions' would imply that the poem was written before his death in August 1637. Interestingly, Suckling and his fellows seem not to have recognised Ben Jonson's status as the reigning poet laureate.
4. A 'tierce' was one-sixth of a 'tun', or roughly 42 gallons/190 litres.

Chapter 13. Shakespears Vncle

1. Two of Mulcaster's pupils, Thomas Jenkins and John Cottam, became schoolmasters in Stratford-upon-Avon; they probably taught William Shakespeare.
2. In 1597, Shakespeare purchased New Place in Stratford-upon-Avon from a member of the Underhill family.
3. The lips, chin and left eyebrow compare with those in the later Faithorne engraving of Davenant, and the high cheekbones seem to match. The portrait might have been painted when Davenant was 16: he inherited £40 in cash from his father, and yet when the tailor John Urswick presented him with a bill for £14 soon afterwards, Davenant was unable (or unwilling) to pay it. Perhaps he had blown his legacy on a portrait – something for his tutor, Daniel Hough, to remember him by.
4. It is possible that the vault was constructed at the same time as the chapel to serve as a 'priest hole' for the use of those (illegally) celebrating Mass in the event of a raid. The adjoining ossuary might then have been a secret repository for Catholic items: rosaries, prayer books, etc.
5. The Beoley skull was described as 'undersized' by Rev. C. J. Langston, suggesting – if it is Shakespeare's skull – that Shakespeare was of modest stature. The possibility that Shakespeare was 'quite short' was entertained by Charles Nicholl in *The Lodger: Shakespeare on Silver Street* (2007). More recently, Professor Hildegard Hammerschmidt-Hummel, discussing the 'Boaden' portrait of Shakespeare, remarked, 'We can see he wasn't a very tall man.' Notably, William Davenant referred to himself as 'small Poet' and 'puny Poet' in two of his poems of the mid-1630s.
6. The Unique First Proof is a high-quality copy of the First Folio engraving that once belonged to the Shakespeare scholar J. O. Halliwell-Phillipps. I am indebted to Lee Durkee for bringing it to my attention.

7. John Overall was Bishop of Coventry and Lichfield at the time of Shakespeare's death. Thomas Egerton was Lord Chancellor and Lord Keeper of the Great Seal – one of the most senior government officials – at the time.

8. 'Cales' (Cadiz) and the Île de Ré were two disastrous military expeditions led by Buckingham against the Spanish and the French.

9. Davenant would have encountered this 'universal patroness of poets' when he was page to the Duchess of Richmond.

10. Drayton's correspondent, William Drummond, revealed that Jonson had characterised himself as 'Alkin' or Alcon in his lost pastoral, *The May-Lord*.

Chapter 14. W. H.

1. Susan, Countess of Montgomery, was another of the great ladies Davenant would have seen at the Duchess of Richmond's house.

2. In *The Shakespeare Conspiracy* (Century, 1994).

3. A letter, dated 20 December 1585 and signed 'Your Majesty's loyal and devoted true servant, W. H.', was sent to Queen Elizabeth I by one 'whose present necessities crave to be provided for'. The writer offered to make a sudden attack on Calais – much like Davenant, with his later scheme to blow up the magazine at Dunkirk – and complained of having been blacklisted and stigmatised by persons of influence. He also made suggestions concerning the planting of colonies in Virginia; this was just two months after an expedition to Virginia, organised by Sir Walter Raleigh, had returned to London (I suggested in *Who Killed William Shakespeare?* that Shakespeare had taken part in that expedition, travelling as a musician on the *Tyger*). Years later, in 1606, *A Four-Fold Meditation of the Four Last Things* by the martyred Jesuit, Robert Southwell, was printed by George Eld, who went on to print *Shake-speares Sonnets* in 1609. The Catholic text was dedicated to 'the Right Worshipfull and *Vertuous Gentleman, Mathew Saunders*' – an associate of the Earl of Southampton – and signed, 'Your Worships unfained affectionate W. H.' Father Robert Southwell was a distant kinsman of Shakespeare's and the 'W. H.' dedication, in this instance, was almost certainly intended as a menacing reminder of Shakespeare's Catholic connections.

4. The smooth transition from Tudor queen to Stuart king confounded the doomsayers, who had predicated anarchy, so that 'the sad Augurs mock their owne presage' and 'Incertainties now crowne them-selves assur'de'.

5.   'From fairest creatures we desire increase,
        That thereby beauties *Rose* might never die.'

6. Russell's half-brother, Sir John Russell, was the son-in-law of Ralph Sheldon of Beoley, in whose funerary urn the 'veritable skull of William Shakespeare' was discovered in 1884. Sir John's grandson, Sir William Russell, would come to the rescue when Davenant urgently needed to raise funds for his theatre company in 1661.

7. Compare the similar couplet from Davenant's poem, '*To my Friend Mr. Ogilby, Upon the Fables of Æsop Paraphras'd in Verse*':
        Though Verses are but Fetters deem'd by those
        Who endless journeys make in wandring Prose

8. For example: 'how false we Lords of Numbers are', from Davenant's elegy 'To the Countesse of *Carlile*, on the death of the Earle her husband' (March 1636).

9. Sonnet 144: 'To winne me soone to hell, my Female evill / Tempteth my better Angell from my side' (Benson's edition).

10. Sonnet 154: 'The little Love-God lying once a sleepe, / Laid by his side his heart in flaming brand'.
11. Davenant substituted his own song, 'Wake all the dead! what hoa! what hoa!', in his *Law against Lovers* adaptation of *Measure for Measure*.
12. Speed added, in a marginal note, 'Papists and Poets of like conscience for fictions'.

Chapter 15. Babes and Beggers

1. *The Cruel Brother, Albovine, The Colonel/Siege, The Just Italian, Love and Honour* and *The Unfortunate Lovers. The Law against Lovers* would also be set in this region.
2. A name Davenant borrowed for a 'young Count' in *Love and Honour*.
3. An error – John Davenant died on 19 April 1622 and was buried on 23 April. Shakespeare, of course, died on 23 April 1616.
4. Walter Dennis, 'parson of Durham', died there in 1577.
5. One of these daughters might have been the 'Natural' (i.e. illegitimate) daughter for whose benefit Shakespeare wrote his 'lost' *Cardenio* play 'in the Time of his Retirement from the Stage'. A copy of *Cardenio*, in the handwriting of the prompter John Downes, apparently belonged to Davenant's theatre company.
6. Davenant would also refer to 'the dayes of *Edgar* … When they coyn'd Leather' in *The Wits*.
7. Anthony Wood's close friend and benefactor was 'The Great Sheldon', Ralph (1623–84), grandson of the Ralph Sheldon whose funerary urn allegedly contained the skull of William Shakespeare. Wood attended his patron's burial 'in a vault situate & being under the Chappell of our Lady joining to St Leonards Church of Beoly' – so did he see Shakespeare's skull in the adjacent ossuary?
8. Sonnet 128, 'How oft when thou my musike musike playst', suggests that Shakespeare's 'Dark Lady' played the virginals with skill and grace.
9. Davenant's version:
   To us fair weather's foul, and foul is fair!
   Come hover through the foggy, filthy Air.
10. Marcus Antonius would die ten years later. By a strange coincidence, so would Shakespeare.
11. He would pay for this, posthumously, when the Duke of Buckingham and others mercilessly lampooned Davenant and John Dryden in their theatrical spoof *The Rehearsal*.

Chapter 16. A Lover's Complaint

1. The ardently Royalist Captain William Sheldon (1609–80) might have been the 'Captaine' of Davenant's poem. Another candidate would be Sir John Suckling, who had returned from military service in Germany in 1632.
2. It is possible that Davenant and company also visited Beoley, 14 miles from Hindlip, to see Shakespeare's skull. They had been in Sheldon territory at Childswickham, where Captain William Sheldon was heir to the manor (Sheldon's neighbour and kinsman owned a copy of Shakespeare's *Poems*, which Davenant perhaps edited). Anthony Langston, who served as steward of Wickhamford Manor before Robert Dover, had replaced Shakespeare's cousin, Thomas Greene, as town clerk of Stratford-upon-Avon; he witnessed a deed in 1619 by which Shakespeare's colleague,

Henry Condell, transferred property near Childswickham to Edward Sheldon of Beoley. In 1884, Rev. C. J. Langston revealed that the 'veritable skull of William Shakespeare' was in the Sheldon vault at Beoley church.

3. The double standard here is that of the sonnets, with their accusations that the 'Dark Lady' had sealed 'false bonds of love as oft as mine' and robbed 'others beds revenues of their rents', and of *Antony and Cleopatra*'s 'mouth-made vowes'.

4. Jane Clifford's family crest also featured two dragons.

5. In early 1600 a book called 'Amours by J. D. with certen o[the]r sonnetes by W.S.' was registered by the stationer Eleazar Edgar. It was probably never published. Perhaps William Shakespeare put the kibosh on this unauthorised collaboration with 'J. D.'

6. 'Shyppard' in William Worcestre's notes of 1480.

7. The feigned name 'Avisa' betrays a Bristolian connection. John 'Lackland', youngest son of King Henry II, married Isabella, Countess of Gloucester, in 1189, thereby assuming the earldom of Gloucester and lordship of Bristol. On becoming King John in 1199 he abandoned his first wife, although he kept her lands. Isabella was variously known as Haweis, Hawisia and Avisa.

8. Sheppard's son Nathan went to work for the Petre family at Ingatestone Hall in Essex. In 1611, Elizabeth, the daughter of the second Lord Petre, married William Sheldon of Beoley, the grandson of the Ralph Sheldon in whose funerary urn Rev. C. J. Langston allegedly discovered Shakespeare's skull.

9. Further hints that Shakespeare was in love with a witty, dark-eyed woman can be found in *Love's Labour's Lost* (c.1594). Berowne, the most Shakespeare-like character in the play, falls for Rosalind, who is 'borne to make blacke, faire'. The character of Don Armado, meanwhile, owes much to Sir Walter Raleigh, then exiled from the Court for having married Bess Throckmorton, a relative of Shakespeare's by marriage. A visit to Raleigh's Sherborne estate in Dorset, early in 1593, would explain the jealousy of the 'Rival Poet' sonnets, which pun on Raleigh's nickname, 'Ocean'.

10. Shakespeare may have had relatives there: a 'John Shakesperye' was buried at Christ Church, Bristol, in 1540.

11. Several close friends of Shakespeare's, including Augustine Phillips and John Heminges, co-editor of the First Folio, went on tour in 1593 with Lord Strange's company, which produced Shakespeare's *Henry VI* trilogy and *Titus Andronicus* (published in 1594). Their lead actor, Edward Alleyn, received a letter at Bristol from his wife, delivered by Richard Cowley, and sent a reply via a kinsman of Thomas Pope (Cowley and Pope were listed with Phillips and Heminges among the 'Principall Actors' in Shakespeare's plays in the First Folio of 1623). Edward Alleyn's letter to his wife included a postscript asking her to 'Lett my orayng tawny stokins of wolen be dyed a very good blak'. Shakespeare seems to have found the term 'orange tawny' amusing – twice he put it in the mouth of the ham actor, Nick Bottom, in *A Midsummer Night's Dream* (1594): 'I will discharge it, in … your orange tawnie beard' (Act 1, Scene 2); and 'The Woosell cocke, so blacke of hew, / With Orenge-tawny bill' (Act 3, Scene 1). Davenant picked up on the joke in *The Platonic Lovers* (1635), referring to the airy 'Spirits' that engender love: 'Their Colour's Orange Tawny sir, as I conceive'.

12. Known as the Swan in 1738, and since 1764 as the White Bear, the Green Dragon stood by the gate which marked the boundary of the County of Bristol, on the road to Aust and the ferry to Wales. It was part of a tenement which included Oldbury House, the earliest known tenant of which was (in 1689) Lady Philippa Gore. She bought the property in 1692, before her second marriage (her first husband, Sir Thomas Gore,

having died in 1675). Sir Thomas was the grandson of Sir John Gore, Lord Mayor of London in 1624, who became free of the Merchant Taylors' Company on the same day – 22 June 1590 – as his first cousin, John Davenant, the father of Sir William.

13. In *Shakespeare Rediscovered* (1938), Clara Longworth, Comtesse de Chambrun, argued that Jane Davenant was referred to jokingly in a letter from Elizabeth, Countess of Southampton, to her husband the earl in June or July 1599: '*All the news I can send you that I thinke will make you merry is that I reade in a letter from London that Sir John Falstaffe is by his mrs. dame pintpot made father of a godly millers thumb, a boye thats all heade and a litel body – but this is a secret.*' The allusion was to Shakespeare's *The First Part of King Henry the Fourth* (c.1596), in which Falstaff says to the Hostess of the Boar's-Head Tavern, 'Peace good Pint-pot'. The Countess of Southampton was perhaps relaying to her husband, Henry Wriothesley, the gossip that the relationship between Shakespeare ('Sir John Falstaffe') and Jane ('dame pintpot') was back on in 1599, before the Davenants left London for Oxford.

14. Garnet was educated at Winchester College, where he gained a reputation as a keen debater or 'blusterer'; his first job was as 'corrector of the common law print' for Richard Tottel, who specialised in printing legal texts – he knew the 'ruffle' of the City and the Inns of Court. Garnet travelled to Rome at the age of 25 and was received into the Society of Jesus in September 1577; he was therefore required to celebrate the Divine Office, also known as the Liturgy of the Hours. He returned to England as a missionary in 1586, crossing the Channel with Shakespeare's kinsman, Father Robert Southwell.

15. As Angelo, the Puritanical 'deputy', says in *Measure for Measure* (1604): 'Oh cunning enemy, that to catch a Saint, / With Saints doth bait thy hooke'.

Index

If you enjoyed this book, you may also be interested in …

9780752487250